W9-CMH-040

ENGLISH
HUMOUR

J.B.PRIESTLEY

ENGLISH HUMOUR

STEIN AND DAY/*Publishers*/New York

First published in the United States of America, 1976
Copyright © 1976 by J. B. Priestley
All rights reserved

This book was designed and produced by George Rainbird Ltd
36 Park Street, London W1Y 4DE

Picture Research: Mary Anne Norbury
Design: Pauline Harrison
Index: Ellen Crampton

The text was set and printed and the book was bound by
Jarrold & Sons Limited, Norwich, Norfolk, England

The colour plates and jacket were originated and printed by
Westerham Press Limited, Westerham, Kent, England

Stein and Day/*Publishers*/Scarborough House,
Briarcliff Manor, N.Y. 10510

Library of Congress Cataloging in Publication Data
Priestley, John Boynton, 1894–
    English humour.

    Includes index.
    1. English wit and humour——History and criticism.
I. Title.
PR931.P74   827'.009   76–12982
ISBN 0-8128-2093-6

Illustrations on reverse of frontispiece by Pont

Illustration on frontispiece: 'How to Dispense with
Servants in the Dining Hall' by Heath Robinson

Contents

Acknowledgments

Quotations in the text
have been taken from the following copyright works
and acknowledgment is made to:

A. D. Peters & Company Limited
for the quotations from *Love in a Cold Climate*,
The Pursuit of Love, and *The Blessing* by Nancy Mitford,
Diary of a Provincial Lady and *The Provincial Lady
in War-Time* by E. M. Delafield,
and *The Best of Beachcomber* edited by Michael Frayn.

William Heinemann Limited and Dodd, Mead & Company
for the quotations from *Zuleika Dobson*
by Max Beerbohm.

Garnstone Press Limited
for the quotation from *Kai Lung* by Ernest Bramah.

The Bodley Head
for the quotation from *My Autobiography*
by Charles Chaplin.

TO MY TWO
INVALUABLE COLLEAGUES
OVER THE YEARS
JOHN HADFIELD
MARY ANNE SANDERS

Preface

Nearly fifty years ago I was invited to write a book for the *English Heritage* series. My contribution was a modest volume called *English Humour*, now long out of print. I am using the title again because it best describes this new book on the very same subject. Though I cannot help sharing some material, what I am not doing is merely bringing up to date the book I wrote so long ago. God knows I am no longer fresh; but this book tries to be.

We English are now so often rejected, despised, banged about, by our neighbours in the United Kingdom, perhaps we ought to try a little nationalism of our own. We can make a start here. Our subject is *English* humour, so the Scots, Welsh, Irish (alas!) must keep out. We can laugh at ourselves without their help. We have been doing it since the fourteenth century. True, it may be harder work now, as I write this. Humour at its best has some root in affection; and while affection is still easy to find among the private lives of the people, we now have some quarters, advanced and unsmiling in art or politics, where affection seems to be missing – and intolerance reigns.

As a final note, I must add that I happen to possess certain useful volumes in which important writers, down the centuries, deliver their opinions of other important writers. I laid out these volumes for reference, but then, after some hesitation, decided not to go near them. I would trust as far as possible my own judgment. This may mean that here and there I have made a fool of myself. But, after all, this will do no great harm in a book on English Humour.

J.B.P.

CHAPTER I

Our First Great Humorist

The atmosphere in which we English live is favourable to humour. It is so often hazy, and very rarely is everything clear-cut. True humour, as distinct from what is merely laughable, comes out of a mixture of many ingredients, though even these may be hazily gathered and compounded. Not all the following are absolutely essential, but the mixture will be richer if they are all found in it: a feeling for irony; a sense of the absurd; a certain contact with reality, one foot at least on the ground; and, perhaps at first sight surprising, affection. Both the irony and the relish of absurdity perhaps share the same deep root into good sense and an idea of proportion. A true humorist is never a shallow frivolous man, giggling away. Humour itself has been described, with some truth, as 'Thinking in fun while feeling in earnest'. A true humorist like Lamb might amuse himself making dozens of jokes, but he is not in essence a joker, simply a determined funny man, and his real humour comes from well below the surface.

The contact with reality is important. The true humorist may indulge himself with some wild inventions but he never takes us up into the air to leave us there. He is not lost in fantasy. Humour comes out of our common life on this earth, out of the interplay of our characters down here. It would be impossible without some recognised society. So Thoreau alone in his wood seems to us a remarkable fellow, but he is not a humorist and is never caught laughing at himself: he takes to his hut in deadly earnest. On the other hand, the true humorist is rarely found grinning away: he is adept at keeping a straight face while poking his fun. (Chaucer is particularly good at this, probably nobody better.) But then irony plays its part too here. These essential elements run into each other.

Now for affection, which must not be confused with love, which is entirely serious, though affection can be a by-product of love in its less passionate and more domesticated phase. Affection not only brings warmth into humour but also insight into character, so creating more humour. The people to whom we are bound by real affection are always, to some extent, comic characters, and we begin to feel this even in childhood. (We are always glad to see Uncle Joe or Aunt Mary but they can't help being rather funny. Much of the best humour, notably in Dickens, depends upon recapturing the impressions of childhood.) Now humour can be quite effective without this warmth of affection – and I can think of some modern examples of this – but, all the same, something is missing that ought to be there, and *is* there in the finest humour; and to enjoy a cold detachment for its own sake reflects a certain arrogant weakness in both the writer and his admiring readers, all of them at odds with life.

However, obeying my general title, I must move down the centuries, trying to single out and salute every writer of any importance who has made us laugh or even broadly smile. While eager to welcome a genuine true humorist, I must also consider wits, various odd funny men, any creators of wild nonsense, itself an English speciality. But right at the beginning of our literature, we are in luck, for here as its father-figure we have a great poet who is also a great humorist – Chaucer, who in his *Canterbury Tales* combines all the necessary qualities that give us rich true humour. So here he is, actually proving every point I have made so far in this chapter.

Unless we think hard about Chaucer or learn more, we tend to accept an image of him as a quaint little medieval figure, somebody in a dim pageant. This is all wrong. We must take a closer look at him. To begin with, no English writer of anything like his stature had such a varied career. He was a courtier, a soldier in two wars, a diplomat undertaking important missions abroad, later a Controller of different Customs, and a hard-reading scholar in several languages. In middle age he had his ups-and-downs, moving from comparative affluence to periods, however brief, of startling poverty. As a writer he was astoundingly copious. (The Oxford Edition of his Complete Works which I have in front of me is set in double columns of alarmingly small print, and even so it runs to over seven hundred pages – a copious writer indeed!) Finally – and above all – in his *Canterbury Tales*, the work of his maturity, he set, in that far-distant fourteenth century, a style that other true English humorists, even if they never gave a thought to Chaucer, have followed ever since. The Englishness, the island manner and outlook and values, are there from the start.

The twin roots of Chaucer as a great poetic humorist are his enormous zest and his tolerant and even affectionate realism. Walter Raleigh points to this zest in his notes for a professorial lecture on Chaucer. (These notes, edited by my old friend, George Gordon, can be found in *On Writing and Writers*, which I hope is still in print for it is crammed with wit and good critical sense and has long been one of my favourite books.) 'Anything fair to see or hear awakes Chaucer's enthusiasm,' Raleigh declares. And after giving examples, he continues:

Anything on a large and generous scale, such as the housekeeping of the Franklin ('It snewed in his hous of mete and drinke'), or the marriages of the Wife of Bath, arouses Chaucer's sympathy. He loves a rogue, so that the rogue be high-spirited and clever at his trade, and not a whey-faced bloodless rascal. The Pardoner, in describing his own preaching, says:

Myn hondes and my tonge goon so yerne,
That it is joye to see my bisinesse,

And so Chaucer felt it. His joy is chronic and irrepressible . . .

'Canterbury Pilgrims', painted about 1809, by William Blake

This has long been out of literary fashion. Writers who suggested that at times they have enjoyed themselves and their 'scene' would be under suspicion at once, as so many mere entertainers. A Chaucer could be equally delighted by the daisies in the grass and by the sheer variety of his travelling companions. This would never do now. Zest, gusto, an unusual capacity for enjoyment, these are handicaps in advanced literary circles.

What I have called his 'tolerant and even affectionate realism' needs some explanation. Here I am not suggesting he sees his characters through a haze of sentiment. He sees them quite clearly and sharply. What he has even an affection for is reality itself, the world as it displayed itself before him. He enjoys the way in which people are tremendously themselves. Here is the Prioress pecking daintily at her dinner; and there is the Miller shovelling and swilling down his grub. Here are various characters mild as milk, and glaring at them, out of his big red frightening face, is the dreaded Summoner. The tales they tell range from the bawdy rough stuff of the Miller and the Reeve to legends and fables of undaunted and (we must confess) rather tedious virtue. Chaucer smilingly presents them all, people and tales, though not without frequent glints of irony.

It would be impossible for a contemporary author to offer us such a motley array of characters at once so realistically and tolerantly. We are too divisive in spirit, too much at the mercy of our ideologies, now the curse of our age. However, we must remember that this company, from the Knight to the ploughman, share a common purpose – to go on a pilgrimage together, all the children of God. If we judge by our largest buildings, our god is now money, for which we have a steadily increasing greed; and a Chaucer would not know what to make of us. Or am I wrong here?

After all, he was a great humorist as well as a great poet, and though the poet might fail, the humorist might deal with us roundly.

Like all true humorists – and unlike all the people who loudly congratulate themselves on their sense of humour – he could laugh at himself. The Host noisily insists upon this man (Chaucer) being given a chance to shine:

> He in the waste is shapen as wel as I:
> This were a popet in an arme to embrace
> For any woman, smal and fair of face.
> He seemeth elvish by his countenance,
> For unto no wight doth he dalliance –

But his 'Tale of Sir Thopas' is so boring he is not allowed to go on with it, and I cannot help feeling that Chaucer knew that what he put in its place, the virtuous moral 'Tale of Melibeus', was only a shade less tedious. We never know for certain if Chaucer is not only laughing at himself but laughing at us, his readers, too. And though the Host's definition of 'elvish' would not be ours, I think it is better to let the term stand in its present sense, even if it suggests something small, mischievous, elfin, about a man of original genius. For in his *Canterbury Tales*, at which he worked long in his last years and even then left uncompleted, he gave the humorous realist in him even more freedom than the poet, as he had not done earlier.

In doing this, I feel, Chaucer set a course that has been followed by English Humour, naturally with many individual variations, ever since his time. I am not assuming now a direct influence. The point is, that what came easily to him – a humorous realism – something not too far removed from the ordinary life of their age – also came easily to a number of English humorists long after him. Something in the national character encouraged these writers not to go too far away from the familiar scene and not to take refuge in wild fantasy. (How homely most of Shakespeare's humour is if we compare it with the huge daft antics of Rabelais or the gravely ironic inventions of Cervantes!) But finally we must not confuse this realism with the much narrower interpretation of it found in so much criticism of novels and plays during the last hundred years, and indeed often used in a pejorative sense. It is not tied to the kitchen sink or the garbage pail. It is how a really sensible man takes the immediate world he knows. The visionaries (however inspiring), the fanatics, the idiots, have no place here. Chaucer was a great poet and a great humorist. He was also a very sensible man. We are equally indebted to all three.

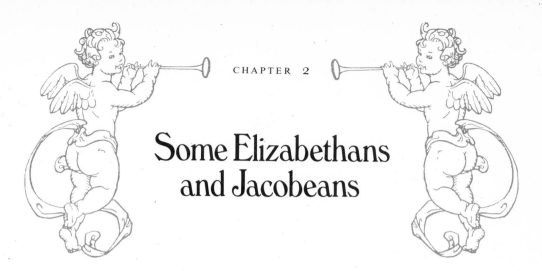

CHAPTER 2

Some Elizabethans and Jacobeans

From the lean season between Chaucer and the Elizabethans there emerges the odd figure of John Skelton, poet, satirist, eccentric. He was a Norfolk man, rather vainglorious for an East Anglian but having his share of that region's stiff courage. At first an Establishment poet-scholar – he was tutor to Henry VIII – he cut loose in middle life and became a ferocious satirist, finally clawing at Wolsey in his prime and, being in holy orders, having to take refuge in sanctuary to keep out of prison. His verse, with its short lines and multiple rhyming, easily runs into doggerel, though even then it is sharp enough to be pointedly satirical, often ferocious. His closest approach to charm and touches of genuine humour can be found in his *Phylyp Sparowe* (praised by Coleridge), supposed to be the lament – half-burlesque, half-tender – of a girl whose pet bird had been killed by a cat.

As a parson, at Diss, he was very much a 'character', preaching some extraordinary sermons and creating a scandal in the parish because he kept a mistress and had several children by her. When his parishioners complained to the Bishop, the next Sunday he faced them boldly and held up in the pulpit the naked baby recently born out of wedlock, and told them it was 'as fair as is the best of all yours'. (Laurence Sterne ought to have celebrated this fellow clergyman.) This was a humorist at least in action. Skelton's reputation survived the Elizabethan Age but declined rather rapidly afterwards, and I doubt if anybody reads him now except a few English scholars. But he had his fierce, wilful day.

To us the Elizabethan and Jacobean dramatists are out of luck. Every time they light their lanterns they have to hold them against the steady blaze of Shakespeare, about whom I shall be writing in the next chapter. Moreover, they seem to me – and I am certainly not alone here – to be far more effective and memorable in tragedy than in their comedy, which tends to be rough bustling stuff, often brought in because there had to be some comic scenes, even if heart and imagination took little account of them. The near-masterpieces, such as Middleton's *Changeling* or Webster's *White Devil*, are all tragedies; though I am now setting aside Ben Jonson. Oddly enough, the sunniest of these dramatists collaborated with these two darker spirits: this was Thomas Dekker, not a lucky man in his career but fortunate enough to be a good poet and a genuine humorist. I have never seen his *Shoemaker's Holiday* on the stage – and some present-day director should show us this lively picture of Elizabethan city life – but remember with something of the affection Dekker must have felt for his shoemaker-in-chief, Simon Eyre, all bustle and hasty commands and strange epithets but kind at heart: 'Give me thy hand; th'art welcome. Hodge, entertain him; Firk, bid him welcome; come, Hans. Run, wife, bid your maids, your trullibubs, make ready my fine men's breakfasts . . .'. Again, I have never seen his *Honest Whore* on the stage, but at least share some of Hazlitt's delight in its oddest character, old Friscobaldo:

> . . . I am not covetous, am not in debt; sit neither at the duke's side, nor lie at his feet. Wenching and I have done; no man I wrong, no man I fear, no man I fee; take heed how far I walk, because I know yonder's my home; I would not die like a rich man, to carry nothing away save a winding sheet; but like a good man, to leave Orlando behind me. I sowed leaves in my youth, and I reap books in my age. I fill this hand, and empty this; when the bell shall toll for me, if I prove a swan, and go singing to my nest, why so! If a crow! throw me out for carrion, and pick out mine eyes. May not old Friscobaldo, my lord, be merry now! Ha?

The scene is supposed to be Milan, but it is long odds that in one of his London taverns Dekker overheard some fantastic old boy explaining himself. I find real humour as well as good poetry in Tom Dekker, about whom we know too little.

There is a point worth making here. When people want to prove that Shakespeare was really somebody else – Bacon, Southampton or even an aristocratic committee – they always tell us we know so little about this actor from Stratford. They should take a look at some of Shakespeare's contemporaries – Dekker for example, whose works both in verse and prose we know about, but that is all we do know for certain. Exactly when was he born and when did he die and in what style did he live? We can't be sure or simply don't know. We are told how Shakespeare disposed of his second-best bed. We don't know if poor Dekker even possessed a bed. So much for that familiar foolish argument!

Both as reader and playgoer I have a warm regard for that boisterous comedy, *The Knight of the Burning Pestle*, long attributed to Beaumont and Fletcher but now held to be by Beaumont alone, the younger and more high-spirited of the pair. We need only remember that lively Induction before the play begins. The speaker of the Prologue is interrupted by an indignant grocer who leaps upon the stage to protest that his trade is ignored: 'I will have a grocer, and he shall do admirable things.' His wife calls from below, 'Let him kill a lion with a pestle', and then joins her husband on the stage. When they are told there is no actor to spare for this heroic part, they bring up their apprentice, Ralph, who 'will go beyond them all'. The wife continues:

> I'll be sworn, gentlemen, my husband tells you true: he [Ralph] will act you sometimes at our house, that all the neighbours cry out to him; he will fetch you up a couraging

part in the garret, that we are all as feared, I warrant you, that we quake again: we'll fear our children with him; if they be never so unruly, do but cry, 'Ralph comes, Ralph comes' to them, and they'll be as quiet as lambs. – Hold up thy head, Ralph; show the gentlemen what thou canst do; speak a huffing part; I warrant you, the gentlemen will accept of it.

The eager enthusiastic dame's voice rings true though more than three and a half centuries separate us, and though some wild work follows in the play, together with

Scene from *The Knight of the Burning Pestle*, Greenwich Theatre, 1975

some instructions from the grocer's wife what Ralph ought to do next, the note of humorous realism is never lost. Chaucer would have enjoyed it.

We must now approach a most impressive figure, a kind of giant, and I must confess I do it with some hesitation. Nobody can deny Ben Jonson talent of a very high order. He was a lord of language and in his comedies had more stagecraft than his contemporaries (Shakespeare, as usual, excepted). I have seen productions of some of them – two of them, *The Alchemist* and *Volpone*, several times – and their action has held my attention and they have made me laugh. Yet I find it hard to give them and their brilliant author a high place in any account of English Humour. Jonson, it seems to me, was a wit and satirist and clever plotter rather than a true humorist. There was as a rule a cutting edge to his mind that rarely allowed him to indulge his comic figures, out of a certain affection, transforming them into gushing springs of forgivable folly. They seem to exist not in ordinary life but in some mysterious desert of absurdity, where there are more monsters than men. The true humorist may make fun of his fellow men, but he does not regard them with contempt. This Jonson does all too often, after rising high above manual labour by the force of his personality and his great gift. He lacked what Shakespeare had in abundance – a genial tolerance, breadth and depth of sympathy.

I can no longer give marks for humour, as I did once, years ago, to the swaggering Bobadill in *Every Man in His Humour.* His famous account, so often quoted, of his plan for substituting the duello for general warfare – nineteen stout experts like himself challenging twenty after twenty after twenty of the enemy army – may be good tomfoolery but does not linger in the memory as excellent humour. Far closer to my taste – and indeed an unusual figure in Jonson – is the innocent Abel Drugger the young tobacco-man in *The Alchemist*, so trusting and foolish as he introduces himself:

Henry Woodward as Bobadill in Act 1 of *Every Man in His Humour*, Theatre Royal, Drury Lane, 1751

This, an't please your worship;
I am a young beginner, and am building
Of a new shop, an't like your worship, just
At corner of a street: Here is the plot on't –
And I would know by art, sir, of your worship,
Which way I should make my door, by necromancy,
And where my shelves; and which should be for boxes,
And which for pots. I would be glad to thrive, sir:
And I was wished to your worship by a gentleman,
One Captain Face, that says you know men's planets,
And their good angels, and their bad.

All as innocent as a talking egg. It is no accident that clever actors, from David Garrick to Cedric Hardwicke, have preferred to play this apparently small part. As they toddled on and off they knew that here was a character not hard-edged but asking for some sympathy in the laughter.

Though I have seen several productions of *Volpone*, I remember only one that retained the character named Sir Politick Would-Be. Yet he seems to me one of Jonson's best comic inventions. He is the much-travelled international-affairs kind of Englishman, seemingly deep in mysterious plots and secret-service nonsense:

I knew him one of the most dangerous heads
Living within the state, and so I held him . . .
    While he lived, in action,
He has received weekly intelligence,
Upon my knowledge, out of the Low Countries,
From all parts of the world, in cabbages;
And those dispensed again to ambassadors,
In oranges, musk-melons, apricots,
Lemons, pome-citrons, and such-like; sometimes
In Colchester oysters, and your Selsey cockles . . .
. . . Sir, upon my knowledge.
Nay, I've observed him, at your public ordinary,
Take his advertisement from a traveller,
A concealed statesman, in a trencher of meat;
And instantly, before the meal was done,
Convey an answer in a tooth-pick.

This is rich fooling. It might be a burlesque, centuries in advance, of our popular elaborate tales of espionage and counter-espionage. So let us leave big Ben with his Sir Politick Would-Be, praying that no other director would be stupid enough to cut him out of the next production of *Volpone*.

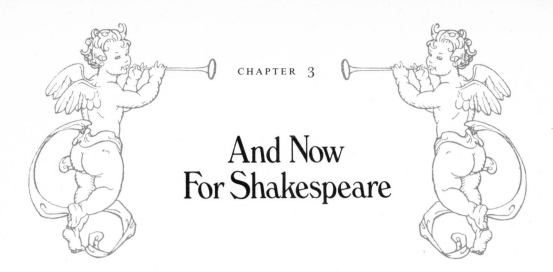

CHAPTER 3

And Now
For Shakespeare

If Shakespeare had not had a large share of humour, he would not have been Shakespeare but Bacon or Marlowe or even a committee of aristocrats, as some foolish people would have us believe. In other words, how could this extraordinary man be the most broadly based, the most far-reaching, the most universal of all dramatic poets, as the world acknowledges him to be, unless he had humour too – and to spare? Certainly he could move away from it and forget it for a time, when his own moods and the themes he chose had little or no place for it, when the amazed and suffering spirit of man found itself confronted by conflagrations and volcanic eruptions of elemental forces, when the small cosy world in which humour flourishes was on fire and turning into cinders. But humour had been there before these flames and abysses, and would return again, softened and perhaps chastened, rather like people exchanging tentative smiles after a catastrophe.

The pure comedies of Shakespeare do not belong to humour, though they may give us glimpses of it. They exist in a poetical world, well away from common reality, to which humour is attached. Each comedy has its own highly poetic and unworldly atmosphere – the magic wood in *A Midsummer Night's Dream*; the amiable forest in *As You Like It*; the stately gardens in *Twelfth Night*; and so forth – but in all of them potential lovers advance, retreat, advance again, in a dance of glittering speeches. When humour arrives, as it does with the artisan-players in the *Dream*, with Touchstone and the rustics in *As You Like It*, with Sir Toby and Sir Andrew Aguecheek in *Twelfth Night*, it might be said *to break in*, coming from some other world. It was probably there to please 'the groundlings', needing a change from the delicate sunlight and moonshine of these comedies. Therefore I feel that while I am entitled to consider some characters from these shimmering silken pieces, just because they belong to humour, I can safely ignore the comedies themselves. We need stronger and tastier meat here.

Shakespeare's humorous characters can be roughly divided into two groups. They are the sophisticated and the unsophisticated. There are the wits, the wags, the comedians, and there are the innocents who have no idea that they are droll. We notice that there are not many of the first kind, though they can boast a monarch of humorists in Falstaff. On the other hand, the innocents are all over the place. I think Shakespeare, with his immensely broad and deep sense of humanity, together with his smiling tolerance, had a special relish and tenderness for them. He can breathe life into characters that seem on the edge of nothing, that never before had a light shone on them. There is little to compare with this among his fellow dramatists. He can create faintly whispering innocents who are unique, just as Hamlet or Cleopatra is unique. They are as triumphant in their way as King Lear or Macbeth. In its incredible breadth of humour, the same mind that can show us the huge glaring sun of Falstaff can also pick out for us dimmer and dimmer moons somewhere within the system. I don't know which is the greater marvel.

Setting aside Falstaff – not an easy thing to do – let us take a closer look at these innocents, who reveal some variety in their sort. Here for example is Feeble, the woman's tailor, suddenly piping up, out of some unexpected depth of humanity, among Falstaff's grotesque recruits:

> By my troth, I care not; a man can die but once; we owe God a death: I'll ne'er bear a base mind: an't be my destiny, so; an't be not, so: no man's too good to serve his prince; and, let it go which way it will, he that dies this year is quit for the next.

And Feeble has moved into great literature. We can even turn to the *Merry Wives*, Shakespeare's laziest play and no favourite of mine. Even so, here we find Slender, young, silly, divided between the bashful and the boastful, trying to cope with sweet Anne Page:

Anne. Will't please your Worship to come in, sir?

Slender. No, I thank you, forsooth, heartily; I am very well.

Anne. The dinner attends you, sir.

Slender. I am not a-hungry, I thank you, forsooth. Go, sirrah, for all you are my man, go wait upon my cousin Shallow. *(Exit Simple.)* A justice of peace sometime may be beholding to his friend for a man. I keep but three men and a boy yet, till my mother be dead: but what though? yet I live like a poor gentleman born.

Anne. I may not go in without your worship: they will not sit till you come.

Slender. I'faith, I'll eat nothing; I thank you as much as though I did.

Anne. I pray you, sir, walk in.

Slender. I had rather walk here, I thank you. I bruised my shin th' other day with playing at sword and dagger with a master of fence; three veneys for a dish of stew'd prunes; and, by my troth, I cannot abide the smell of hot meat since. Why do your dogs bark so? be there bears i' the town?

Anne. I think there are, sir; I heard them talk'd of.

Slender. I love the sport well; but I shall as soon quarrel at it as any man in England. You are afraid, if you see the bear loose, are you not?

Anne. Ay, indeed, sir.

Slender. That's meat and drink to me, now. I have seen Sackerson loose twenty times, and have taken him by the chain; but, I warrant you, the women have so cried and shriek'd at it, that it pass'd; but women, indeed, cannot abide 'em; they are very ill-favour'd rough things.

This may seem slight and easy, but there is to my mind a touch of genius in it. But we can find more than a touch if we go to the other extreme of age, to discover the humble Silence proudly attending upon that vain old prattler, Justice Shallow:

Shallow. The same Sir John, the very same. I saw him break Skogan's head at the court-gate, when 'a was a crack not thus high: and the very same day did I fight with one Sampson Stockfish, a fruiterer, behind Gray's Inn. Jesu, Jesu, the mad days that I have spent! and to see how many of my old acquaintance are dead!
Silence. We shall all follow, cousin.
Shallow. Certain, 'tis certain; very sure, very sure: death, as the Psalmist saith, is certain to all; all shall die. How a good yoke of bullocks at Stamford fair?
Silence. Truly, cousin, I was not there.
Shallow. Death is certain. Is old Double of your town living yet?
Silence. Dead, sir.
Shallow. Jesu, Jesu, dead! 'a drew a good bow; and dead! 'a shot a fine shoot: John o' Gaunt loved him well, and betted much money on his head. Dead! 'a would have clapped i' the clout at twelve score; and carried you a forehand shaft a fourteen and fourteen and a half, that it would have done a man's heart good to see. How a score of ewes now?
Silence. Thereafter as they be: a score of good ewes may be worth ten pounds.
Shallow. And is old Double dead?

This is at once comical and yet almost terrible, laying bare, in the confusion of old age, the roots of our existence.

After those two, it seems idle to bring on any more innocents. We do not need even the masterful and idiotic Bottom, eager to play everybody and everything – and finally achieving a magnificent role in Elfland. Nor even Sir Andrew Aguecheek, often so self-revealing: 'Methinks sometimes I have no more wit than a Christian or an ordinary man has: but I am a great eater of beef, and I believe that does harm to my wit.' However, we can make an exception of a woman of experience suddenly transformed into an innocent. Hostess Quickly, in charge of a tavern, cannot help being a woman of great experience, but under the spell of Falstaff she is yet another innocent:

Falstaff. What is the gross sum that I owe thee?
Hostess. Marry, if thou wert an honest man, thyself and the money too. Thou didst swear to me upon a parcel-gilt goblet, sitting in my Dolphin-chamber, at the round table, by a sea-coal fire, upon Wednesday in Wheeson week, when the prince broke thy head for liking his father to a singing-man of Windsor, thou didst swear to me then, as I

was washing thy wound, to marry me and make me my lady thy wife. Canst thou deny it? Did not goodwife Keech, the butcher's wife, come in then and call me gossip Quickly? coming in to borrow a mess of vinegar; telling us she had a good dish of prawns; whereby thou didst desire to eat some; whereby I told thee they were ill for a green wound? And didst thou not, when she was gone down stairs, desire me to be no more so familiarity with such poor people; saying that ere long they should call me madam? And didst thou not kiss me and bid me fetch thee thirty shillings? I put thee now to thy book-oath: deny it if thou canst.

Falstaff. My lord, this is a poor mad soul; and she says up and down the town that her eldest son is like you; she hath been in good case, and the truth is, poverty hath distracted her. . . .

Speaking as one who has worked hard and long in this trade, I declare that such scenes as these are marvels of both detailed comic invention and imagination. They come out of the breadth and depth of Shakespeare's sense of and feeling for humanity. In their own way they are as triumphant as his tragedies.

Falstaff shows us Shakespeare at his best and at his worst. We will take a look at the worst, if only to get rid of it. This famous character grows and grows until he dominates *Henry IV Part Two*. But this is to be followed by *Henry V*. Falstaff would burst this play wide open. The audience would be waiting for the fat knight to appear, not the king. So now it is as if the cautious actor-manager, with plans for property-development in Stratford, took over from the poet, the dramatist, the *maker*. (Among all the arguments about Shakespeare, has it ever been suggested that as soon as he began to write, a nobler spirit actually took possession of him?) So Falstaff has suddenly to behave stupidly, rush to his destruction, and then be killed off. Not only that, but a mere travesty of the character we know is pushed into a rather silly comedy, whose Merry Wives would never have had a hope of hoodwinking our Falstaff. It is really as if two quite different minds and temperaments had been at work here – one to create and the other to destroy. A masterpiece has been lovingly developed and crowned, only to be torn to pieces. I could not understand this in my youth; it still puzzles me now. How could *our Shakespeare*, this wonder of a man, do it?

The Falstaff who fully emerges in *Henry IV Part Two* is not simply a fat knight who drinks too much, borrows money, takes a whore on his knee. He is a great man, the greatest in this play, where nobody else is so clear-sighted or speaks his mind so frankly. Moreover, he is an extraordinary great man. He is not driving on and on towards greater power or more useful knowledge. He does not want, in the larger sense, to make use of us, but to entertain us, to make us laugh, to conjure up ease and merriment. He is a king in a tavern not a palace, with a treasury, a menacing armed guard, any number of severe statutes. He goes to war but has no illusions about war. He understands people, seeing through Justice Shallow in one glance. But he himself is not always understood, not even by persons who ought to know better. For example, in one academic paper I read I was told that in the 'men in buckram' scene

Ralph Richardson as Falstaff and Laurence Olivier as Justice Shallow
in *Henry IV Part Two*, Old Vic, 1945

with the Prince and Poins, Falstaff was actually trying to *deceive* them, and in despair multiplied the men in buckram. But this is not Falstaff. He is talking to be *found out*, to add to his companions' joy and laughter. This is always his way among boon companions. He is their fountain of humour, not only witty in himself but the cause that wit is in other men. If he keeps drinking, it is not to stupefy himself and lose his senses, but, as he tells us in his praise of sherrissack, to make the brain 'apprehensive, quick, forgetive, full of nimble, fiery and delectable shapes'.

Between Falstaff and the other wits, wags, comedians, from aristocratic Sir Toby to the very democratic Autolycus, the gap is so immense that I feel it is far more rewarding to stay with him. There is more breadth and depth of humour in one wave of his mind than in all their fooling. But I prefer to meet him in print to seeing him on the stage. (An exception is Ralph Richardson's performance of him with the Old Vic in 1945.) The over-padded actors are so busy being a fat old man, puffing away, wheezing and grunting. The spirit of the great creature is missing. He is being contracted and weighed down when he is always expanding. He is not heavily armoured by his bulk and his years. He wears them both as if they were a comic uniform, using them as material for more humour; all the best jokes about his bulk are his own. He is really a poetical creation, perhaps belonging to some haunting masculine dream, as old as drink and firelight, of a gigantic wonderful night out, a hell of a party.

When he says to the Chief Justice, 'You that are old consider not the capacities of us that are young', he is not simply being astoundingly impudent, he is speaking out of something the Chief Justice has lost, a youthful spirit, alight with zest and mirth. This can be missing in a young man, like Prince John of Lancaster, cold and ruthless, capable of putting down a rebellion by an appalling act of treachery, who can say as he goes, 'Fare you well, Falstaff. I in my condition, Shall better speak of you than you deserve.' To which Falstaff, alone now, retorts, 'I would you had but the wit: 'twere better than your dukedom . . .'. Even when he acknowledges his age, he separates himself from it. So after seeing through Shallow and Silence at a glance, he tells us, 'Lord, Lord, how subject we old men are to this vice of lying!' And we feel that a spirit alive in him is dead in them, that his eye is still clear and bright while theirs are misty with age, self-deception and foolishness.

We have from time to time here glanced at the various elements that together create humour. How do we consider Falstaff in these terms? A sense of irony and of the absurd? He has these in abundance. A certain contact with reality, so that we have not left this earth for pure fantasy? Well, he is to my mind the supreme realist in the play *Henry IV Part Two*, filled with clanking notables half out of their minds. But now – the final ingredient, affection? This may seem doubtful. Falstaff does not express affection – there is no laughter in it – but he frequently behaves as if it were there: 'Gallants, lads, boys, hearts of gold, all the titles of good fellowship come to you! What, shall we be merry?' When Prince Hal and Poins, disguised, go to play the last of their poor farce tricks, we should remember the warning of Poins: 'My lord, he will drive you out of your revenge and turn all to a merriment, if you take not the heat.' And what a wonderful gift this is – to dissolve thoughts of revenge and turn all into a merriment! What a different world we should have now if this gift were common and found among men of great influence and power.

Doll Tearsheet's tough little heart is moved to a certain tenderness: 'Come, I'll be friends with thee, Jack: thou art going to the wars; and whether I shall ever see thee again or no, there is nobody cares.' But is she right in her conclusion? Bardolph has been his butt for years, but he can cry when he hears that Falstaff is dead: 'Would I were with him, wheresom'er he is, either in Heaven or in Hell!' But – alas – those who don't seem to care include not only Prince John and his like and Henry V but also Master William Shakespeare. Is it my fancy that when Falstaff hurries to his doom, in everything he says and in everything said to him afterwards, Shakespeare is writing in haste and poorly, far from the level at which he created Falstaff? What is certain – and very ironical – is that the big scene in Shallow's orchard, before Falstaff is made to lose his wits, displays to us, better than any other single scene, the wide range of Shakespeare's humour.

Falstaff and Bardolph are there, at ease, with the innocents, Shallow, Silence, Davy. Too much sack has been drunk at supper, and Silence is under its influence and is quite bold for once, insisting upon singing; though not discouraged by the others, who drink his health. Shallow is happily fussing away. Bardolph and Davy, Shallow's man, discuss a possible meeting in London. Falstaff presides over the group, occasionally throwing out an encouraging remark. It is a fine night in a Gloucestershire orchard. And, as Silence declares: 'And we shall be merry: now comes in the sweet o' the night.'

But what does come, bursting in like a rocket, is the fantastic figure of Ancient Pistol. And with him there arrives a quite different kind of humour, not met here before. It is the humour of deliberate and literary and dramatic burlesque. An over-written old play might have entered the scene:

Pistol. . . . Sweet knight, thou art now one of the greatest men in this realm.
Silence. By'r Lady, I think 'a be, but goodman Puff of Barson.
Pistol. Puff! Puff in thy teeth, most recreant coward base!
Sir John, I am thy Pistol and thy friend,
And helter-skelter have I rode to thee;
And tidings do I bring and lucky joys
And golden times and happy news of price.
Falstaff. I pray thee, now, deliver them like a man of this world.
Pistol. A foutra for the world and worldlings base! I speak of Africa and golden joys.
Falstaff. O base Assyrian knight, what is thy news? Let King Cophetua know the truth thereof.
Silence. (sings) And Robin Hood, Scarlet, and John.
Pistol. Shall dunghill curs confront the Helicons?
And shall good news be baffled?
Then, Pistol, lay thy head in Furies' lap.
Shallow. Honest gentleman, I know not your breeding.
Pistol. Why then, lament therefore.
Shallow. Give me pardon, sir: if, sir, you come with news from the Court, I take it there's but two ways, either to utter them, or to conceal them. I am, sir, under the King in some authority.
Pistol. Under which king, Besonian? speak or die.
Shallow. Under King Harry.
Pistol. Harry the Fourth? or Fifth?

Shallow. Harry the Fourth.

Pistol. A foutra for thine office!

Sir John, thy tender lambkin now is king;

Harry the Fifth's the man. I speak the truth:

When Pistol lies, do this; and fig me, like

The bragging Spaniard.

Falstaff. What, is the old King dead?

Pistol. As nail in door: the things I speak are just.

Falstaff. Away, Bardolph! saddle my horse. Master Robert Shallow, choose what office thou wilt in the land, 'tis thine. Pistol, I will double-charge thee with dignities.

Bardolph. O joyful day! I would not take a knighthood for my fortune.

Pistol. What, I do bring good news?

Falstaff. Carry Master Silence to bed. Master Shallow, my Lord Swallow, be what thou wilt; I am Fortune's steward. Get on thy boots: we'll ride all night. O sweet Pistol! Away, Bardolph! *(Exit Bardolph.)* Come, Pistol, utter more to me; and withal devise something to do thyself good. Boot, boot, Master Shallow: I know the young King is sick for me. Let us take any man's horses; the laws of England are at my commandment. Blessed are they that have been my friends; and woe to my Lord Chief Justice!

Now let us take a quiet look at the end of this scene, refusing to be rushed and bamboozled by Shakespeare, in his hurry to rid himself of Falstaff. We know that while Falstaff enjoys playing the fool, he is no fool at all, being an acute observer of men and situations. We know that he will make every allowance for Pistol's ultra-romantic and dramatic exaggerations. We know that he has been well acquainted with Prince Hal, and not only as a boon companion. In view of all this, can we accept that now Hal is King, with a monarch's responsibility – Falstaff can believe he will be allowed to do anything he wants to do? This seems to me ridiculous. It is turning a very clever, clear-sighted man into a reckless idiot. The mind that created Falstaff was not working at the end of this scene. Our Shakespeare was somewhere else.

However, when he was not somewhere else, when he was in full creation, what a world of wit and high spirits, foolish innocence and happy laughter, he left in our keeping! Scene after scene, face after face, illuminate the haze of memory. Mad Mercutio and the prattling Nurse; Bottom and his fellow artisan-players and the fairies in the magic wood; Rosalind and Touchstone matching wits; Sir Toby, Sir Andrew and the clown at their catches; Benedick and Beatrice fencing with love, and Dogberry addressing the watch; Slender and Sir Hugh Evans at Windsor; Pistol and Fluellen at the war; Autolycus cozening the shepherds; Falstaff in the tavern or marching his ragged regiment into immortality – what a world indeed! And what a breadth and depth of humanity are here, all from a great master of whom it was said he 'takes up the meanest subjects with the same tenderness that we do an insect's wing, and would not kill a fly'. But then there is no real humour without empathy, a liberal imagination, tolerance, some measure of affection.

CHAPTER 4

After the Puritans

Leaving the theatre for a few moments I want to offer a note on some of the prose-writers of the seventeenth-century – men as varied as Aubrey, Izaak Walton, Sir Thomas Browne, Thomas Fuller. There is about them a sort of elfin quaintness, belonging to this century and no other, that makes them hover on the edge of humour. We are never sure if they are smiling, often secretly laughing, or are as solemn as owls.

There can be no such doubt about Samuel Butler (1612–80), a satirist and wit with a strong humorous side to him. He had served as clerk to various Puritan justices during the Commonwealth, and took his revenge after the Restoration by writing his mock-heroic poem, *Hudibras*, with Puritanism his main target. A final irony was that while the Puritans had bullied him, the Court, which he welcomed and served, neglected him, so that he died in poverty. There is some humour, as well as wit, in the cheerful impudence of his images and rhymes:

> The sun had long since in the lap
> Of Thetis, taken out his nap,
> And like a lobster boil'd, the morn
> From black to red began to turn.
>
> He was in logic a great critic,
> Profoundly skill'd in analytic.
> He could distinguish and divide
> A hair 'twixt south and south-west side.
> On either which he would dispute,
> Confute, change hands, and still confute.
>
> He could raise scruples dark and nice,
> And after solve 'em in a trice:
> As if Divinity had catch'd
> The itch, of purpose to be scratch'd.

> What makes all doctrines plain and clear?
> About two hundred pounds a year.
> And what which was prov'd true before,
> Prov'd false again? Two hundred more.

Some of his sharpest couplets went long ago into the common stock of worldly wisdom:

> Compound for sins, they are inclin'd to
> By damning those they have no mind to.
>
> He that complies against his will,
> Is of his own opinion still.

So that a host of people still quote Butler when they have never set eyes on his *Hudibras*. But, after all, that is one kind of lasting fame. And indeed, the Restoration, which brought in the wits, cannot show us one better endowed than poor neglected Samuel Butler.

'And so to bed'. These four well-remembered words bring us to the strangest case in the long history of English Humour, that of Samuel Pepys. He is our great *unconscious* humorist, the man who never intended to amuse distant generations of readers, who simply kept a diary in code from 1660 to 1669 (when he had trouble with his eyesight), reminding himself what he had done, where he had been, what he had felt. And this was no ordinary man. He was an important civil servant, hobnobbing with the great until he was out of public favour, President of the Royal Society for two years, a recognised connoisseur of music, pictures, books and manuscripts. And yet he turns up, two centuries later, as a famous comic character. He has some value, of course, as a social historian, but it is the unconscious humour of his diary, so frankly revealing, that keeps him alive. (Could there be – we ask wistfully – some important civil servant, some solemn figure high up in the Admiralty, who is busy even now explaining his private life? The odds are heavily against it: Pepys is a warning against intimate confidences.) I shall not bother with quotation here; Pepys should be enjoyed at length; moreover, his characteristic manner has been imitated too often by funny journalists. But before leaving him, we might ask ourselves one question. On this level of naïve self-revelation, hiding nothing that could be set down in print at last, wouldn't we all turn ourselves into comic characters – unless of course we proved to be horrible fellows? And when we are tempted to take ourselves too seriously and be self-important, might it not be a good idea to remember the droll close-up Pepys offers us, simply by being entirely frank?

Now we come to the group loosely called the 'Restoration Dramatists', though they all outlived that age. In his famous account of the characters in this Artificial Comedy, Lamb tells us: 'They have got out of Christendom into the land – what shall I call it – of cuckoldry – the Utopia of gallantry, where pleasure is duty, and the manners perfect freedom. It is altogether a speculative scene of things, which has no reference whatever to the world that is.' But a closer look at these plays proves that this is not true. There is something else besides sex in them – something belonging to the world we know – and that is money. People who live for pleasure, men or women, cannot risk anything like poverty. So the bank may be important as well as bed. For my part I would have welcomed more financial intrigue in these comedies, for endless ungallant gallantry, against a chorus of sniggering, soon becomes tedious and silly. Again, I find it hard to believe that 'the town', Charles II's London, was as delightful as so many of these characters declare it to be. There must have been much to be said for the life in the country that they all seem to dread.

Wycherley's *The Country Wife*, which owes something to two Molière comedies, is still revived, chiefly because Mrs Margery Pinchwife is a superb part for an attractive actress, preferably small. It is reasonably well constructed and succeeds in bustling us through the evening. But we do not need to be prudish, shocked by references to 'pox' and 'clap', to find it coarse and tasteless. Though he had talent and a fair wit, Wycherley is coarse in grain. There is about him a brutal masculinity, a late-night smoke-room atmosphere, that soon becomes offensive, especially in mixed company; even though there are touches in his drawing of Margery Pinchwife that suggest something better might be arriving. He lived long enough to become the friend of Pope in his teens, and longer still, we are told, to sink into a lecherous dotage. He must have spent too much time re-reading his plays.

Judi Dench as Mrs Margery Pinchwife in *The Country Wife*, by William Wycherley, Nottingham Playhouse, 1966

Congreve is very different (though not an admirable character, being cold, selfish and affected). His comedies, all produced when he was still young, are sadly deficient in elementary stagecraft. He is in fact better to read than to see performed. I have seen several productions of *The Way of the World* and still do not remember what the play is about. He is better to read because his dialogue is superb. In artificial comedy it has never been matched. (The two Irishmen, Sheridan and Wilde, never achieve his cool perfection.) It is significant, as I shall explain later, that what was just another scene in Congreve's idea of his play is now to our eyes and ears easily the best thing in it. It is the scene in which Mirabell is courting Millamant, and though it has been quoted often enough, I cannot resist giving it another airing:

Mrs Millamant. Oh, I hate a lover than can dare to think he draws a moment's air, independent of the bounty of his mistress. There is not so impudent a thing in nature, as the saucy look of an assured man, confident of success. The pedantic arrogance of a very husband has not so pragmatical an air. Ah! I'll never marry, unless I am first made sure of my will and pleasure.

Mirabell. Would you have 'em both before marriage? Or will you be contented with the first now, and stay for the other 'till after grace?

Mrs Millamant. Ah! don't be impertinent – My dear liberty, shall I leave thee? My faithful solitude, my darling contemplation, must I bid you then adieu? Ay-h adieu – my morning thoughts, agreeable wakings, indolent slumbers, all ye *douceurs*, ye *sommeils du matin*, adieu? – I can't do't, 'tis more than impossible – positively, Mirabell, I'll lie abed in a morning as long as I please.

Mirabell. Then I'll get up in a morning as early as I please.

Mrs Millamant. Ah! Idle creature, get up when you will – and d'ye hear, I won't be called names after I'm married; positively I won't be called names.

Mirabell. Names!

Mrs Millamant. Ay, as wife, spouse, my dear, joy, jewel, love, sweetheart, and the rest of that nauseous cant, in which men and their wives are so fulsomely familiar – I shall never bear that – good Mirabell, don't let us be familiar or fond, nor kiss before folks, like my Lady Fadler and Sir Francis: nor go to Hyde-park together the first Sunday in a new chariot, to provoke eyes and whispers, and then never to be seen there together again; as if it were proud of one another the first week, and ashamed of one another ever after. Let us never visit together, nor go to a play together; but let us be very strange and well bred: let us be as strange as if we had been married a great while; and as well bred as if we were not married at all.

Mirabell. Have you any more conditions to offer? Hitherto your demands are pretty reasonable.

Mrs Millamant. Trifles! – As liberty to pay and receive visits to and from whom I please; to write and receive letters, without interrogatories or wry faces on your part; to wear what I please; and choose conversation with regard only to my own taste; to have no obligation upon me to converse with wits that I don't like, because they are your acquaintance: or to be intimate with fools because they may be your relations. Come to dinner when I please; dine in my dressing-room when I'm out of humour, without giving a reason. To have my closet inviolate; to be sole empress of my tea-table, which you must never presume to approach without first asking leave. And lastly, wherever I am, you shall always knock at the door before you come in. These articles subscribed, if I continue to endure you a little longer, I may by degrees dwindle into a wife.

And the scene still holds when Mirabell brings out his own masculine provisos, most of them, Millamant declares, 'odious' to his fair companion.

The reason why this particular scene appears to dominate the play is that something has been added. Below the usual sparkle there is a new warmth. There are, we feel, two real people here, not the usual cardboard figures of gallants and their prey. Congreve has gone some way from sheer wit and cold and complicated plotting towards real humour. It is significant that in our own later age this scene has become increasingly important. I think Congreve would have been surprised. But authors often write better than they know, unconsciously adding a dimension to a character or scene.

Writing plays was a sideline to Vanbrugh's triumphant career as an architect. Though still concerned with elaborate seduction, he moves on from Wycherley and Congreve, to come closer to the real world. Some of his people talk quite sensibly. There is more air in his plays. (There is more still in Farquhar's, but he – alas – was an Irishman.) Vanbrugh can still be bawdy, of course, to suit the taste of his audiences, but his people are not always pointing, whispering and sniggering. He kept his place in the Theatre because he created some rich acting parts.

One of them is Lord Foppington in *The Relapse*, whose opinion of reading is still worth quoting:

Amanda. Well, I must own I think books the best entertainment in the world.
Lord Fop. I am so much of your ladyship's mind madam, that I have a private gallery, where I walk sometimes, is furnished with nothing but books and looking-glasses. Madam, I have gilded them and rang'd 'em so prettily, before Gad, it is the most entertaining thing in the world to walk and look upon 'em.
Amanda. Nay, I love a neat library too; but 'tis, I think, the inside of a book shou'd recommend it most to us.
Lord Fop. That, I must confess, I am not altogether so fond of. Far to my mind the inside of a book, is to entertain one's self with the forc'd product of another man's brain. Naw I think a man of quality and breeding may be much diverted with the natural sprauts of his own. But to say the truth, madam, let a man love reading never so well, when once he comes to know this tawn, he finds so many better ways of passing away the four-and-twenty hours, that 'twere ten thousand pities he should consume his time in that. . . .

We know that Sir John Brute, in *The Provok'd Wife*, was one of Garrick's favourite parts; and Vanbrugh introduces Sir John in what must be one of the surliest scenes in all Comedy:

Lady Brute. Do you dine at home today, Sir John?

Sir John. Why, do you expect I should tell you what I don't know myself?

Lady Brute. I thought there was no harm in asking you.

Sir John. If thinking wrong were an excuse for impertinence, women might be justify'd in most things they say or do.

Lady Brute. I'm sorry if I have said anything to displease you.

Sir John. Sorrow for things past is of little importance to me, as my dining at home or abroad ought to be to you.

Lady Brute. My enquiry was only that I might have provided what you lik'd.

Sir John. Six to four you had been in the wrong there again; for what I lik'd yesterday I don't like today; and what I like today, 'tis odds I mayn't like tomorrow.

Lady Brute. But if I had ask'd you what you lik'd?

Sir John. Why then there wou'd have been more asking than the thing was worth.

Lady Brute. I wish I did but know how I might please you.

Sir John. Ay, but that sort of knowledge is not a wife's talent.

Lady Brute. Whate'er my talent is, I'm sure my will has been ever to make you easy.

Sir John. If women were to have their wills, the world wou'd be finely govern'd.

Lady Brute. What reason have I given you to use me as you do of late? It once was otherwise: You marry'd me for love.

Sir John. And you me for money: so you have your reward, and I have mine.

Lady Brute. What is it that disturbs you?

Sir John. A parson.

Lady Brute. Why, what has he done to you?

Sir John. He has married me. . . *(Exit Sir John)*

If we were attending the play, we could sit back at this point and look forward to many unpleasant things happening to this Sir John Brute.

A note in passing. Does it worry other people – as it does me – that this brute has to be called Brute and his two companions called Lord Rake and Colonel Bully, while Rasor is a valet and Treble a singing master? It is surprising how long it lasted, this morality-play style of naming characters. Even Trollope could call a parson with a large family Mr Quiverful.

The periodical essayists of the *Tatler* and *Spectator* are of course very different from the dramatists who preceded them. The hard wit and bawdy have gone. We have arrived at family reading. We are treated to comic figures – Sir Roger de Coverley, Will Wimble, and the rest – but they are of no great stature. Moreover, such humour as there was in these pieces came from Steele, an Irishman. The stately Addison, his partner, was English enough but far removed from the comic genius of our nation. His praise of cheerfulness offers a key to his character.

I have always preferred cheerfulness to mirth. The latter I consider as an act, the former as an habit of mind. Mirth is short and transient, cheerfulness fixed and permanent.

Those are often raised into the greatest transports of mirth who are subject to the greatest depression of melancholy; on the contrary, cheerfulness, though it does not give the mind such an exquisite gladness, prevents us falling into any depths of sorrow. Mirth is like a flash of lightning that breaks through a gloom of clouds, and glitters for a moment; cheerfulness keeps up a kind of daylight in the mind, and fills it with a steady and perpetual serenity.

This is Safety First counsel that no poet or any true humorist would accept. It explains why the works of Addison are – in the American's account of Matthew Arnold's lectures – 'nowhere to go for a laugh'. If we only saunter along a safe highway, we may escape trouble but we are going to miss the breadth and heights and depths of experience. I am reminded of those doctors of ours, perhaps the new Puritans, who would forbid children to touch fireworks because they might occasionally injure themselves. My memories of childhood tell me that the excitement and glory of fireworks were well worth the risk.

Though we associate Dean Swift with Ireland, he was an Englishman. But only on rare occasions was he a humorous man. For the most part he was about as tolerant and affectionate as a hungry tiger. Embittered by an unhappy childhood and a youth starved of opportunity; aware of his great gifts – impossible to deny – and fiercely ambitious and then cruelly disappointed, though not without loving women and clever friends, he regarded his fellow men not only with contempt but with a terrible disgust. What happened to his Gulliver is one of the supreme ironies of English literary history. How diabolically clever he had been, taking Gulliver to a race of mini-creatures, to mock all regal and State pretences, and then to show him among giants whose immensely enlarged bodies appear obscene! And then, instead of deepening misanthropy, he began to amuse generations of children, delighted by his grave details of life among pygmies and giants. But it is only fair to add that there is still fun, together with much satirical wit, in his account of Laputa, an advance burlesque of our own scientific and technological age.

Such humour as he has is best discovered in his occasional pieces, written at odd moments and probably at high speed. I am thinking now of such things as his *Directions to Servants* and odd verses and his elaborate bantering of the astrologer Partridge, whose death he predicted and then solemnly announced later, in spite of the protests of poor Partridge. He could even laugh at himself, if rather grimly, as in the lines on his own dissolution:

> See, how the dean begins to break!
> Poor gentleman! he droops apace!
> You plainly find it in his face.

(*opposite*) Illustration by Rex Whistler to the 1930 edition of
Gulliver's Travels, by Dean Swift

The Lord Munodi
takes him in his chariot
to see the town of LAGADO.

That old vertigo in his head
Will never leave him till he's dead.
Besides his memory decays:
He recollects not what he says;
He cannot call his friends to mind;
Forgets the place where he has dined;
Plies you with stories o'er and o'er –
He told then fifty times before.
How does he fancy we can sit
To hear his out-of-fashion wit?

Lines that are not altogether farcical, I can tell you, to one octogenarian commentator.

John Gay

It was Swift who suggested to his young friend John Gay that there might be something in a burlesque opera about the rogues and trulls of London. So Gay, already an accomplished writer of witty light verse, created *The Beggar's Opera*, produced successfully by John Rich in 1728 – making, the town said, 'Gay rich and Rich gay.' (The splendid revival, with designs by Lovat Fraser, in the 1920s at the Lyric Theatre, Hammersmith, ran for 1,463 performances.) I owe some of my happiest hours to this famous ballard-opera, either in the theatre or roaring it out round the piano with friends. That very masculine chorus still rings in my head:

Fill ev'ry glass for wine inspires us,
    And fires us
With courage, love and joy.
Women and wine should life employ,
Is there aught else on earth desirous?
Fill ev'ry glass *(etc.)*

(*opposite*) Designs by Lovat Fraser for the production at the Lyric, Hammersmith, of *The Beggar's Opera*, 1920, from the edition of the work published by Heinemann in 1921.
(above) Captain Macheath and Peachum, (below) Lockit and the Beggar

Costume designs by Lovat Fraser;
(left) Mrs Peacham,
(right) Polly Peachum, for the
production at the Lyric,
Hammersmith, of *The Beggar's
Opera*, 1920

I would say that, taken as a whole, there is real humour filtering through this piece – the very idea of it is humorous – but that most of Gay's individual contributions, here as elsewhere, are marked by a light cynical wit. As, for example:

> Do you think your mother and I should have liv'd comfortably so long together, if ever we had been married?
> One wife is too much for one husband to bear,
> But two at a time there's no mortal can bear.
> This way, and that way, and which way I will,
> What would comfort the one, t'other wife would take ill.
> What then in love can women do?
> If we grow fond they shun us;
> And when we fly them, they pursue,
> And leave us when they've won us.
> An inconstant woman, tho' she has no chance to be very happy, can never be very unhappy.

And now to leave Woman for our own contemporary social and political life, this final shaft:

> Fools may our scorn, not envy raise,
> For envy is a kind of praise.

Bravo, John Gay!

Scene from John Gay's *The Beggar's Opera*,
at the Lyric, Hammersmith, 1920

Fifty years ago I introduced to the general reading public *The Diary of Thomas Turner*. He was a humble grocer in East Hoathly, Sussex. He was born in 1729 and his diary runs from 1754 to 1765. He was as candid as Pepys though of course on a much lower social level. On that level he was in many respects a typical eighteenth-century figure, alternating between gloomy introspection, with many thoughts about death (all too frequent in his circle), and uproarious drunken parties, which left him full of remorse. Though wild in his spelling, he was a reading man, fond of Tillotson's *Sermons* and Sherlock's *On Death*. He also alternated between praise of his wife and dismay over her bad temper:

Nov. 2 – Oh! how transient is all mundane bliss! I who, on Sunday last, was all calm and serenity in my breast, am now nought but storm and tempest. Well might the wise man say, 'It were better to dwell in a corner of the house-top, than with a contentious woman in a wide house.'

He had traditional trouble with her mother too, this dame:

Having a very great volubility of tongue for invective, and especially if I am the subject; tho' what the good woman wants with me I know not, unless it be that I have offended her by being too careful of her daughter, who, poor creature, has enjoyed but little pleasure of her life in her marriage state, being almost continually to our great misfortune, afflicted with illness.

She died at twenty-seven, and a few years later Turner married again.

However, we need a longer quotation to give us a clearer picture of the local scene and of the remorseful Thomas Turner. I must add that the Mr Porter, to be discovered in these prolonged binges, was in fact the local parson.

Wednesday, 22nd – About four p.m., I walked down to Whyly. We played at bragg the first part of the even. After ten we went to supper on four boiled chicken, four boiled ducks, minced veal, sausages, cold roast goose, chicken pasty, and ham. Our company, Mr. and Mrs. Porter, Mr. and Mrs. Coates, Mrs. Atkins, Mrs. Hicks, Mr. Piper and wife, Joseph Fuller and wife, tho. Fuller and wife, Dame Durrant myself and wife, and Mr. French's family. After supper our behaviour was far from that of serious, harmless mirth; it was down right obstreperious, mixed with a great deal of folly and stupidity. Our diversion was dancing or jumping about, without a violin or any musick, singing of foolish healths, and drinking all the time as fast as it could be well poured down; and the parson of the parish was one among the mixed multitude. If conscience dictates right from wrong, as doubtless it sometimes does, mine is one that I may say is soon offended; for, I must say, I am always very uneasy at such behaviour, thinking it not like the behaviour of the primitive Christians, which I imagine was most in conformity to our Saviour's gosple. Nor would I be thought to be either a cynick or a stoick, but let social improving discourse pass round the company. About three o'clock, finding myself to have as much liquor as would do me good, I slipt away, unobserved, leaving my wife to make my excuse. Though I was very far from sober, I came home, thank GOD, very safe and well, without even tumbling; and Mr. French's servant brought my wife home, at ten minutes past five.

Thursday, Feb. 25 – This morning about six o'clock just as my wife was got to bed, we was awakened by Mrs. Porter, who pretended she wanted some cream of tartar; bus as soon as my wife got out of bed, she vowed she should come down. She found Mr. Porter, Mr. Fuller and his wife, with a lighted candle, and part of a bottle of wine and a glass. The next thing was to have me down stairs, which being apprized of, I fastened my door. Up stairs they came, and threatened to break it open; so I ordered the boys to open it, when they poured into my room; and, as modesty forbid me to get out of bed, so I refrained; but their immodesty permitted them to draw me out of bed, as the common phrase is, topsy-turvey; but, however, at the intercession of Mr. Porter, they permitted me to put on my . . . and, instead of my upper cloaths, they gave me time to put on my wife's petticoats; and in this manner they made me dance, without shoes and stockings, untill they had emptied the bottle of wine, and also a bottle of my beer. . . . About three o'clock in the afternoon, they found their way to their respective homes, beginning to be a little serious, and, in my opinion, ashamed of their stupid enterprise and drunken preambulation. Now, let any one call in reason to his assistance, and seriously reflect on what I have before recited, and they will join with me in thinking that the precepts delivered from the pulpit on Sunday, tho' delivered with the greatest ardour, must lose a great deal of their efficacy by such examples.

Sunday, March 3 – We had as good a sermon as I ever heard Mr. Porter preach, it being against swearing.

Tuesday, March 7 – We continued drinking like horses, as the vulgar phrase is, and singing till many of us were very drunk, and then we went to dancing and pulling wigs, caps, and hats; and thus we continued in this frantic manner, behaving more like mad people than they that profess the name of Christians. Whether this is consistent to the wise saying of Solomon, let any one judge: 'Wine is a mocker, strong drink is raging, and he that is deceived thereby is not wise.'

March 10 – Supped at Mr. Porter's, where the same scene took place, with the exception that there was no swearing and no ill words, by reason of which Mr. Porter calls it innocent mirth, but I in opinion differ much therefrom.

Saturday, March 11 – At home all day. Very piteous.

I am not setting up poor little Thomas Turner as a rival to Pepys. He is on a lower and narrower level, a village grocer against an important civil servant. But if that diary I edited and introduced fifty years ago can still be found I recommend it as occasional bedside reading. It is at once absurd and rather touching, like much of our life.

CHAPTER 5

Eighteenth-century Giants

Henry Fielding, both as a man and as a writer, is an old favourite of mine. After a reckless youth – he was a big man with large appetites – he matured to be tender-hearted and tough-minded, to have a hard head and a soft heart, unlike some more recent literary figures, who seem to have soft heads and hard hearts. (The film of *Tom Jones*, typical of our time, shows us a Fielding robbed of his very formidable intellect.) It is no part of my task here to show what he did to the English Novel, how he immensely broadened its whole base, how in *Tom Jones* his complicated grand design gives us irony within irony as well as bustling scenes and a crowd of characters.

'Partridge interrupts Tom Jones in his protestations to Lady Bellaston';
engraving by Thomas Rowlandson, from the 1791 edition of *Tom Jones*, by Henry Fielding

Admittedly, he has some devices – notably his trick of describing an alehouse scuffle in mock-epic terms – that seem tedious to us now. But we must approach him here as a humorist, and in this capacity he is best represented by his earlier and slighter novel, *Joseph Andrews*.

This was begun as a burlesque of Richardson's highly successful *Pamela: or, Virtue Rewarded*. Pamela, the beautiful and virtuous maidservant, resists all her master's attempts to seduce her and finally marries him. (A calculating minx really, who if she had been all that virtuous would have left his service for that of a better man.) Elaborate seduction, passing the time for idle men who lacked such recreations as golf and bridge, became meat and drink to Richardson, as it did to whole generations of popular journalists, who worked the same trick as he did, that is, sexually titillating their readers while also arousing their righteous indignation. Fielding showed what he thought about Pamela by taking the same situation but reversing the sexes. Lady Booby became the predator and her handsome young footman, Joseph Andrews, the prey. But this could not last long: Fielding soon burst out from mere burlesque.

However, there is a good ironic scene coming in one of the early chapters. Joseph has been robbed, beaten and left, bleeding and naked, in a ditch. The passengers in a coach hear his cries, and, after a good deal of argument, it is agreed he shall be taken into the coach. But the lady there objects to the presence of a naked man:

> Though there were several greatcoats about the coach, it was not easy to get over this difficulty which Joseph had started. The two gentlemen complained they were cold, and could not spare a rag; the man of wit saying, with a laugh, that charity began at home; and the coachman, who had two greatcoats spread under him, refused to lend either, lest they should be made bloody; the lady's footman desired to be excused for the same reason, which the lady herself, notwithstanding her abhorrence of a naked man, approved: and it is more than probable poor Joseph, who obstinately adhered to his modest resolution, must have perished, unless the postilion (a lad who hath been since transported for robbing a henroost) had voluntarily stripped off a greatcoat, his only garment, at the same time swearing a great oath (for which he was rebuked by the passengers), 'That he would rather ride in his shirt all his life than suffer a fellow-creature to lie in so miserable a condition.'

The two sly remarks in brackets are typical of Fielding.

But the tale is soon dominated by Parson Adams, himself without a glimmer of humour and yet a great comic character. Such characters are either themselves rich humorists, like Falstaff, or are various sorts of innocents and simpletons. Parson Adams might be described – and I think Fielding, who loved Cervantes, would not

(*opposite*) 'Parson Adams's miraculous escape', engraving by J. Hulett, from *The Adventures of Joseph Andrews and his friend Mr Abraham Adams*, by Henry Fielding, 1743

have objected – as a smaller, rural, Church-of-England Don Quixote. The world he often sees is not the real world, which now and again gives him a sharp rap. But it never knocks him down, if only because Fielding has an affection for this character. (Such affection, combined with droll irony, creates the atmosphere in which Adams, as a comic character, grows and flourishes.) An early example of his innocence and absentmindedness is the affair of the sermons. He is taking them to London in a bag, and tries to borrow money with them as security. 'There were in that bag no less than nine volumes of manuscript sermons, as well worth a hundred pounds as a shilling was worth twelve-pence.' The landlord will not accept such security; a fellow parson and a bookseller say that sermons are a drug on the market; but this does not deter Adams. What does is the discovery that there are no sermons in the bag, his wife having replaced them by shirts and other useful articles.

Better still is that talk on vanity. Adams's companion, Wilson, has just savagely denounced vanity, the 'worst of passions, and more apt to contaminate the mind than any other'. This sets Adams alight:

> Adams now began to fumble in his pockets, and soon cried out, 'Oh la! I have it not about me.' Upon this the gentleman asking him what he was searching for, he said he searched after a sermon, which he thought his masterpiece against vanity. 'Fie upon it, fie upon it!' cries he. 'Why do I ever leave that sermon out of my pocket? I wish it was within five miles; I would willingly fetch it to read it to you.' The gentleman answered there was no need, for he was cured of the passion. 'And for that very reason,' quoth Adams, 'I would read it, for I am confident you would admire it; indeed, I have never been a greater enemy to any passion than that silly one of vanity.'

So Adams is vain enough to be ready to walk ten miles in order that his sermon denouncing vanity should be admired. But we are also told that Wilson merely smiled at this display of what he had fiercely attacked as 'the worst of passions'. It is obvious then that vanity is not the worst of passions, and that these moralists are a pair of geese. They are no worse than that because they are innocent at heart. Elsewhere, as Fielding often shows us, sugary humbug and cant may come from a hard heart and act as a cover for downright villainy. And I think that here Fielding exerted a considerable influence on Dickens in his earlier work.

There is a splendid long scene, too long to be quoted in full, that sharply but amusingly contrasts Adam's preaching and practice, his professional codes and his natural heartfelt impulses. The scene is set in the Adams house. Joseph Andrews is impatient to marry his Fanny, and for this he is rebuked by Adams, who produces quite a sermon on marriage, fear as a want of confidence in the Supreme Being, and the danger of setting the affections on a fellow creature. Then a man rushes in to tell Adams that his youngest son is drowned, and Adams is immediately overwhelmed and half-crazy with grief. Joseph in his turn tries to comfort him and even uses some of his own argument. But Adams will have none of them and continues to cry out his loss. However, the boy has been saved, and the joy of Adams is now as wild as his grief had been. But when he has calmed down, he turns moralist again, telling Joseph he must not give way too easily to his earthly affections. Joseph points out that it is easier to give this kind of advice than to act upon it. Adams retorts by declaring that Joseph does not understand the tenderness of fatherly love and that the loss of a child is an unusually great trial. Joseph counters this by saying that it may be as bad to lose a well-beloved mistress, so that Adams, cornered, has to declare:

'Yes, but such love is foolishness and wrong in itself, and ought to be conquered; it savours too much of the flesh.' 'Sure, sir,' says Joseph, 'it is not sinful to love my wife, no, not even to doat upon her to distraction!' 'Indeed, but it is,' says Adams: 'Every man ought to love his wife, no doubt; we are commanded to do so; but we ought to love her with moderation and discretion.' 'I am afraid I shall be guilty of some sin in spite of all my endeavours,' says Joseph; 'for I shall love without any moderation, I am sure.' 'You talk foolishly and childishly,' cried Adams. 'Indeed,' says Mrs. Adams, who had listened to the latter part of their conversation, 'you talk more foolishly yourself. I hope, my dear, you will never preach any such doctrines as that husbands can love their wives too well. If I knew you had such a sermon in the house, I am sure I would burn it; and I declare, if I had not been convinced you had loved me as well as you could, I can answer for myself, I should have hated and despised you. Marry, come up! Fine doctrine indeed! . . .'

But while these extracts are all very well, readers who do not know the novel should meet Parson Adams where he lives, old wig and torn cassock and all, in that work, where he can be brave too on occasion, commanding our respect. When Lady Booby, the village dictator, tells him he must not publish the banns between Joseph and Fanny, he defies her. When the hunting squire and his friends play tricks on and make a fool of this poor bedraggled parson, when at last out of patience, Adams rebukes them manfully. But even in this speech, there are touches that are half-comical, half-pathetic, as for example:

' . . . My appearance might very well persuade you that your invitation was an act of charity, though in reality we were very well provided; yes, sir, if we had had an hundred miles to travel, we had sufficient to bear our expenses in a noble manner.' (At which words he produced the half-guinea which was found in the basket.) 'I do not show you this out of ostentation of riches, but to convince you I speak truth.'

There is all Adams's innocence in that 'ostentation of riches', yet the long speech in which it appears, manfully rebuking the company, has its own essential dignity and courage. The creation of such a character as Parson Adams, born out of irony, absurdity and affection, is a triumph of humour. There is a good deal in Fielding we could now do without – the horseplay and scuffles, the stinking ponds and pigsties, the tedious mock-epic accounts of such things – but what arrives straight from his sense of character, his hard head and generous heart, is so much rare gold. He was a moralist in an age of moralists, but one of a special sort, sweeping away sham, humbug and cant. A last word to readers who have not spent much time in the eighteenth century: Fielding's intellectual rigour, his irony and humour, deserve – and amply reward – more than one reading.

I am always surprised when I remember that Fielding (born April 1707) and Sterne (born November 1713) came into the world so close together. As writers there seems to be an immense gulf between them. This is partly because Fielding looks back to Cervantes while Sterne looks forward to twentieth-century fiction. Perhaps I ought to declare here that while Laurence Sterne was born and passed his childhood in County Tipperary, this was simply because his father's regiment happened to be stationed over there; he is an Englishman. (But there may have been some leprechaun influence at work on his childhood.) He was educated at Halifax and at Cambridge and then spent his time as a parson in Yorkshire. (Incidentally, as readers we rarely acknowledge our enormous debt to the Church of England.) Possibly an early upbringing in Ireland followed by many years in Yorkshire might together explain his dazzling career as a humorist; I don't know; I merely offer a suggestion, knowing something of Ireland and a great deal about Yorkshire, whose people have their full share of unprofessional humorists. I can also declare with more confidence that his *Tristram Shandy* was the combined effort of a determined funny man – asking his printers to play tricks with him: blank or blackened pages; innumerable dots and dashes – and a great original humorist.

Tristram Shandy succeeds by being what an ordinary sensible novel shouldn't be. We expect a steady narrative but Sterne makes no attempt to give us one. So in one place Mr Shandy begins a little speech to his brother Toby, but two chapters go by before he is allowed to finish it. The author is always pretending that he is anxious to press forward to record some crisis, but, being equally anxious to tell us everything, he is perpetually being held up by tiny incidents, odd thoughts, flashes of feeling. This is not mere whimsicality. Indeed, it is this attention to minute details that makes Sterne the father of so much later and deeply subjective fiction. But unlike most of that fiction, his huge daft narrative, in which ordinary time hardly seems to exist, comes out of a humorous vision of this life of ours. The misunderstandings and exasperation in the Shandy household are comic, not sour and bitter as they are in much modern fiction. Sterne asks us to enjoy them. He is not protesting against life but laughing at it, at the same time imploring us not to take ourselves too solemnly. (We have now a number of small but fanatical and very active political groups that ought to stop 'infiltrating' for a few nights, to read *Tristram Shandy*.) These people at Shandy Hall, as we would say now, have a problem, needing, we might add, the help of social workers, sociologists, psychiatrists: they lack effective communication. But this inability to communicate, in Sterne, leads neither to savage satire nor bitter frustration but to rich humour, as I shall explain later.

(*opposite*) Laurence Sterne, by Sir Joshua Reynolds

However, for those readers who do not know their Sterne, a few other explanations should come first. The narrator we meet in the quotations is Tristram
Shandy himself, though we are taken through scores of chapters waiting for him to
be born. Mr Shandy, his father, a retired merchant, is an amateur philosopher, busy
putting together the most intricate arguments and always hoping, though in vain,
that they will be challenged. But his wife either instantly agrees with them or ignores
them; and it is the same with his brother Toby, the retired captain, whose mind is
filled with reminiscences of army life and military history. (He and his servant,
Corporal Trim, two enormous children, spend most of their time conducting mimic
sieges on the bowling-green.) So now we can take a peep or two into Shandy Hall.

> It was a consuming vexation to my father, that my mother never asked the meaning of a
> thing she did not understand. – That she is not a woman of science, my father would say
> – is her misfortune – but she might ask a question. – My mother never did. – In short,
> she went out of the world at last without knowing whether it turned round, or stood still.
> – My father had officiously told her above a thousand times which way it was, – but she
> always forgot . . .

Any practical question she decided at once, not allowing her husband to change her
mind by simply never understanding any of his elaborate arguments:

> Amongst the many and excellent reasons, with which my father had urged my mother
> to accept of Dr. Slop's assistance preferably to that of the old woman, – there was one of
> a very singular nature; which, when he has done arguing the matter with her as a
> Christian, and came to argue it over again with her as a philosopher, he had put his
> whole strength to, depending indeed upon it as his sheet-anchor. – It failed him; tho'
> from no defect in the argument itself; but that, do what he could, he was not able for his
> soul to make her comprehend the drift of it. – Cursed luck! – said he to himself, one
> afternoon, as he walked out of the room, after he had been stating it for an hour and a
> half to her, to no manner of purpose; – cursed luck! said he, biting his lip as he shut the
> door, – for a man to be master of one of the finest chains of reasoning in nature, – and
> have a wife at the same time with such a headpiece, that he cannot hang up a single
> inference within side of it, to save his soul from destruction. . . .

Mr Shandy is no better off with his brother Toby. Indeed, he is worse off because
Toby has a trick of showing some faint gleam of interest in various speculations and
conclusions, but then, when Mr Shandy delightedly warms to the work, hoping to
bring out at last all his proofs, the faint gleam will have vanished, so that when Mr
Shandy has arrived at some astounding paradox, Toby's mind is once more a blank
and he is quietly whistling 'Lillabullero'. When there is some mention of the passage
of time, Mr Shandy asks eagerly, 'Do you understand the theory of that affair?' 'Not
I,' Toby replies, 'But you have some ideas of what you talk about,' Mr Shandy
persists. 'No more than my horse,' Toby tells him. When Mr Shandy, believing

himself to be appallingly ill-used, takes to his bed in despair, a single metaphor of his plunges Toby into reminiscence of army life:

> Did ever man, brother Toby, cried my father, raising himself upon his elbow, and turning himself round to the opposite side of the bed, where my uncle Toby was sitting in his old fringed chair, with his chin resting upon his crutch – did ever a poor unfortunate man, brother Toby, cried my father, receive so many lashes? – The most I ever saw given, quoth my uncle Toby (ringing the bell at the bed's head for Trim) was to a grenadier, I think in Mackay's regiment. – Had my uncle Toby shot a bullet through my father's heart, he could not have fallen down with his nose upon the quilt more suddenly.
> – Bless me! said my uncle Toby.
> – Was it Mackay's regiment, quoth my uncle Toby, where the poor grenadier was so unmercifully whipped at Bruges about the ducats? – Oh Christ! he was innocent! cried Trim, with a deep sigh. – And he was whipped, may it please your honour, almost to death's door . . .

And Mr Shandy, still with his nose upon the quilt, might then have realised that there are lashes and *lashes*.

As I have said elsewhere, there is perhaps nothing richer in the whole book than the scene that follows the one above. Trim talks of his brother Tom, who was tortured upon the rack for nothing but marrying a Jew's widow who sold sausages. Uncle Toby rewards his Corporal with a pension for his long service and goodness of heart. Mr Shandy, in a Socratic posture, holding fast his forefinger between a finger and the thumb of his other hand, discourses on Man and his Destiny with Toby, seated in his old fringed chair, valanced round with parti-coloured worsted bobs. Then the two lovable creatures go downstairs, discussing the name Trismegistus; and Toby catches Mr Shandy on the shinbone with his crutch. However, Mr Shandy forgets his pain in the double success of his repartees. They arrive below in time to ask the maid, Susannah, how her mistress does in childbirth. They are snubbed, and shake their heads together, the married man remarking how all the women in a household give themselves airs when the mistress is brought to bed in childbirth, the bachelor, Toby, pointing out that it is 'we who sink an inch lower. – If I meet but a woman with child – I do it.' So the scepticism and restless intellectual vanity of the one, and the innocence and simple faith of the other, in the face of these mysteries of birth and sex and death, run together and forget their differences in a concerted head-shaking.

Though they find it difficult – or even impossible – to communicate with one another, these people cope with their differences above a depth of steady and tender affection. Without this there would be no humour but satire, possibly – as we often get now in fiction – with some tragedy of frustration and loneliness. Sterne draws us into this atmosphere of affection with great skill, just as he creates with equal skill not only the members of the household but also the various people outside it. But this affection, real and true, must not be confused with his moments of all-too-determined sentimentality, when we can almost see him standing aside, ready to grin at the tears he hopes to see in our eyes. This is one of his faults, like his sniggering indecencies, far more embarrassing than honest bawdy. Indeed, he has so many faults – an overdone whimsicality, sly plagiarisms, all narrative broken and held up by a desire to show off – that I have often wondered if there could not be at least one version of *Tristram Shandy* fairly severely edited, clearing away a good deal of rubbish. There would be plenty of real gold in what remained. Sterne must be given a very high place indeed among English humorists. And there is more than mere whimsicality in his insistence upon the importance of tiny details, the way in which our lives are affected by little accidents, odd thoughts, sudden flashes of feeling. We have seen his close-up method and manner repeated over and over again in the later fiction of a dozen different countries. What has been chiefly lacking is the atmosphere of affection he was able to create, an atmosphere in which a true humorist can flourish. We are now living in a world that has made immense gains in discovery, invention, know-how, but is hardly impressive in its gross national products of affection.

(*opposite*) Four watercolour drawings for *Tristram Shandy*, by John Nixon, 1786

Toby's Courtship with Widow Wadman

CHAPTER 6

Some 'Characters'

In my book on *The English*, where I discussed Dr Johnson as one of our great national figures, I was compelled to point out that many of his famous sayings were now unacceptable, sheer nonsense to any sensible man. For example, his idea that people could be content under any form of government. How long would he have lasted under Hitler or Stalin? But with Humour our subject, we need another approach. Johnson was certainly no professional humorist. He became a humorist late in life and, so to speak, after hours, when he could leave his dark brooding over the ills of this life and our dreaded entry into the next, for what he liked best of all – good company in a good tavern and plenty of rousing talk. (Doesn't he tell us that when we are solitary we must not be idle, and when we are idle we must not be solitary?) Now though we owe a huge debt to Boswell, he is apt to cheat us when we are looking for Johnson as a boon companion, ready to welcome nonsense and laughter:

> I passed many hours with him on the 17th, of which I find all my memorial is, 'Much laughing.' It should seem he had that day been in a humour for jocularity and merriment, and upon such occasions I never knew a man laugh more heartily. We may suppose, that the high relish of a state so different from his habitual gloom, produced more than ordinary exertions of that distinguishing faculty of man, which has puzzled philosophers so much to explain. . . .

This is maddening. The grand old man frolics away and we are not allowed to be there, Boswell being so anxious to show us the disputatious sage and social philosopher. Yet Sir John Hawkins could say, of Johnson, 'He was the most humorous man I ever knew.'

(*opposite*) Detail from 'Dr Johnson at Vauxhall', exhibited 1784, watercolour by Thomas Rowlandson

Favouring the more humorous, I take a handful out of the bushel of possible quotations:

Your levellers wish to level *down* as far as themselves; but they cannot bear levelling *up* to themselves.

This was a good dinner enough, to be sure; but it was not a dinner to *ask* a man to.

Nothing is more hopeless than a scheme of merriment.

You must not mind me, madam; I say strange things, but I mean no harm.

It is very strange and very melancholy that the paucity of human pleasures should ever persuade us ever to call hunting one of them.

I do not know, sir, that the fellow is an infidel; but if he be an infidel, he is an infidel as a dog is an infidel; that is to say, he has never thought upon the subject.

I would be loath to speak ill of any person who I do not know deserves it, but I am afraid he is an attorney.

Sir, you have but two topics, yourself and me. I am sick of both.

The Irish are a fair people; they never speak well of one another.

If he does really think that there is no distinction between virtue and vice, why, sir, when he leaves our houses let us count our spoons.

When men come to like a sea life they are not fit to live on land.

Whoever thinks of going to bed before twelve o'clock is a scoundrel.

Are we alive after all this satire!

He [Charles James Fox] talked to me at club one day concerning Cataline's conspiracy – so I withdrew my attention and thought about Tom Thumb.

As I know more about mankind I expect less of them, and am ready now to call a man *a good man*, upon easier terms than I was formerly.

Praise of everybody is praise of nobody.

If I had no duties, and no reference to futurity, I would spend my life in driving briskly in a postchaise with a pretty woman.

However, we cannot leave him there. Don't we find something humorous in *character* itself if there is a massive bulk of it, especially if it is crammed with sense and nonsense, with sturdy qualities mixed with prejudices, whims, sheer oddities, and above all if it is lovable? If the eighteenth century itself were a novel, then Samuel Johnson, taking his ease at last, seeking out good company, expressing himself freely on all topics, would be one of that novel's great comic characters, perhaps its greatest. We remember him when so many of that age's important personages have faded from our memory. We would rather meet him – even if we had to risk one of his crushing retorts – than any of its prime ministers, generals, or admirals. He lives in our affection.

So, too, does his closest rival in terms of humorous personality – Charles Lamb. Unlike Johnson, Lamb never even thought of himself as a literary man, a public author, except perhaps during his later years when he was bringing out his *Essays of Elia*. His humour was not an idle thing, but the white flower plucked from a dangerous nettle. Because his older sister, Mary, was subject to fits of madness – and she stabbed their mother to death – he had to be the responsible member of his family, keeping the home going with his clerkship at the East India Company, combining infinite tender concern with an iron discipline over his own life, forswearing marriage, children, any absence from his desk drudgery until his final retirement. When he knew that his sister was losing her mind again, he would take her to the asylum; they would be seen going there together, arm in arm, weeping. When Carlyle patronised him as a rickety Cockney tomfool, Carlyle never realised that he had been facing a better and stronger man than himself, one who made less fuss about his drudgery and dedicated life than Carlyle did about a stomach ache or a noise in the street. The great writers who were his friends knew all about Lamb. Even the rather priggish Wordsworth, who had seen Lamb tipsy and mischievous more than once, who was there when Lamb insisted upon feeling the bumps of that other Commissioner of Stamps (a solemn bore), could declare, 'O, he was good, if e'er a good man lived!'

Lamb's whimsicality, both in talk and in print, was a holiday from his grave responsibilities. We can occasionally catch glimpses of the dark depths below. 'My waking life has much of the confusion, the trouble and obscure perplexity of an ill dream. In the daytime I stumble upon dark mountains.' Or again: 'I love to lose myself in other men's minds. When I am not walking, I am reading; I cannot sit and think. Books think for me.' (But he was in fact a superb and most subtle critic.) However, he could be blandly impudent about books:

> I can read any thing which I call a book. There are things in that shape which I cannot allow for such. In this catalogue of books which are no books – biblia a-biblia – I reckon Court Calendars, Directories . . . the works of Hume, Gibbon, Robertson, Beattie, Soame Jenyns, and, generally, all those volumes which 'no gentleman's library should be without'.

His dislike of the unknown (including all travel to it) was largely whimsical, humorous; his affection for the known and familiar was deep and lasting. He wrote to Wordsworth:

> Separate from the pleasure of your company, I don't much care if I never see a mountain in my life. I have passed all my days in London, until I have formed as many

and intense local attachments, as any of you mountaineers can have done with dead nature. The lighted shops of the Strand and Fleet Street, the innumerable trades, tradesmen and customers, coaches, waggons, playhouses, all the bustle and wickedness round about Covent Garden, the very women of the Town, the watchmen, drunken scenes, rattles. . . . The sun shining upon houses and pavements, the print shops, the old book stalls, the parsons cheap'ning books, coffee houses, steams of soup from kitchens, the pantomimes, London itself as a pantomime and masquerade – all these things work themselves into my mind and feed me, without a power of satiating me. . . .

Dr Johnson would have roared his approval of Lamb's love of London, and might have clapped his hands at this:

A garden was the primitive prison till man with promethean felicity and boldness luckily sinn'd himself out of it. Thence followed Babylon, Nineveh, Venice, London, haberdashers, goldsmiths, taverns, playhouses, satires, epigrams, puns – these all came in on the town part, and the thither side of innocence. Man found out inventions.

Unfailing in his kindness and sympathy when they were really needed, he could be humorously sharp in tedious company. When a woman bored him by praising at length 'a charming man' and ended by exclaiming, 'And well I know him, bless him!', Lamb replied, 'Well, I don't, but damn him, at a hazard.' When Dr Parr asked him how he contrived to puff so much smoke out of his pipe, Lamb said he had 'toiled after it as other men after virtue'. And probably he surprised the stately Macready by declaring that he wished to draw his last breath through a pipe and exhale it in a pun. 'I was at Hazlitt's marriage,' he wrote to Southey, 'and had like to have been turned out several times during the ceremony. Anything awful makes me laugh. I misbehaved once at a funeral.' And to a friend who played whist with him he could cry, 'Martin, if dirt were trumps, what hands you would hold!' But at the loss of an old friend he could ache with regret:

In him I have a loss the world cannot make up. He was my friend and my father's friend all the life I can remember. I seem to have made foolish friendships ever since. Those are friendships which outlive a second generation. Old as I am waxing, in his eyes I was still the child he first knew me. To the last he called me Charley. I have none to call me Charley now. . . .

There are many highly poetic elegies that never distil as much grief and regret as that.

His remarks – e.g. 'The greatest pleasure I know, is to do a good action by stealth, and to have it found out by accident' – and his letters are better than his essays, in which the whimsies are sometimes over-elaborated. Some of his best letters are to his friend, Manning, and when Manning went as far away as China, Lamb pretends to rebuke him for being away for ages, so long that time has brought death and

Charles Lamb, 1798, by Robert Hancock

desolation among the people and places they both knew. It is a lengthy letter, but it is worth quoting because it seems to me a masterpiece of solemn nonsense, grave fooling, with all its scattered points made with superb skill:

Empires have been overturned, crowns trodden into dust, the face of the western world quite changed: your friends have all got old – those you left blooming – myself (who am one of the few that remember you) those golden hairs which you recollect my taking a pride in, turned to silver and grey. Mary has been dead and buried many years, she desired to be buried in the silk gown you sent her. Rickman, that you remember, active and strong, now walks out supported by a servantmaid and a stick. Martin is a very old man. The other day an aged woman knocked at my door, and pretended to my acquaintance; it was long before I had the most distant cognition of her; but at last together we made her out to be Louisa, the daughter of Mrs. Topham, formerly Mrs. Kenney, whose first husband was Holcroft, the dramatic writer of the last century. St. Paul's Church is a heap of ruins; the monument isn't half so high as you knew it, divers parts being successfully taken down which the ravages of time had rendered dangerous; the horse at Charing Cross is gone, no one knows whither, and all this has taken place while you have been settling whether Ho-hing-tong should be spelt with a – or a –. For aught I see you had almost as well remain where you are, and not come like a Struldbug into a world where few were born when you went away. Scarce here and there one will be able to make out your face; all your opinions will be out of date, your jokes obsolete, your puns rejected with fastidiousness as wit of the last age. Your way of mathematics has already given way to a new method, which after all is, I belive, the old doctrine of Maclaurin, new-vamped up with what he borrowed of the negative quantity of fluxions from Euler.

Poor Godwin! I was passing his tomb the other day in Cripplegate churchyard. There are some verses upon it written by Miss Hayes, which if I thought good enough I would send you. He was one of those who would have hailed your return, not with boisterous shouts and clamours, but with the complacent gratulations of a philosopher anxious to promote knowledge as leading to happiness – but his systems and his theories are ten feet deep in Cripplegate mould. Coleridge is just dead, having lived just long enough to close the eyes of Wordsworth, who paid the debt to nature but a week or two before. Poor Col. but two days before he died wrote to a bookseller proposing an epic poem on the 'Wanderings of Cain' in twenty-four books. It is said he has left behind him more than four thousand treatises in criticism and metaphysics, but few of them in a state of completion. They are now destined, perhaps, to wrap up spices. . . . Gather up your wretched reliques, my friend, as fast as you can, and come to your old home. I will rub my eyes and try to recognise you. We will shake withered hands together, and talk of old things, of St. Mary's Church and the barber's opposite, where the young students in mathematics used to assemble. Poor Crisp, that kept it, afterwards set up a fruiterer's shop in Trumpington Street, and for aught I know resides there still, for I saw the name up in the last journey I took there with my sister just before she died. I suppose you heard that I had left the India House, and gone into the Fishmongers' Almhouses over the bridge. I have a little cabin there, small and homely, but you shall be welcome to it. You like oysters, and to open them yourself; I'll get you some if you come in oyster time. . . .

Lamb died before he reached sixty, and his last years, spent too far from his beloved London, brought him little happiness. Everybody and everything were going . . . going . . . gone. He often thought about death, wondering what – '. . . fireside conversations, innocent vanities, and jests, and *irony itself* . . .' – might outlast it. There could be plenty of irony for him to enjoy. His odd remarks and scribblings at his office desk have long outlasted the epics of his friend Southey. The whimsical clerk has been promoted far above the solemn professional authors. He died with few close friends left. Now he has a million.

The only Prime Minister I propose to bring into this chronicle is George Canning. In his high-spirited youth he was chiefly responsible for *The Anti-Jacobin*, in which he and his Tory companions mocked the revolutionary spirit of the age. One of its most famous squibs – and certainly Canning's work – is the encounter between 'The Friend of Humanity' and 'The Needy Knifegrinder', a sad disappointment as a prospective revolutionary:

> I give thee sixpence! I will see thee damn'd first –
> Wretch! whom no sense of wrongs can rouse to vengeance;
> Sordid, unfeeling, reprobate, degraded,
>   Spiritless outcast!
> *(Kicks the knife-grinder, overturns his wheel, and exit in a transport of republican enthusiasm and universal philanthropy.)*

There is some lively fooling in their burlesque of German Romanticism, *The Rovers*, which had songs like this:

> There, first for thee my passion grew,
> Sweet! sweet Matilda Pottingen!
> Thou wast the daughter of my Tu-
> -tor, Law Professor at the U-
> -niversity of Gottingen!
> -niversity of Gottingen!

It also contains my favourite stage direction of all time:

> Several soldiers cross the stage wearily, as if returning from the Thirty Years' War.

One verse of Canning's has come to us down the years, its appeal hardly weakened:

> Give me the avowed, the erect, the manly foe;
> Bold I can meet – perhaps may turn his blow;
> But of all plagues, good Heaven, thy wrath can send,
> Save, save, oh! save me from the Candid Friend!

What a pity there is no Canning to appear on our political party broadcasts!

Even so, I would exchange half a dozen Cannings for one Sydney Smith, one of my favourite characters, for whose sake once again I salute the Church of England. He was the only parson we know of who could be so funny that he could make his fellow guests cry with laughter. (See Tom Moore's Diary.) Yet he could set aside his cap-and-bells – though not for too long – to plead eloquently for toleration, for reform, for a liberal humane outlook; and in his own life was a model of cheerful energy, good sense, fun and wit. If 'thinking in fun while feeling in earnest' is a recipe for humour, then he was – as I believe him to be – a great humorist. Though fond of dining out, especially at a lavish table, he preserved his independence, was never subservient to the powerful and the rich. The famous Whig hostess, Lady Holland, an imperious woman, once cried to him. 'Sydney, ring the bell', to which he replied, 'And shall I sweep the room too.' Whether removed to a remote rural parish ('ten miles from a lemon', he declared) or a Canon of St Paul's, he was always his cheerful, energetic, witty and wise self. One of his amusing anecdotes testifies to his popularity as a guest in London society:

> Lord Dudley was one of the most absent men I think I have ever met in society. One day he met me in the street, and invited me to meet myself. 'Dine with me today; dine with me, and I will get Sydney Smith to meet you.' I admitted the temptation he held out to me, but said I was engaged to meet him elsewhere.

I could probably fill the remainder of this chapter with quotable examples of his wit, humour, and sharp common sense, and while being generous I must restrain myself:

> Bishop Berkeley destroyed this world in one volume octavo; and nothing remained, after his time, but mind; which experienced a similar fate from the hand of Mr. Hume in 1737.

> What makes a fire so pleasant is, I think, that it is a live thing in a dead room.

> The weather is beautiful; but as Noodle says (with his eyes beaming with delight) 'We shall suffer for this, sir, by-and-by.'

> No one minds what Jeffrey says – it is not more than a week ago when I heard him speak disrespectfully of the Equator.

> It is a place with only one post a day. . . . In the country I always fear that creation will expire before tea-time.

> I have seen nobody since I saw you, but persons in orders. My only varieties are vicars, rectors, curates, and every now and then (by way of turbot) an archdeacon.

> How can a bishop marry? How can he flirt? The most he can say is, 'I will see you in the vestry after service.'

> The luxury of false religion is to be unhappy.

> Avoid shame but do not seek glory – nothing so expensive as glory.

> My idea of heaven is eating *pâtés de foie gras* to the sound of trumpets.

> You never expected justice from a company, did you? They have neither a soul to love nor a body to kick.

Macaulay is like a book in breeches. . . . He not only overflowed with learning, but stood in the slop. . . . He has occasional flashes of silence that make his conversation perfectly delightful. . . .

Marriage resembles a pair of shears, so joined that they cannot be separated, often moving in opposite directions, yet always punishing anyone who comes between them.

One evil in old age is, that as your time is come, you think every little illness is the beginning of the end. When a man expects to be arrested, every knock at the door is an alarm.

And now that we have high taxation, heavy duties, VAT, we can appreciate the following:

The schoolboy whips his taxed top – the beardless youth manages his taxed horse, with a taxed bridle, on a taxed road; – and the dying Englishman, pouring his medicine, which has paid seven per cent, into a spoon that has paid fifteen per cent – flings himself back upon his chintz bed, which has paid twenty-two per cent – and expires in the arms of an apothecary who has paid a licence of a hundred pounds for the privilege of putting him to death.

He disliked the Methodists, at that time a narrow Puritanical sect, and castigated their outlook in these memorable terms:

The Methodists hate pleasure and amusements; no theatre, no cards, no dancing, no punchinello, no dancing dogs, no blind fiddlers; – all the amusements of the rich and the poor must disappear, wherever these gloomy people get a footing. It is not the abuse of pleasure they attack, but the interspersion of pleasure, however much it is guided by good sense and moderation. It is not only wicked to hear the licentious plays of Congreve, but wicked to hear Henry the Fifth, or the School for Scandal. It is not only dissipated to run about all the parties in London and Edinburgh, but dancing is not *fit for a being who is preparing himself for Eternity*. Ennui, wretchedness, melancholy, groans and sighs, are the offerings which these unhappy men make to a Deity who has covered the earth with gay colours and scented it with rich perfumes, and shown us, by the plan and order of his works, that he has given to man something better than a bare existence and scattered over his creation a thousand superfluous joys which are totally unnecessary to the mere support of life. . . .

A speech on the Reform Bill would not appear to offer much chance of humour, but here is part of one that Sydney Smith made:

. . . What right has *this* Lord, or *that* Marquis, to buy ten seats in Parliament, in the shape of Boroughs, and then to make laws to govern me? And how are these masses of power re-distributed? The eldest son of my Lord has just come from Eton; he knows a good deal about Aeneas and Dido, Apollo and Daphne; and that is all. And to this boy his father gives a six-hundredth part of the power of making laws, as he would give him a horse or a double barrelled gun. Then Vellum the steward is put in – an admirable man; – he has raised the estates – watched the progress of the family Road and Canal Bills – Vellum shall help to rule over the people of Israel. A neighbouring country gentleman, Mr. Plumpkin, hunts with my Lord – opens him a gate or two while the hounds are running – dines with my Lord – agrees with my Lord – wishes he could rival the South Down sheep of my Lord – and upon Plumpkin is conferred a portion of the government. Then there is a distant relation of the same name, in the County Militia, with white teeth, who calls up the carriage at the Opera and is always wishing O'Connell was hanged, drawn, and quartered – then a barrister, who has written an article in the Quarterly, and is very likely to speak, and refute M'Culloch; and these five people, in whose nomination I have no more agency than I have in the nomination of the toll-keepers of the Bosphorus, are to make laws for me and my family – to put their hands in my purse and to sway the future destinies of this country; and when the neighbours step in and beg permission to say a few words before these persons are chosen, there is an universal cry of ruin, confusion, and destruction; we have become a great people under Vellum and Plumpkin – under Vellum and Plumpkin our ships have covered the ocean – under Vellum and Plumpkin our armies have secured the strength of the Hills – to turn out Vellum and Plumpkin is not Reform, but Revolution.

I have just turned to a life of Sydney Smith by my old friend from Cambridge days, now lost to me, Gerald Bullett, a good writer and a fastidious man. He writes with the enthusiasm his subject deserves. He tells us that even in his last months of sickness and pain, Sydney Smith could describe his condition with humour: 'I am weak, and taking all proper care of myself:,which care consists of eating nothing I like and doing nothing that I wish.' Again: 'If you hear of sixteen or eighteen pounds of human flesh, they belong to me. I look as if a curate had been taken out of me.' I cannot improve upon Bullett's final paragraph; so here it is:

He died on the 22nd February 1845, 'at peace with himself and all the world. . . .' 'And now dear Children I have done,' writes Catherine Smith at the end of her narrative. 'After passing nearly half a century with *such* a man I am alone . . . the Light of my Life is extinguished.' Yet for her as she writes of him, as for us who may still enjoy his ghostly company, his courage and gaiety and goodness, something of that light lives on; and from the shattered lamp there rises, subtle and pervasive, 'the aromatic smell of wisdom'.

I feel as if I am saying Hail and Farewell to two old friends.

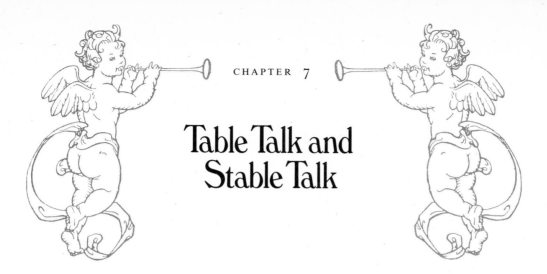

CHAPTER 7

Table Talk and Stable Talk

We have now to tackle a more complicated character – Thomas Love Peacock. If, as some people tell us, Peacock is very much an acquired taste, then all I can say is that I acquired it very early, because I well recall in my youth digging around for second-hand copies of his works. (This was years before I wrote the *English Men of Letters* volume on him.) In my view, he should be seen first of all as a humorist. There is plenty of satire in his work, but it is largely humorous, not sour, not savage, but mostly indulgent, whimsical, genial. His writing was a holiday from his responsible posts with the East India Company, where he rose to be Chief Examiner, succeeding the dour James Mill and finally giving up his place to John Stuart Mill. He had neither the ambition not the vanity of the solemn professional author. Before he amused his readers, he was amusing himself. He cannot be pinned down and neatly labelled, if only because he shows us widely different and, indeed, contradictory opinions, tastes, prejudices, a High Tory at one end of his scale and a Radical at the other. We might say that he could dine happily one night with fellow admirers of Ancient Greece and be equally comfortable the next night with the Utilitarians, Bentham himself being one of his friends. All this is understandable if we discover behind his writing an essential humorist.

The usual reference-book description of him as a novelist has probably done him more harm than good. People looking for another sensible novel have retired, baffled and probably angry. He was not a novelist and never pretended to be. He comes nearest to being one when he describes, often with considerable charm, the remote places where his characters assemble to sit round a dining table and talk and talk while passing and sampling the claret or madeira. Most of these characters – though there are some notable exceptions – tend to be rather sketchily personified opinions, daft obsessions, monstrous prejudices. So far as they are based on real people – as some of them clearly are – his creatures are caricatures of public attitudes, ignoring the private lives of his victims. Among the few sensible persons in his house parties are the best of his young women, very different from the simpering dolls in the novels of his time. In this matter English fiction owes something to Peacock, who greatly influenced his son-in-law, George Meredith.

The table talk that dominates these so-called 'novels' is very good talk indeed. However absurd his characters may be, they not only share the wine that goes round and round but also share Peacock's superb prose style. We can enjoy a taste of it from *Crotchet Castle*, perhaps the best of these table talk books:

> *The Stranger*. I beg your pardon, sir: do I understand this place to be your property?
> *The Rev. Dr. Folliott*. It is not mine, sir: the more is the pity; yet it is so far well, that the owner is my good friend, and a highly respectable gentleman.
> *The Stranger*. Good and respectable, sir, I take it, mean rich?
> *The Rev. Dr. Folliott*. That is their meaning, sir.

And, a moment later:

> *The Stranger*. Young Mr. Crotchet, sir, has been like his father, the architect of his own fortune, has he not? An illustrious example of the reward of honesty and industry?
> *The Rev. Dr. Folliott*. As to honesty, sir, he made his fortune in the city of London; and if that commodity be of any value there, you will find it in the price current. I believe it is below par, like the shares of young Crotchet's fifty companies. . . .

Later, at the dinner table, the assembled theorists all produce manuscripts to explain their schemes to regenerate society, but are defeated by Dr Folliott:

> *The Rev. Dr. Folliott*. See through a wine-glass; full of claret; then you see both darkly and brightly. But, gentlemen, if you are all in the humour for reading papers, I will read you the first half of my next Sunday's sermon. *(Produces a paper)*
> *Omnes*. No sermon! No sermon!
> *The Rev. Dr. Folliott*. Then I move that our respective papers be committed to our respective pockets.

However, I am now going to move away from the table talk books to a work entirely different, a narrative based on old Welsh legends, namely, *The Misfortunes of Elphin*. I do this for two reasons. First, it is a great favourite of mine. Secondly, it is underestimated and indeed too often left unread.

We have two reasons again to explain the Welsh setting. Peacock, who had an eye for landscape, loved the mountain scenery of Wales. Secondly, he married a Welsh girl. The way he set about doing this proves that he could play the whimsical philosopher, probably the humorist, even in his intimate private life. Not for eight years had he seen Jane Gryffydh again or exchanged any words with her, but then he coolly made her an offer of marriage by letter, beginning:

> It is more than eight years since I had the happiness of seeing you. I can scarcely hope that you have remembered me as I have remembered you; yet I feel confident that the simplicity and ingenuousness of your disposition will prompt you to answer me with the same candour with which I write to you. . . .

And then he goes on, in the same stately manner, to explain his new comparative prosperity, the circumstances that confine him to London, and so on and so forth, but also tells her that the greatest blessing the world could bestow on him would be to make her his wife. No man in his senses would bet money on how a girl would receive this astonishing proposal, but it is a fact that five months later they were married near her home and were then on their way to London. It was for many years a good marriage until Jane's health began to break down after the loss of their favourite child, Margaret aged three. It was for her tombstone that Peacock wrote his most touching poem, beginning:

> Long night succeeds thy little day;
>   Oh blighted blossom! can it be,
> That this grey stone and grassy clay
>   Have closed our anxious care of thee?

There are few occasions that a born humorist cannot cope with, but one of them is the death of a favourite daughter at the age of three.

Thomas Love Peacock, about 1805,
by Roger Jean

Life is too short – at least my life is – to describe all that happens in *The Misfortunes of Elphin*. But his introduction to the remote scene offers Peacock ample opportunity for bland sarcasm and irony. Here is a tasting sample:

. . . Of moral science they had little; but morals without science, they had about the same as we have. They had a number of fine precepts, partly from their religion, partly from their bards, which they remembered in their liquor, and forgot in their business.

Political science they had none. The blessings of virtual representation were not even dreamed of; so that when any of their barbarous metallic currency got into their pockets or coffers, it had a chance to remain there, subjecting them to the inconvenience of unemployed capital. Still they went to work politically much as we do. The powerful took all they could get from their subjects and neighbours; and called something or other sacred and glorious, when they wanted the people to fight for them. They repressed disaffection by force, when it showed itself in an overt act; but they encouraged freedom of speech, when it was, like Hamlet's reading, 'words, words, words'.

There is a great deal more in this vein, belonging to the radical side of Peacock's rich nature.

Much of the action is concerned with an enormous embankment that is in danger of being ruined by neglect, because the Lord High Commissioner of Royal Embankment, we are told, 'drank the profits and left the embankment to his deputies, who left it to their assistants, who left it to itself'. This High Commissioner, Prince Seithenyn, is the tale's triumph. He is a huge comic character, and, outside Shakespeare, the best toper, never met out of his cups, in English Literature. He is reeling drunk when we first meet him but is ready to do some debating:

'Prince Seithenyn,' said Elphin, 'I have visited you on a subject of deep moment. Reports have been brought to me that the embankment, which has been so long entrusted to your care, is in a state of dangerous decay.'

'Decay,' said Seithenyn, 'is one thing, and danger is another. Everything that is old must decay. That the embankment is old, I am free to confess; that it is somewhat rotten in parts, I will not altogether deny; that it is any the worse for that, I do most sturdily gainsay. It does its business well: it works well: it keeps out the water from the land, and it lets in the wine upon the High Commission of Embankment. Cup-bearer, fill. Our ancestors were wiser than we: they built it in their wisdom; and, if we should be so rash as to try to mend it, we should only mar it.'

'The stonework,' said Teithrin, 'is sapped and mined: the piles are rotten, broken, and dislocated: the floodgates and sluices are leaky and creaky.'

'That is the beauty of it,' said Seithenyn. 'Some parts of it are rotten, and some parts of it are sound.'

'It is well,' said Elphin, 'that some parts are sound: it were better that all were so.'

'So I have heard some people say before,' said Seithenyn; 'perverse people, blind to venerable antiquity: that very unamiable sort of people who are in the habit of indulging their reason. But I say, the parts that are rotten give elasticity to those that are sound: they give them elasticity, elasticity, elasticity. If it were all sound, it would break by its own obstinate stiffness: the soundness is checked by the rottenness, and the stiffness is balanced by the elasticity. There is nothing so dangerous as innovation. See the waves in the equinoctial storms, dashing and clashing, roaring and pouring, spattering and battering, rattling and battling against it. I would not be so presumptuous as to say, I could build anything that would stand against them half-an-hour; and here this immortal old work, which God forbid the finger of modern mason should bring into jeopardy, this immortal work has stood for centuries, and will stand for centuries more, if we let it alone. It is well: it works well: let well alone. Cupbearer, fill. It was half rotten when I was born, and that is a conclusive reason why it should be three parts rotten when I die.'

The whole body of the High Commission roared approbation.

'And after all,' said Seithenyn, 'the worst that could happen would be the overflow of a springtide, for that was the worst that happened before the embankment was thought of; and, if the high water should come in, as it did before, the low water would go out again, as it did before. We should be no deeper in it than our ancestors were, and we could mend as easily as they could make.'

'The level of the sea,' said Teithrin, 'is materially altered.'

'The level of the sea!' exclaimed Seithenyn. 'Who ever heard of such a thing as altering the level of the sea? Alter the level of that bowl of wine before you, in which, as I sit here, I see a very ugly reflection of your very good-looking face. Alter the level of that: drink up the reflection: let me see the face without the reflection, and leave the sea to level itself.'

'Not to level the embankment,' said Teithrin.

'Good, very good,' said Seithenyn. 'I love a smart saying, though it hits at me. But whether yours is a smart saying or no, I do not very clearly see; and, whether it hits at me or no, I do not very sensibly feel. But all is one. Cupbearer, fill.'

To contemporary readers, Seithenyn's defence of the embankment was a broad parody of Canning's defence of the British Constitution, but it seems to me that to us, who care nothing about Canning's tactics, this scene is welcome for its own sake. It has a tiny encore when Seithenyn turns up again after being missing for twenty years:

The stranger goggled about his eyes in an attempt to fix them steadily on Taliesin. . . . After a silence, which he designed to be very dignified and solemn, the stranger spoke again: 'I am the man.'

'What man?' said Taliesin.

'The man,' replied his entertainer, 'of whom you spoke so disparagingly: Seithenyn ap Seithyn Saidi.'

'Seithenyn,' said Taliesin, 'has slept twenty years under the waters of the western sea, as King Gwythno's *Lamentations* have made known to all Britain.'

'They have not made it known to me,' said Seithenyn, 'for the best of all reasons, that one can only know the truth: for, if that which we think we know is not truth, it is something which we do not know. A man cannot know his own death; for, while he knows anything, he is alive; at least, I never heard of a dead man who knew anything, or pretended to know anything; if he had so pretended, I should have told him to his face he was no dead man.'

With this example of ripe and reeling logic we leave Peacock, not everybody's man, but a rare find to readers who delight in wit, humour and good writing.

We come a long way down the scale to reach Marryat, a capital story teller, given to knockabout fun, but only on rare occasions a real humorist. There is some acceptable drollery in his Mr Easy, that domestic philosopher, with his theory of names and his proposed system of improving upon nature by compressing or enlarging men's bumps. But his Mr Chucks, the genteel bosun, is even better. He too is an authority upon names:

'No name can be too fine for a pretty girl, or a good frigate, Mr. Simple; for my part I'm very fond of these hard names. Your Bess, and Poll, and Sue, do very well for the Point, or Castle Rag; but in my opinion they degrade a lady. Don't you observe, Mr. Simple, that all our gunbrigs, a sort of vessel that will certainly damn the inventor to all eternity, have nothing but low, common names, such as Pincher, Thrasher, Boxer, Badger, and all that sort, which are quite good enough for them; whereas all our dashing, saucy frigates have names as long as the maintop bowling, and hard enough to break your jaw – such as Melpomeny, Terpsichory, Arethusy, Baccanty – as long as their pennants which dip alongside in a calm.'

'Very true,' replied I; 'but do you think then, that it is the same with family names?'

'Most certainly, Mr. Simple. 'When I was in good society, I rarely fell in with such names as Potts, or Bell, or Smith, or Hodges; it was always Mr Fortesque, or Mr FitzGerald, or Mr FitzHerbert; seldom bowed, sir, to anything under *three* syllables.'

'Then I presume, Mr Chucks, you are not fond of your own name?'

'There you touch me, Mr Simple; but it is quite good enough for a boatswain,' replied Mr Chucks with a sigh.

No heights or depths there, but it will pass as humour.

A number of Early Victorian writers, dazzled by the immense success of *Pickwick Papers*, tried to do something of the same sort. It is only fair to Surtees – and I want to be fair because I don't care for him – to point out that he came before Dickens in the comic sporting line, set up the *New Sporting Magazine* in 1831 and then introduced Jorrocks to his readers. His *Handley Cross*, the saga of Jorrocks as Master of Foxhounds, has been reprinted over and over again right down to our own time. Its popularity amazes me. It must extend far beyond hunters and huntresses. Yet what is the general reader offered? One little scene has been quoted often enough, and if I include it here, this is chiefly in view of what will follow:

The fire began to hiss, and Mr. Jorrocks felt confident his prophecy was about to be fulfilled. 'Look out of the winder, James, and see wot-un a night it is,' said he to Pigg, giving the log a stir, to ascertain that the hiss didn't proceed from any dampness in the wood.

James staggered up, and after a momentary grope about the room – for they were sitting without candles – exclaimed: 'Hellish dark, and smells of cheese!'

'Smells o' cheese!' repeated Mr. Jorrocks, looking round in astonishment: 'smells o' cheese! – vy, man, you've got your nob i' the cupboard – this be the winder!'

'Mr Jorrocks has a Bye Day', illustration by John Leech to *Handley Cross, or Mr Jorrocks' Hunt*, by Robert Smith Surtees, 1854

Now for a confession. Hoping to improve upon this familiar scene, I began, after half a century, to re-read *Handley Cross*. Somewhere about the middle of it, I gave up, having had enough.

There is plenty of energy and movement, together with an occasional real sense of hunters and hounds in the open air, but these do not seem to me to excuse the book's crudities, vulgarities and repetitions. It is facetious not genuinely humorous. Surtees is not a humorist but a relentless, determined funny man: a kind of writer that was to prosper from his time onwards. Hunting people may rejoice in Jorrocks, but he does not begin to satisfy me. I cannot accept him as a great comic character. He may be comic now and again, but I do not believe in him as a character. He is something pasted together to meet the funny occasion. He seems to me to have no root in reality. Here is a wholesale grocer steady and sharp enough to acquire a comfortable fortune in the City, yet we find him behaving like an idiot. (For example – only one of a great many – he was 'all delight' after receiving a letter, inviting him to be Master of Foxhounds at Handley Cross, signed by the following: Captain Miserrimus Doleful, Duncan Nevin, Alfred Boltem, Simon Hookem, Walter Fleeceall, Judas Turnbill, Michael Grasper. Surtees is trying to turn us into idiots too.) No, relentless facetiousness plus heavy-handed satire cannot give us a memorable comic character or a genuine humorous novel.

CHAPTER 8

The Wonderful World of Dickens

The humour of Dickens is on such a gigantic scale that at first we can only stare at it, and then wonder where to begin. It is as if we had asked to see a little salt water and had then been taken to the seaside. We seem to be looking at an ocean of the comic. Not half a chapter but a whole book could be written on the humour of Dickens. Consider one story alone: *Pickwick Papers*, for example. It does not offer us some comic characters but *a crowd of them*, bewildering if warming the memory, which begins to recall humorous scenes by the dozen. But it will not do simply to sort out this humour, finally deciding what is closest to the secret of Dickens's enduring appeal.

Clearly some division is necessary; so we might make a start by dividing this humour into three kinds. The first is the passing humour, found in all the novels, whatever tales they may tell, of scene and situation, in which we would have to include even accounts of streets and houses, products of Dickens's extraordinary vitality. We need not stop to examine these; every reader has at one time or another fallen under their spell, which belongs to the special world that Dickens, half consciously and half unconsciously, was able to create for himself. In one aspect it is intensely real – coming out of a memory and power of observation that were phenomenal – and yet it has another aspect that seems to be surreal, almost as if we were moving towards a fairy tale. It is this double aspect, quite apart from other features of his work we shall arrive at later, that separates him from other good or even great novelists. In one sense he is not a novelist at all, as for example Thackeray or Trollope were novelists. Indeed, I have suggested elsewhere that we could think of Dickens writing grotesque prose poems.

Within this special world, nourished by this unique atmosphere, are characters, a whole host of them, who largely contribute to the humour, being very funny at times, though they have also various parts to play in the story. They have not been created simply to make us laugh. Offhand one can think of Sam Weller, Winkle, Dick Swiveller, Toots and his Susan Nipper, Guppy (with his extraordinary proposal), or a much later character like Lammle. These must be distinguished – though I am not saying this is always easy – from the characters who belong to the

'First appearance of Mr Samuel Weller', illustration by Phiz
to *Pickwick Papers*, by Charles Dickens, 1837

third and most glorious stage of Dickensian humour, the characters we might describe as the Giant Drolls, generally best remembered. Obvious examples are Pecksniff, Mr and Mrs Micawber, Mrs Gamp. It may seem a strange statement, but I believe that Dickens created these astonishing creatures without quite understanding what he was doing. He would insist, so to speak, in dragging them into the plot, when they didn't really belong to that world at all but to some timeless Giant Droll kingdom, where everybody is gloriously and immortally daft.

This kingdom, I suggest, has no hard frontiers; all is shifting and meeting around there. In other words, it may be difficult to decide where Dickensian humour Stage Two (funny characters who can be used in the plot) ends and Stage Three begins, with its Giant Drolls who ought to be kept out of the plot. Readers must depend on their own judgment. As an example of my own opinion, I will say that Sam Weller is a fine specimen of a Stage Two character, ready to be involved in any plot, whereas his father – bless him – is a Stage Three character, a Giant Droll. And please notice this about the elder Weller – it is *what he says,* often so unexpected, that endears him to us through our laughter. Here we arrive at the secret of the Dickensian Giant Drolls: it is not what they are nor what they do but *exactly what they say* that is so entrancing and memorable.

There was a time when some critics, with minds wearing full armour, dismissed these astonishing creations as so many caricatures based on some particular quality, hypocrisy for Pecksniff, vague optimism for Micawber, and so forth. Their attention should have been drawn to Mrs Sapsea's powerful epitaph, concluding with, 'Stranger, pause. And ask thyself this question, Canst thou do likewise? If not, with a blush retire.' And all these critics, together with their novelist friends, should have with a blush retired. Fiction is full of comic characters of a sort based on caricature formulas, ruling passions, repetitions, but they do not exist alongside the Dickensian Giant Drolls. These creatures of wild absurdity are not carefully built up but come into being out of a tremendous gushing spring of high spirits and an unusual and rather childlike kind of imagination. It is almost as if they arrived out of some comic mythology. Like mythological figures they are timeless and unchanging, and that is why Dickens was wrong when he tried to pull them, quite unconvincingly, into his plots: they do not belong down there. They exist in the separate kingdom of Giant Drolls. They are at once larger and dafter than life.

There are moments when these characters make us feel we are in a huge unique theatre, where they are being uproariously played by wonderful comedians. Is Mr Pecksniff really an architect of sorts, who takes and swindles pupils, pretends to be uncommonly virtuous and moralistic, and drinks too much brandy? All we are sure of is that he can talk like this when he is in a coach with his daughters:

'What are we?' said Mr. Pecksniff, 'but coaches. Some of us are slow coaches.'
'Goodness, Pa!' cried Charity.
'Some of us, I say,' resumed her parent with increased emphasis, 'are slow coaches; some of us are fast coaches. Our passions are the horses; and rampant animals, too!'

'Really, Pa!' cried both the daughters at once. 'How very unpleasant.'

'And rampant animals, too!' repeated Mr. Pecksniff, with so much determination, that he may be said to have exhibited, at the moment, a sort of moral rampancy himself: 'and Virtue is the drag. We start from The Mother's Arms, and we run to The Dust Shovel.'

When he had said this, Mr. Pecksniff, being exhausted, took some further refreshment. When he had done that, he corked the bottle tight, with the air of a man who had effectually corked the subject also; and went to sleep for three stages.

'Meekness of Mr Pecksniff and his charming daughters', illustration by Phiz to *Martin Chuzzlewit*, by Charles Dickens, 1844

We have to follow him to London, staying at Mrs Todgers's establishment, where he gets drunk and has to be carried to bed, only to rise again to make one immortal remark:

. . . A vision of Mr. Pecksniff, strangely attired, was seen to flutter on the top landing. He desired to collect their sentiments, it seemed, upon the nature of human life.

'My friends,' cried Mr. Pecksniff, looking over the banisters, 'let us improve our minds by mutual inquiry and discussion. Let us be moral. Let us contemplate existence. Where is Jinkins?'

'Here,' cried that gentleman. 'Go to bed again!'

'To bed!' said Mr. Pecksniff. 'Bed! ''Tis the voice of the sluggard, I hear him complain, you have woke me too soon, I must slumber again.'' If any young orphan will repeat the remainder of that simple piece from Dr. Watts's collection an eligible opportunity now offers.'

Nobody volunteered.

'This is very soothing,' said Mr. Pecksniff, after a pause. 'Extremely so. Cool and refreshing; particularly to the legs. The legs of the human subject, my friends, are a beautiful production. Compare them with wooden legs, and observe the difference between the anatomy of nature and the anatomy of art. Do you know,' said Mr. Pecksniff, leaning over the banisters, with an odd recollection of his familiar manner among new pupils at home, 'that I should very much like to see Mrs. Todgers's notion of a wooden leg, if perfectly agreeable to herself!'

This is the very poetry of absurdity.

These beings exist only in their own atmosphere or in that kingdom of their own. That is why Dickens should never have sent the Micawbers to Australia – or to anywhere else – to become affluent and respected citizens. This was a sad mistake, just as it was a stroke of genius to plant Micawber, with his 'artistic temperament', not in any Bohemian circle, among artists, but in the seedy fringes of commerce and salesmanship and obscure little agencies, living on hope and domestic oratory. It is here we find romance, even among petty calculations; and being essentially a romantic, Mr Micawber really enjoys himself in all situations:

'I say,' returned Mr. Micawber, quite forgetting himself, and smiling again, 'the miserable wretch you behold. My advice is, never do tomorrow what you can do today. Procrastination is the thief of time. Collar him! . . . My other piece of advice, Copperfield,' said Mr. Micawber, 'you know. Annual income twenty pounds, annual expenditure nineteen nineteen six, result happiness. Annual income twenty pounds, annual expenditure twenty pounds ought and six, result misery. The blossom is blighted, the leaf is withered, the God of Day goes down upon the dreary scene, and – and in short you are for ever floored. As I am!'

To make his example the more impressive, Mr. Micawber drank a glass of punch with an air of great enjoyment and satisfaction, and whistled the College Hornpipe.

The last sentence gives us the key to the scene and the actor in it. He is never really 'floored' and every new opportunity arises like a transformation scene in an old pantomime and offers a chance for more rich oratory:

'. . . Whatever station in society I may attain, through the medium of the learned profession of which I am about to become an unworthy member, I shall endeavour not to disgrace, and Mrs. Micawber will be safe to adorn. Under the temporary pressure of pecuniary liabilities, contracted with a view to their immediate liquidation, but remaining unliquidated – through a combination of circumstances, I have been under the necessity of assuming a garb from which my natural instincts recoil – I allude to spectacles – and possessing myself of a cognomen, to which I can establish no legitimate pretensions. All I have to say on that score is, that the cloud has passed from the dreary scene, and the God of Day is once more high upon the mountain tops. On Monday next, on the arrival of the four o'clock afternoon coach at Canterbury, my foot will be on my native heath – my name, Micawber!'

Mr. Micawber resumed his seat at the close of these remarks, and drank two glasses of punch in grave succession. . . .

Incidentally, we must never forget or overlook Mrs Micawber, who exists in the same upper air of absurdity as her husband. But while he is the romantic adventurer and orator, she is the clear-sighted practical helpmate, quite severe in her reasoning, letting nothing escape her – except that she is a logician in a moonstruck existence:

'To coals,' said Mrs. Micawber. 'To the coal trade. Mr. Micawber was induced to think, on inquiry, that there might be an opening for a man of his talent in the Medway Coal Trade. Then, as Mr. Micawber properly said, the first step to be taken clearly was, to come and *see* the Medway. Which we came and saw. I say,' "we," Master Copperfield; for I never will,' said Mrs. Micawber with emotion, 'I never will desert Mr. Micawber.'

I murmured my admiration and approbation.

'We came,' repeated Mrs. Micawber, 'and saw the Medway. My opinion of the coal trade on that river, is, that it may require talent but that it certainly requires capital. Talent, Mr. Micawber has; capital, Mr. Micawber has not. We saw, I think, the greater part of the Medway; and that is my individual conclusion. . . .'

Later she has to clear the air again, before throwing down the gauntlet to society on Mr Micawber's behalf:

'. . . For corn, as I have repeatedly said to Mr. Micawber, may be gentlemanly, but it is not remunerative. Commission to the extent of two and ninepence in a fortnight cannot, however limited our ideas, be considered remunerative. . . . Then I ask myself this question. If corn is not to be relied upon, what is? Are coals to be relied upon? Not at all. We have turned our attention to that experiment, on the suggestion of my family, and we find it fallacious. . . . The articles of corn and coals being equally out of the question, Mr. Copperfield, I naturally look round the world, and say, "What is there in which a person of Mr. Micawber's talent is likely to succeed?" And I exclude the doing of anything on commission, because commission is not a certainty. What is best suited to a person of Mr. Micawber's peculiar temperament, is, I am convinced, a certainty. . . .'

Notice that it does not worry us at all that the Micawbers (with a taste for punch) find only two and ninepence coming in a fortnight. We feel that they don't really live in our world, possibly feeding on honey-dew and drinking the milk (punch) of Paradise.

'Restoration of mutual confidence between Mr and Mrs Micawber', illustration
by Phiz to *David Copperfield*, by Charles Dickens, 1850

This brings me to a point I have made before; but it is worth making again. If we take the general run of these Giant Drolls, we cannot help feeling, if only vaguely, that we have met characters rather like these before. I am assuming now that we spent our childhood and early youth (as I did) in a house where friends of our parents were always coming and going. If some of these visitors were at all odd and comic, they made rather the same impression upon us that these Dickensian characters do. They were tremendously themselves; they seemed to be timeless, unchanging; they did not really belong to our world; they were mythologically comic, their drollery larger than life. And it is my belief that the memory and imagination of childhood found their way into Dickens's work, stoking up, we might say, his creative unconscious. And it is significant that the Giant Drolls, his highest pitch of humour and extreme absurdity, are discovered in his early novels and are almost absent from his later work. True, vitality itself, tearing high spirits, played a great part here, the last novels, though more impressive as works of art, being the work of a man who was busy wearing himself out and at odds with almost everybody and everything around him. And Dickensian humour of the kind we are praising here demands enormous vitality, a fierce creative energy.

To enlarge this theme, let us compare two novels from the beginning and the end of his career, namely, *Nicholas Nickleby* and *Our Mutual Friend*. As contributions to the art of fiction, as real novels, any comparison seems ridiculous. *Our Mutual Friend* has breadth and depth, all the dust-heap symbolism, a wealth of social comment and criticism, an attempt to bring into focus a whole ailing society. Moreover, it has its own humour, mainly satirical, as we remember the Veneerings and their circle of new 'old friends' and Mr Podsnap and his pronouncements to guests, not forgetting the young man who could only say 'Esker' to encourage the French. But what it does not have, what has been lost along the darkening way, is the wild, wonderful, unique humour of the young Dickens, dizzy with success and ready to pour out tales by the dozen. And as Humour is our subject, this is very important indeed. We cannot allow ourselves to be crushed by the vastly superior weight of *Our Mutual Friend*. Brushing aside academic criticism and values – always a pleasure for us laity – we can allow ourselves a fresh look at the youthful *Nicholas Nickleby*.

Opening my Volume Two at random, somewhere near the middle, I find the villainous Ralph Nickleby alone, grinding his teeth and saying, 'There is some spell about that boy. Circumstances conspire to help him. Talk of fortune's favours! What is even money to such Devil's luck as this!' A little later, having left Mr Mantalini defeated, Ralph is telling himself, 'Oho! Sets the wind that way so soon? Half knave and half fool, and detected in both characters? I think your day is over, sir.' But of course no man in his senses talks to himself in this style. Ralph is really spouting to an audience; we are not in a novel but in a theatre – and in a second-rate theatre at that. And Sir Mulberry Hawk and Lord Verisopht and lecherous old Gride all belong to the same theatre. In other words, when *Nicholas Nickleby* is serious, getting on with the plot, it is mostly quite silly.

But its humour is glorious. Even that brute, Squeers, is allowed his moments, as when he smacks his lips over his wretched mixture of milk and water, crying 'Here's richness!' We are offered a wide range of what I have called Stage Two characters, necessary for the action but quite funny in themselves. Floating above them are various Giant Drolls, among whom we must include that great holder-up of the story, Mrs Nickleby:

'Your poor dear papa . . . looking at me while I was talking to him about his affairs, just as if his ideas were in a state of perfect conglomeration. . . . He never knew, till it was too late, what I would have him do. . . . However, this has nothing to do, certainly, nothing whatever to do – with the gentleman in the next house. . . . There can be no doubt that he is a gentleman, and has the manners of a gentleman, and the appearance of a gentleman, although he does wear smalls and grey worsted stockings. That may be eccentricity, or he may be proud of his legs. I don't see why he shouldn't be. The Prince Regent was proud of his legs, and so was Daniel Lambert, who was also a fat man; *he* was proud of his legs. So was Miss Biffin: she was – no, I think she had only toes, but the principle is the same. . . . The bottom of his garden joins the bottom of ours, and of course I had several times seen him sitting among the scarlet-beans in his little arbour, or working at his little hot-bed. I used to think he stared rather, but I didn't take any particular notice of that, as we were newcomers, and he might be curious to see what we were like, but when he began to throw his cucumbers over our wall. . . . Yes, his cucumbers over our wall. And vegetable marrows likewise. . . .'

Then there is Vincent Crummles, actor-manager, who surely belongs to the higher reaches of the absurd. He is discussing the arrival of Miss Petowker from Drury Lane:

'. . . As much talent as was ever compressed into one young person's body . . . "The Blood Drinker" will die with that girl; and she's the only sylph I ever saw, who could stand upon one leg, and play the tambourine on her other knee, like a sylph . . . Mrs. Crummles saw what she could do – always knew it from the first. She taught her, indeed, nearly all she knows, Mrs. Crummles was the original Blood Drinker. . . . Some new proof of talent bursts from that astonishing woman every year of her life. Look at her, mother of six children, three of 'em alive, and all upon the stage! . . . I pledge you my professional word I didn't even know she could dance, till her last benefit, and then she played Juliet, and Helen Macgregor, and did the skipping-rope hornpipe between the pieces. The very first time I saw that admirable woman, she stood upon her head upon the butt-end of a spear, surrounded with blazing fire-works. . . . Such grace, coupled with such dignity! I adored her from that moment!'

But we could venture further into the secrets of the playhouse. Nicholas has told Crummles he must leave the company:

'We can have positively your last appearance, on Thursday – re-engagement for one night more, on Friday – and, yielding to the wishes of numerous influential patrons, who were disappointed in obtaining seats, on Saturday. That ought to bring three very decent houses.'

'Then I am to make three last appearances, am I?' inquired Nicholas, smiling.

'Yes,' rejoined the manager, scratching his head with an air of some vexation; 'three is not enough, and it's very bungling and irregular not to have more, but if we can't help it we can't, so there's no use in talking. You couldn't sing a comic song on the pony's back, could you?'

'No,' replied Nicholas, 'I couldn't indeed.'

'It has drawn money before now,' said Mr. Crummles, with a look of disappoint-ment. 'What do you think of a brilliant display of fireworks?'

'That it would be rather expensive,' replied Nicholas, drily.

'Eighteenpence would do it,' said Mr. Crummles. 'You on the top of a pair of steps with the phenomenon in an attitude; "Farewell," on a transparency behind; and nine people at the wings with a squib in each hand – all the dozen and a half going off at once – it would be very grand – awful from the front, quite awful.'

Apart from the downright villains, Mr Mantalini is one of the least admirable persons in *Nicholas Nickleby*: a spendthrift, a liar, unfaithful to the wife whose hard-earned money he cadges and flings away. Yet there are moments when, if we welcome a height of absurdity, he offers us pure joy. One of these moments is when Madame Mantalini puts him on to a fixed allowance of £120 a year.

'Demmit! – it is a horrid reality. She is sitting there before me. There is the graceful outline of her form; it cannot be mistaken – there is nothing like it. The two countesses

'Theatrical emotion of Mr Vincent Crummles', illustration by Phiz
to *Nicholas Nickleby*, by Charles Dickens, 1839

had no outlines at all, and the dowager's was a demd outline. Why is she so excruciat-ingly beautiful that I cannot be angry with her, even now?'

'You have brought it upon yourself, Alfred,' returned Madame Mantalini – still reproachfully, but in a softened tone.

'I am a demd villain!' cried Mr. Mantalini, smiting himself on the head. 'I will fill my pockets with change for a sovereign in halfpence and drown myself in the Thames; but I will not be angry with her even then, for I will put a note in the twopenny post as I go along, to tell her where the body is. She will be a lovely widow. I shall be a body. Some handsome women will cry; she will laugh demnedbly.'

'Alfred, you cruel, cruel creature,' said Madame Mantalini, sobbing at the dreadful picture.

'She calls me cruel – me – me – who for her sake will become a demd, damp, moist, unpleasant body!' exclaimed Mr. Mantalini.

'You know it almost breaks my heart, even to hear you talk of such a thing,' replied Madame Mantalini.

'Can I live to be mistrusted?' cried her husband. 'Have I cut my heart into a demd extraordinary number of little pieces, and given them all away, one after another, to the same little engrossing demnition captivator, and can I live to be suspected by her! Demmit, no, I cant . . . I don't want any sum. I shall require no demd allowance. I will be a body.'

But I must resist the temptation to quote, not without danger, because a reader may be ready to consider humour without being in the mood to laugh at it.

A solemn critical person may easily – and appallingly – underrate Dickens. His faults, which are on a large scale, will probably be obvious to such a person. His astounding gifts may be taken for granted or even ignored. This is particularly true of his gigantic and infinitely varied humour. Most men – and I mean *men*, not women – imagine that they have a lot of humour at their command, if they should stoop to use it, when in fact they have nothing of the kind. You have only to listen to after-dinner speeches to realise how men deceive themselves in this matter, sure they can be funny whenever an audience is waiting to laugh. They are certain they could be humorists if they really wanted to be. (They are related to all the people who tell us they could write novels and plays *if they had the time*.) But making readers laugh, all over the world, and on and on, can be hard and wearing. It was no problem to the younger Dickens, who had tearing high spirits and a furnace of creation at his service; but it is easy to see how the older Dickens, all his early optimism gone, at odds with his society, began to find it harder and harder to be comical when he felt he ought to be. So, if our emphasis is entirely on humour, we have to reverse general critical opinion on Dickens; we go back to his own time and the years immediately following it, when it was felt that his later novels were inferior to his earlier tales. They are not of course *as novels*, but as rich hampers of Dickensian humour certainly they are. It is the Dickens up to and including *David Copperfield* who continually makes us laugh.

Humour on such a gigantic scale and so wonderfully varied, with almost enough characters to fill a small town, cannot be faultless. There must be elements of caricature, exaggeration, repetition. But I suggest that such elements are far smaller than most rather humourless critics have imagined. I claim as a witness here no less a person than Santayana, no Englishman but a Spanish-American philosopher. He declared firmly that when people say that Dickens exaggerates, it seemed to him they could have no eyes and ears, never really looking at and listening to their fellow human beings but existing in a vague world of abstractions. This is particularly true of the host of what I called the Stage Two characters, as distinct from the Giant Drolls who are deliberately created larger than life, reaching some upper air of absurdity. (There may have been somebody rather like Mr Mantalini, but the Mantalini we know, in his daft glory, would have to be *created*.) Somewhere behind any long comic novel, crowded with characters, as I know myself from experience, there must be not only uncommon energy and vitality but also a large fund or pool of closely observed experience, much of it passing into the unconscious until it is needed. And everything we are told about Dickens confirms his ability *to notice*, to observe closely and continually, together with his remarkable memory. Humour can be a hard task-master, even if you have a genius for it like Dickens. Gradually, with vitality ebbing, with all that editing, public reading, travelling, party-going and speechifying, his years, longer and harder than other men's, wore him down. So while there are glints and sparkles of comedy to the end, shades of weariness and melancholy creep over the scene. Any riot of humour belongs to the early years, to the rather handsome, beardless young man with the sharp bright eyes.

Noticing that Dickens and his characters seem to be rarely mentioned nowadays, I wondered if his popularity were vanishing at last. I asked a local librarian, always helpful, what was happening. He replied at once that Dickens was not being forgotten in this Free Library. A new complete set of his works had been acquired, only a few years ago. After examining the shelves, the librarian told me that of all these volumes – probably thirty-odd – only two were not out on loan. This seemed to me good news, even after remembering that there is a renewed interest in Victorian life and times. We need the humour of Dickens in all its various phases. It makes us laugh – at a time when most people find less and less to laugh about. It takes us into an atmosphere that is truly and even passionately democratic. This means something very different from obtaining a majority – by fair means or foul – to pass a resolution. There is nothing abstract and statistical about Dickens's democracy. It involves attending closely to real people, not mere units but living, hopeful or despairing, human beings. It is the kind of democracy that is rapidly disappearing. More and more we seem to live in a world dominated by blindly unfeeling humourless types, by fanatics, ideologues, power-mongers, faceless bureaucrats. In his day, Dickens would have laughed them off the scene. In our day, we can at least echo his laughter, and find some solace and refreshment, both for heart and mind, in the rich heritage of his humour.

CHAPTER 9

The Facetious and the Funny

I want to call a halt here in my chronicle of authors and books. The time is round about the middle of the nineteenth century. From now on there will be more and more hard-working funny men and fewer and fewer notable humorists. Comic weeklies – with *Punch* leading them – are now popular. Novelists are busy trying to imitate the earlier successes of Dickens. There are even comic lecturers. Laughter, especially if suitable for the family circle, is in great demand. To supply this demand there is and will be a large output of professional and determined facetiousness. Now *facetious* is a curious word. It has greatly changed its meaning. Once it meant polished, elegant or agreeable. (My authority here is the last *Webster* but one, my favourite dictionary.) Then it described the jocose, the sportive – etc. Here, as readers may have already noticed, I give it a lower place still, setting it against what I regard as real humour. I see it as anything for a grin, giggle or easy laugh, making use of a familiar bundle of tricks. These were grimly described, many years ago, by the Brothers Fowler in their *The King's English*, under the heading 'Airs And Graces' – largely out of date now, probably because the Fowlers were so ruthless.

One Victorian facetious device will serve as an example. We find it over and over again among the funny men. An occasion that could be described in plain words is offered to us, for comic effect, in solemn polysyllables. Let me improvise a sample. 'The individual with the elongated proboscis thereupon commenced his oration.' In other and better words: 'The man with the long nose then began his speech.' And it is ten to one that the true humorist would write something like that, and would certainly avoid the facetious long-word trick. But the funny man who is not really a humorist depends on comic tricks. We might say he is messing about with the surface of life, capering and posturing without any sustained vision of our existence, often so absurdly out of proportion, so disturbing to our pride and vanity. The genuine humorist of any size seldom deals in small jokes: he is fascinated by huge enduring jokes, which may begin with birth and end with death. There seem to me three elements necessary to the outlook and the work of a great humorist. One is an ever-present sense of irony. Another is affection. The third is some contact with reality. This last must be widely interpreted. Thus, for instance, Lewis Carroll's Humpty

Dumpty and White Knight, though wildly ridiculous, have a reality of their own sort that Surtees's Jorrocks cannot discover for me: he is a fake and they are not. But now we must be on our way again.

My nearest reference book describes Richard Harris Barham as a 'humorous poet'. He seems to me nothing of the kind, but an ingenious comic versifier, whose *Ingoldsby Legends* were enormously popular for several decades and encouraged later funny men to try their hands at the same sort of thing, often sharing his taste for the grotesquely gruesome:

> Oh! 'tis shocking to view
> The sight which the corpse reveals!
> Sir Thomas's body, it looks so odd – he
> Was half-eaten up by the eels!
> His waistcoat and hose, and the rest of his clothes,
> Were all gnawed through and through;
> And out of each shoe an eel they drew;
> And from each of his pockets they pull'd out two,
> And the Gardener himself had secreted a few,
> As well we may suppose;
> For when he came running to give the alarm,
> He had six in the basket that hung on his arm . . .

And the widow herself reaches a climax of tasting and tastelessness:

> Eels a many I've ate; but any
> So good ne're tasted before!
> They're a fish, too, of which I'm remarkably fond,
> Go – pop Sir Thomas again in the pond,
> Poor dear! HE'LL CATCH US SOME MORE!

The joke is there, but, even more than the eels, it demands a strong stomach to digest it. However, Barham's gusto and impudent rhyming brought him some followers – W. S. Gilbert for one.

What can we say about Thackeray? He is a difficult subject for this book – and indeed, I would say, for any other. In the Christmas Books of his maturity, holiday pieces, he can go rollicking along, full of fun. On the other hand, his early work, meant to be partly comic, has always seemed to me too gritty and rather repulsive. There is of course genuine humour glinting through his major work. He can create a comic character, a Costigan or a Foker, but he does not indulge and enlarge his droll characters, but dismisses them with a smile and a shrug, wincing a little perhaps. A great novelist no doubt; certainly in *Vanity Fair* and *Henry Esmond*; and probably undervalued nowadays, perhaps because of an atmosphere of weary stuffiness, as if everybody were sitting in a room too long. But with due respect – as the politicians like to say – I cannot give him a secure place as a humorist. He has the capabilitity but not the right temperament. He is not sufficiently positive and indulgent. He is not a cynic: that was always a silly charge. But he is too wincingly self-conscious for splendid enjoyment of this life.

He had plenty to wince about: the early loss of his fortune through gambling and silliness; the much greater loss of his wife through insanity, though she outlived him by nearly thirty years; his extreme sensitiveness to hostile criticism or any misunderstandings; the way in which he aged fast, ready to call himself an old man while still in his forties; his rapidly failing health after successfully launching the *Cornhill Magazine* in 1860 – he died in 1863. He was a man who liked his clubs and could enjoy social occasions, but I feel he was unhappy when alone, haunted by regrets or forebodings. And it may be that the born humorist is most himself when he is alone, with humour rising from his depths. Thackeray had the gifts of the humorist except that something central, the yeast for his bread, was missing, not allowing him to expand, to laugh at the world and at himself. In his delightful late essays he could smile at himself and ask us to smile too, but melancholy and regret are always close at hand. He ought to have been granted another and luckier life.

Trollope admired Thackeray to the point of hero worship. Yet we are coming to realise now that Trollope was equally gifted – except as a stylist in prose – and probably as an all-round novelist far more greatly gifted. He was also the sturdier character, overcoming an unhappy childhood and youth. (Whatever we may say, this is something that sheer character can do.) Moreover, he combined hard work and a wide knowledge of the world with an unexpected deeply intuitive sense of character, both male and female. He lost shoals of readers when he told them in his *Autobiography* how and when he did his writing – regular stints of it early in the morning, possibly with the help of a stopwatch. But it was foolish to make a fuss about this. A man may write regularly long before breakfast or start at midnight with lashings of coffee and brandy: what chiefly concerns us as readers is the quality of the work that reaches us. Trollope may be unequal, like all copious writers, but his best is very good indeed.

He is not of course a humorist. But exploring characters in some depth, bringing them together in a wide variety of situations, he arrives at humour often along the way. But if he aims at humour on a broad scale, he fails disastrously, becoming heavily facetious. To present scenes of his that bring us to genuine humour would involve more explanation than I have room for here. But a fairly early scene seems to me better than facetious: it is that in which poor Bishop Proudie, desperately clinging to his dignity, has to cope with cheeky and persistent Bertie Stanhope:

'Do you like Barchester, on the whole?' asked Bertie.
The bishop, looking dignified, said he did like Barchester.
'You've not been here very long, I believe,' said Bertie.
'No – not long,' said the bishop, and tried again to make his way between the back of the sofa and a heavy rector, who was staring over it at the grimaces of the signora.

'You weren't a bishop before, were you?'

Dr. Proudie explained that this was the first diocese he had held.

'Ah – I thought so,' said Bertie; 'but you are changed about sometimes, a'nt you?'

'Translations are occasionally made,' said Dr. Proudie; 'but not so frequently as in former days.'

'They've cut them all down to pretty nearly the same figure, haven't they?' said Bertie.

To this the bishop could not bring himself to make any answer, but again attempted to move the rector.

'But the work, I suppose, is different?' continued Bertie. 'Is there much to do here, at Barchester?' This was said exactly in the tone that a young Admiralty clerk might use in asking the same question of a brother acolyte at the Treasury.

'The work of a Bishop of the Church of England,' said Dr. Proudie, with considerable dignity, 'is not easy. The responsibility which he has to bear is very great indeed.'

'Is it?' said Bertie, opening wide his wonderful blue eyes. 'Well, I never was afraid of responsibility. I once had thoughts of being a bishop myself.'

'Had thoughts of being a bishop!' said Dr. Proudie, much amazed.

'That is, a parson – a parson first, you know, and a bishop afterwards. If I had once begun, I'd have stuck to it. But, on the whole, I like the Church of Rome the best.'

The bishop could not discuss the point, so he remained silent.

'Now, there's my father,' continued Bertie. 'He hasn't stuck to it. I fancy he didn't like saying the same things over so often. By the bye, Bishop, have you seen my father?'

The bishop was more amazed than ever. Had he seen his father? 'No,' he replied; 'he had not yet had the pleasure: he hoped he might'; and, as he said so, he resolved to bear heavy on that fat, immovable rector, if ever he had the power of doing so.

'He's in the room somewhere,' said Bertie, 'and he'll turn up soon. By the bye, do you know much about the Jews?'

At last the bishop saw a way out. 'I beg your pardon,' said he; 'but I'm forced to go round the room.'

'Well, I believe I'll follow in your wake,' said Bertie.

But now I have decided I must read some of Trollope's later novels again. Surely there must be some humour, conscious or unconscious, among these politicians of his?

A Load of Nonsense

It must be a long time since I first read Chesterton's *Victorian Age In Literature*, which brought a firework display to the sedate avenues of the *Home University Library of Modern Knowledge*. I was delighted by the book then – and I was quite right – for though it contains some impudent generalising, it also gives us some fine intuitive judgments. But it can be caught out. So, for example, Chesterton says, 'Of the Victorian Age as a whole it is true to say that it did discover a new thing: a thing called Nonsense.' If this means there was no nonsense before the Victorian Age, it is wildly untrue, ignoring various kinds of nonsense we can discover in three previous centuries. It is only true if we agree that the Victorian public welcomed nonsense with more enthusiasm and large rewards than any other earlier public. In many respects this was a far grimmer age than any known before, and its large middle class, perhaps not always feeling comfortable, wanted to laugh.

The two great names in Victorian nonsense are of course Edward Lear and Lewis Carroll. Lear was a very odd fish indeed, whose life and career were crammed with sharp contradictions. He was an epileptic who also suffered from asthma; a man who could weep copiously when he felt lonely and neglected, as he often did; a kind of spiritual homosexual who could yet be warmly attracted by women and their children; hypersensitive and moody and yet capable of prodigious bouts of close hard work, and courageous and resolute enough to undertake long and rather dangerous journeys in the Near East. (Here I must acknowledge my debt to Mrs Vivien Noakes's *Edward Lear: The Life of a Wanderer*, a splendid book.) He could be trying to friends and acquaintances, both in talk and letters, by a constant facetiousness, in which he used some of the devices popular among American funny men: 'I have gained a great amount of health bodily and mentle, and also trust to benefit obliquily of many of my felly creatures who will hereafter peeroase my jurnles, and admyer my pigchers.' But this facetiousness must not be confused with his Nonsense, mostly in print and going through many editions. Here again I for one would make a distinction between his limericks (with their weak concluding lines) and his true Nonsense poems.

The power of these largely comes from something that he shared with his friend

Tennyson – a feeling for words, and especially for strange haunting names. In spite of their wild surrealism, many of them seem like melancholy news from some remote planet. Or some of them might be the love poetry of people we have never encountered, in scenes we cannot ever have visited; as in this sad little song:

> She sits upon her Bulbul
> Through the long long hours of night –
> And o'er the dark horizon gleams
> The Yashmack's fitful light.
> The lone Yaourt sails slowly down
> The deep & craggy dell –
> And from his lofty nest, loud screams
> The white plumed Asphodel.

Even the daft tale of 'The Jumblies':

> They went to sea in a Sieve, they did,
> In a sieve they went to sea:
> In spite of all their friends could say
> On a winter's morn, on a stormy day
> In a sieve they went to sea!

has a strangely mournful refrain:

> Far and few, far and few,
> Are the lands where the Jumblies live;
> Their heads are green, and their hands are blue,
> And they went to sea in a Sieve.

The Yonghy-Bonghy-Bo is only a short distance away from a memorable pathetic character:

> On the coast of Coromandel
> Where the early pumpkins blow,
> In the middle of the woods
> Lived the Yonghy-Bonghy-Bo.
> Two old chairs, and half a candle,
> One old jug without a handle,
> These were all his worldly goods:
> In the middle of the woods,
> These were all the worldly goods
> Of the Yonghy-Bonghy-Bo,
> Of the Yonghy-Bonghy-Bo.

'Lady Jingly Jones and the
Yonghy-Bonghy-Bo', about 1867,
by Edward Lear

How he can start with a striking image!

> The Owl and the Pussy-Cat went to sea
> In a beautiful pea-green boat.

And bring in cunning names and terms –

> They sailed away for a year and a day
> The land where the Bong-tree grows.
> They dined on mince, and slices of quince,
> Which they ate with a runcible spoon;
> And hand in hand, on the edge of the sand,
> They danced by the light of the moon.

We begin to feel that if we went far enough in our galaxy, we should find the Dong with the Luminous Nose, the Pobbles and their Aunt Jobiska, oblong oysters and runcible hats and bottles of Ring-Bo-Ree, and Ploffskin, Pluffskin, Pelican jee, the sunset isles of Boshen, and the hills of the Chankly Bore.

Almost always there is – at least to adult minds and not in those of the children, who adored him and immediately accepted him as their Uncle – below the mounting absurdities an undercurrent of melancholy and regret. Except when he was working hard, which was often enough, and when he was entertaining children, Lear was an unhappy man, robbed of any permanent close attachment, visited by a loneliness that could leave him walking a room with his face streaming with tears. From all his worries and disappointments, the Nonsense provided him with some sort of escape. And because, however daft its surface may be, there is a kind of poetry in it, innumerable other people for a little while have found escape by the same extraordinary route.

I seem to remember that Chesterton, discussing Victorian nonsense, put Lear above Lewis Carroll. I cannot agree with this. To be set against Lear's genius for names and his haunting melancholy are Lewis Carroll's sustained invention, his creation of moonstruck characters for ever remembered, his dream worlds bristling with topsy-turvy logic and mad metaphysics. I can jump back seventy years and recall myself as a small boy first exploring these magic *Alice* tales. What I have read since about the Reverend Charles Lutwidge Dodgson, mathematician and don, with his prudishness, his conventional piety, his fussiness, his endless notes and cross-indexing, I cannot help feeling that somehow he, who started it all, is really himself a character out of the *Alice* stories, who might easily have asked the Mad Hatter or Humpty Dumpty to dine with him.

I have of course dipped into these books, to re-read favourite passages, scores of times, but what I have just done (probably as an excuse to stop working at my desk) is to read *Wonderland* and *Looking-Glass* all through, almost as if they were new books. Now I find – as I certainly didn't once – that *Wonderland* begins too slowly and clumsily, though something is redeemed by the Dodo's profound reply to the question about the caucus race: '*Everybody* has won, and *all* must have prizes.' That is how life should be, though – alas! – we must remember the Dodo has long been extinct. Alice's changes of size now seem to me heavy-going, and the droll magic hardly starts to work until we come to 'Pig and Pepper'. The Mad Tea Party is better still, an old favourite that wears well. The croquet game is nearly as good, and the reappearance of the Duchess, bent on moralising, is grand. The Mock Turtle itself is a good idea, but there really are too many puns and donnish fooling in the scene with it and the Gryphon. However, the trial is glorious fun, and I found I was still exceptionally fond of that verse beginning:

> They told me you had been to her,
> And mentioned me to him;
> She gave me a good character,
> But said I could not swim.

With its equally mysterious ending:

> Don't let him know she liked them best,
> For this must ever be,
> A secret, kept from all the rest,
> Between yourself and me.

The frequent burlesques of well-known poems are easy work, often done by funny men, but these bewildering laconic verses here and in *Looking-Glass* are touched with genius. This cannot be said about the ending of *Wonderland*, in which the Reverend Charles Dodgson seems to have snatched the pen from Lewis Carroll.

The opening of *Looking-Glass* I now find embarrassing. However, I have discovered all over again that it is a far better book than *Wonderland*. (Cards *v*. Chess, with Chess to win.) It is a far richer and more rewarding tale. When people quote Carroll, it is probably about ten to one that they are remembering *Looking-Glass*.

85

The 'Walrus and the Carpenter', illustration by John Tenniel
to *Through the Looking-Glass and What Alice Found There*, by Lewis Carroll, 1872

During the seven years between the two books, Carroll ripened, no matter what happened to Dodgson. As soon as Kitty is out of the way and we are through the looking-glass, the daft magic starts with the chess pieces. And with 'Jabberwocky' I think Carroll beats Lear at his own game. Then we have the wild flight with the Red Queen, all that tremendous effort to stay in the same place. The Looking-Glass insects and the railway-carriage scene don't work for me, but Tweedledum and Tweedledee are soon with us. Through them we arrive at the immortal 'Walrus and the Carpenter', that saga of deceit and greed, making us feel that whether the Walrus and the Carpenter are really respectable financiers or political adventurers, certainly we – almost all of us – are the doomed oysters. (My wife tells me that when she was a little girl she felt so sorry for the hopeful little oysters, all dressed up for the walk and talk, the poem brought her close to tears.) Then, next, the 'Wool and Water' chapter has some claim to be considered the best dream scene in all our literature. Notice the way in which Alice, trying to concentrate on some object on the shelves, is always defeated, the object always escaping. Over fifty years later, J. H. Dunne, the Time theorist, explained this dream effect in terms of conflicting dimensions.

We are now in the presence of Humpty Dumpty, a great character in every respect, dictatorial and arrogant and occasionally suggesting to my mind some literary critics, pillars of our English Departments. He is excellent 'teaching' 'Jabberwocky', and even better when he gives us another of those mysterious laconic poems:

I sent a message to the fish:
I told them 'This is what I wish.'

The little fishes of the sea,
They sent an answer back to me.

The little fishes answer was
'We cannot do it, Sir, because – '

The confused talk between Alice and the White King suggests to me that our
linguistic philosophers are already on the way to us:

'The other Messenger's called Hatta. I must have *two*, you know – to come and go.
One to come, and one to go.'
'I beg your pardon?' said Alice.
'It isn't respectable to beg,' said the King.
'I only meant that I didn't understand,' said Alice. 'Why one to come and one to go?'
'Didn't I tell you?' the King repeated impatiently. 'I must have *two* – to fetch and
carry. One to fetch, and one to carry.'

There is some rich fooling throughout this scene. But what follows is better still, for
now we have the White Knight, that mild, clumsy, but ever-hopeful amateur
inventor. It is here that Nonsense merges into smiling compassionate humour, as
Carroll really tells us:

Of all the strange things that Alice saw in her journey Through the Looking-Glass, this
was the one that she always remembered most clearly. Years afterwards she could bring
the whole scene back again, as if it had been only yesterday – the mild blue eyes and
kindly smile of the Knight – the setting sun gleaming through his hair, and shining on

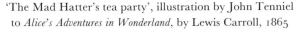

'The Mad Hatter's tea party', illustration by John Tenniel
to *Alice's Adventures in Wonderland*, by Lewis Carroll, 1865

his armour in a blaze of light that quite dazzled her – the horse quietly moving about, with the reins hanging loose on his neck, cropping the grass at her feet – and the black shadows of the forest behind – all this she took in like a picture, as, with one hand shading her eyes, she leant against a tree, watching the strange pair, and listening, in a half-dream, to the melancholy music of the song.

There is some fine Nonsense work in the daft examination of Alice by her fellow Queens. There is too in the crazy feast that follows, in which the leg of mutton makes a little bow when introduced and thereafter cannot be cut and eaten. But it is the plum pudding that provides the climax to this scene, if only because it offers the Red Queen the chance to utter a sublime rebuke:

> ∴ It was so large that she couldn't help feeling a *little* shy with it, as she had been with the mutton; however, she conquered her shyness by a great effort, and handed a slice to the Red Queen.
>
> 'What impertinence!' said the Pudding. 'I wonder how you'd like it, if I were to cut a slice out of *you*, you creature!'
>
> Alice could only look at it and gasp.
>
> 'Make a remark,' said the Red Queen: 'it's ridiculous to leave all the conversation to the pudding!'

This is Nonsense raised to some peak of solemn drollery. If there is a richer rebuke than this – '*It's ridiculous to leave all the conversation to the pudding!*' – within the whole range of English Humour, I don't know where to find it. Blessings – and thanks all over again – to Lewis Carroll!

But there is still *The Hunting of the Snark*. (In spite of a few good jokes, I prefer to ignore *Sylvie and Bruno*.) In many people's minds this poem is haunted by a sense of failure and defeat, though it is in fact a brilliantly original piece of work. The truth is this. While it is 'Inscribed To A Dear Child', unlike the *Alice* tales it is not intended to make an immediate appeal to children. What can they make out of its curious refrain:

> They sought it with thimbles, they sought it with care;
> They pursued it with forks and hope;
> They threatened its life with a railway share;
> They charmed it with smiles and soap.

What has a railway share to do with childhood? What have the passages about the Banker and Barrister to do with it? And there is something else, more important.

(*opposite*) 'The Beaver brought paper, portfolio, pens', illustration by Swain after Henry Holiday to *The Hunting of the Snark*, by Lewis Carroll, 1876

Beneath the wild nonsense of the impatient Bellman and his crew of B's and his map of the ocean without any land shown on it, there is a faintly dark undercurrent of the sinister. We cannot help feeling that we are on our way into the world of Jabberwock, the Jubjub bird, the frumious Bandersnatch. We may know that the common Snark will do us no harm, even though it is oddly eccentric, with its habit of getting up too late and its fondness for bathing machines, to say nothing of its peculiar flavour – 'meagre and hollow, but crisp, like a coat that is too tight in the waist'. But if it should turn out to be Boojum, there can be a dreadful sequel – we could vanish away. Which is what happened to the Baker (who could cope only with bridecake) at the end of the quest:

> They gazed in delight, while the Butcher exclaimed
>   'He was always a desperate wag!'
> They beheld him – their Baker – their hero unnamed –
>   On the top of a neighbouring crag.
>
> Erect and sublime, for one moment of time,
>   In the next, that wild figure they saw
> (as if stung by a spasm) plunge into a chasm,
>   While they waited and listened in awe.
>
> 'It's a Snark!' was the sound that first came to their ears,
>   And seemed almost too good to be true.
> Then followed a torrent of laughter and cheers:
>   Then the ominous words 'It's a Boo –'
>
> Then silence. Some fancied they heard in the air
>   A weary and wandering sigh
> That sounded like ' – jum' but the others declare
>   It was only a breeze that went by.
>
> They hunted till darkness came on, but they found
>   Not a button, or feather, or mark,
> By which they could tell that they stood on the ground
>   Where the Baker had met with the Snark.
>
> In the midst of the word he was trying to say,
>   In the midst of his laughter and glee,
> He had softly and suddenly vanished away –
>   For the Snark *was* a Boojum, you see.

But where had the Baker gone? I think he landed up in *Wonderland* or *Looking-Glass* or both. True, there don't seem to be many marriages in those parts, but even so I fancy he was commissioned to create an enormous bridecake. Among his assistants, perhaps, were the Mad Hatter, the March Hare, and Humpty Dumpty.

CHAPTER II

From *Patience* to Pooter

Above the facetious men contributing to *Punch, Fun* and the rest, there looms the formidable William Schwenck Gilbert. (Was his future already decided when, as a child in Italy, he was captured by brigands and ransomed for £25?) What Gilbert could do, he did very well – nobody better. He could devise comic-operetta plots at once absurd and complicated, filled with situations soon to be called 'Gilbertian'. He was a deft hand at witty or waggish lyrics. He was a lively cynic, often refreshingly disillusioned, never really at his best when called upon to be sentimental or solemn. He has an ingenious bantering line in his best lyrics, as for example in *Patience*:

> Then a sentimental passion of a vegetable fashion
> must excite your languid spleen,
> An attachment *à la* Plato for a bashful young potato,
> or not-too-French bean!
> Though the Philistines may jostle, you will rank as an apostle
> in the high aesthetic band,
> If you walk down Piccadilly with a poppy or a lily
> in your medieval hand,
> And everyone will say,
> As you walk your flowery way,
> 'If he's content with a vegetable love which
> would certainly not suit *me*,
> Why, what a most particularly pure young man
> this young man must be!'

This is good theatrical fooling, even though as genuine satire it is rubbish. Where Gilbert is even better is in his cool development of the absurd ideas and situations, notable in *H.M.S. Pinafore* and *The Pirates of Penzance* and – my own favourite – in the wildly unexpected mixture of peers and fairies we find in *Iolanthe*. But elsewhere, and *The Mikado* and *The Gondoliers* come to mind, he was successfully rescued by the brilliant scores of Sullivan, who had at his best – or so it seems to me – a touch of genius that Gilbert lacked.

There is about Gilbert an aggressive clubman masculinity, together with a lack of that feminine element which brings fertility to the creative artist. We have been told what a severe and intolerant martinet he was when he staged his pieces, which suffered for years from a lack of new and refreshing ideas. He was efficient but too inflexible. As a writer he has none of the tolerance, easy indulgence, compassion of the true humorist. Consider his women, for example. Unless they are pretty young girls, they are unattractive ageing spinsters, plotting to be taken off the shelf where they brood and rage. He can of course do better with men, such as the King in *Princess Ida*, with whom, as a born grumbler, I naturally sympathise:

> Oh, don't the days seem lank and long
> When all goes right and nothing goes wrong,
> And isn't your life extremely flat
> With nothing whatever to grumble at!

If I deny Gilbert a secure place among English humorists I do not want to appear grudging and ungrateful. As a comic librettist, inspiring the best composer of light music our country has had, he did Late Victorian and Edwardian England (and America) a remarkable – and indeed, I would add, a unique – service, illuminating evenings that can never be counted.

There was a time when two writers, utterly different, Meredith and Hardy, were always being paired, like Swan and Edgar or Rodgers and Hart. In the 1920s I wrote the *English Men of Letters* volume on Meredith. And here comes a confession. While I greatly admired his poetry and novels – and I still think his influence on English poetry and fiction has been shockingly underrated – I found I couldn't take to him as a man. (I never met him of course; he was years before my time.) There was no doubt about his brilliance, the speed and reach of his mind; but as a man he appeared to me to be uncommonly vain, affected, and lacking compassion. It was some defect in his character – certainly not any lack of ability – that prevented him from becoming a great humorist. Let us take a quick peep at his *Essay on Comedy*:

> There are plain reasons why the Comic poet is not a frequent apparition; and why the great Comic poet remains without a fellow. A society of cultivated men and women is required, wherein ideas are current and the perceptions quick, that he may be supplied with matter and an audience. The semi-barbarism of merely giddy communities, and feverish emotional periods, repel him; and also a state of marked social inequality of the sexes; nor can he whose business is to address the mind be understood where there is not a moderate degree of intellectual activity. . . .

We may not disagree with what is said there; but I feel certain that many readers will find, as I do, its high and dry manner unattractive. We are being addressed loftily by a rather affected vain man. There is no humorist trying to confide in us here. This is not a man and a brother who will ever laugh at himself. We can expect wit and flashing glimpses of character, which Meredith has in abundance, together (as in *The Adventures of Harry Richmond*, for instance) with tremendous zest and a constant sparkle or with the sharp ironies of *The Egoist*; but there will be only tantalising glimpses of real humour. I am sorry to hurry away from a poet and novelist of impressive stature, whose work has been so under-valued now for half a century; but I must keep to my subject.

It is ironical that Hardy, whose universe was far darker and crueller than Meredith's, can show us more real humour. It comes out of the slow talk of his Dorset rustics:

'Times have changed from the times they used to be,' said Mail, regarding nobody can tell what interesting old panoramas with an inward eye, and letting his outward glance rest on the ground, because it was as convenient a position as any. 'People don't care much about us now! I've been thinking, we must be almost the last left in the country of the old string-players. Barrel-organs, and they next door to 'em that you blow wi' your foot, have come in terribly of late years.'

'Ah!' said Bowman, shaking his head; and old William, on seeing him, did the same thing.

'More's the pity,' replied another. 'Time was – long and merry ago now – when not one of the varmits was to be heard of; but it served some of the choirs right. They should have stuck to strings as we did, and keep out clar'nets, and done away with serpents. If you'd thrive in musical religion, stick to strings, says I.'

'Strings are well enough, as far as that goes,' said Mr. Spinks.

'There's worse things than serpents,' said Mr. Penny. 'Old things pass away, 'tis true; but a serpent was a good old note; a deep rich note was the serpent.'

'Clar'nets, however, be bad at all times,' said Michael Mail. 'One Christmas – yearsagone now, years – I went the rounds wi' the Dibbeach choir. 'Twas a hard frosty night, and the keys of all the clar'nets froze – ah, they did freeze – so that 'twas like drawing a cork every time a key was opened; the players o' 'em had to go into a hedger and ditcher's chimley-corner, and thaw their clar'nets every now and then. An icicle o' spet hung down from the end of every man's clar'net a span long; and as to fingers – well, there, if ye'll believe men, we had no fingers at all, to our knowledge.'

'I can well bring back to my mind,' said Mr. Penny, 'what I said to poor Joseph Ryme (who took the tribble part in High-Story Church for two-and-forty year) when they thought of having clar'nets there. "Joseph," I said, says I, "depend upon't, if so be you have them tooting clar'nets you'll spoil the whole set-out. Clar'nets were not made for the service of Providence; you can see it by looking at 'em," I said. And what cam o't? Why, my dear souls, the parson set up a barrel-organ on his own account within two years o' the time I spoke, and the old choir went to nothing.'

'As far as look is concerned,' said the tranter, 'I don't for my part see that a fiddle is much nearer heaven than a clar'net. 'Tis farther off. There's always a rakish scampish countenance about a fiddle that seems to say the Wicked One had a hand in making o'en; while angels be supposed to play clar'nets in heaven, or som'at like 'em, if ye may believe picters.'

There is rustic genius in some of these phrases. What could be better than 'long and merry ago now'? Are there any richer humorous rural characters than these outside Shakespeare? Thomas Hardy should not have quarrelled so bitterly with a universe that offered him, among other things, such people and such enchanting talk.

We can find many references to 'the New Humour' during the last twenty years of the nineteenth century. There was certainly plenty of rollicking facetiousness, which attracted a large public. Much of it appeared in *Punch*, edited by F. C. Burnand, a desperate punster, whose best book *Happy Thoughts* came as early as 1866. (Here the frustrated diarist's great work in hand is called *Typical Developments*, an inspired absurd title.) Burnand's most popular contributor was probably 'F. Anstey' (Guthrie) who could combine a grave farcical manner with wild invention. But the 'smash hit' of this period came from outside *Punch*, which resented its author's success. This was *Three Men in a Boat* by Jerome K. Jerome. Even when I was young, twenty years after its first appearance, it was still making us laugh, but what today's youth would make of it, I can't imagine. Jerome was not really a humorist in grain; he was a man who took himself seriously (incidentally a good editor) and was at heart a sentimentalist. But once he had those three men on the Thames, he was determined to be funny, and certainly for his own time he succeeded. But in any chronicle of humour he fades away at the mere mention of the Brothers Grossmith, for it was they who wrote the immortal *Diary of a Nobody*.

There is a mystery here that baffles me. George and Weedon Grossmith were two successful funny men on the stage. But their *Nobody*, Charles Pooter, is a middle-aged, ultra-respectable, humourless, socially timid City clerk, living in a gimcrack villa in Holloway. To begin with, I do not understand how they came to be acquainted with the background and style of life of such a man. If they cheerfully made it all up, to provide them with a serial for *Punch* in 1892, then my wonder is all the greater. To be sure, there are comic exaggerations; poor Mr Pooter, who is nothing if not candid, has to record too many mishaps; and some of his acquaintances, towards the end, are unlikely and are obvious caricatures. Even so, making a few allowances, we believe and are held by almost everything he tells us. He comes down all the years to exist as an enduring great comic character, and we share with him his 'dear wife Carrie', his dashing son Lupin, the constant poppers-in, Gowing, not dependable and always 'going too far', the kind but dull Cummings, that ideal among employers, Mr Perkupp, and a host of other figures. Pooter soon becomes more than a butt: he stays comic yet he seems real and touching. We have arrived at last at true humour again, with its mixture of absurdity, irony and affection. I have just read *The Diary of a Nobody* once again, and it seems to me to wear wonderfully well, though I must warn readers who don't know it that it is best enjoyed as a whole. But as I can't begin to quote fifty different passages along the way, I offer as a

'The greengrocer's boy . . .
who pushed into my hands two
cabbages and half-a-dozen
coal-blocks', illustration
by Weedon Grossmith to
Diary of a Nobody, by George
and Weedon Grossmith, 1892

generous tasting sample the memorable evening of the Lord Mayor's reception and
ball:

A big red-letter day; viz., the Lord Mayor's reception. The whole house upset. I had
to get dressed at half-past six, as Carrie wanted the room to herself. Mrs. James had
come up from Sutton to help Carrie; so I could not help thinking it unreasonable that
she should require the entire attention of Sarah, the servant, as well. Sarah kept
running out of the house to fetch 'something for missis,' and several times I had, in my
full evening-dress, to answer the back-door.

The last time it was the greengrocer's boy, who, not seeing it was me, for Sarah had
not lighted the gas, pushed into my hands two cabbages and half-a-dozen coal-blocks. I
indignantly threw them on the ground, and felt so annoyed that I so far forgot myself as
to box the boy's ears. He went away crying, and said he should summons me, a thing I
would not have happen for the world. In the dark, I stepped on a piece of the cabbage,
which brought me down on the flags, all of a heap. For a moment I was stunned, but
when I recovered I crawled upstairs into the drawing-room and on looking into the
chimney-glass discovered that my chin was bleeding, my shirt smeared with the coal-
blocks, and my left trouser torn at the knee.

However, Mrs. James brought me down another shirt, which I changed in the drawing-room. I put a piece of court-plaster on my chin, and Sarah very neatly sewed up the tear at the knee. At nine o'clock Carrie swept into the room, looking like a queen. Never have I seen her look so lovely, or so distinguished. She was wearing a satin dress of sky-blue – my favourite colour – and a piece of lace, which Mrs. James lent her, round the shoulders to give a finish. I thought perhaps the dress was a little too long behind, and decidedly too short in front, but Mrs. James said it was *à la mode*. Mrs. James was most kind, and lent Carrie a fan of ivory with red feathers, the value of which, she said, was priceless, as the feathers belonged to the Kachu eagle – a bird now extinct. I preferred the little white fan which Carrie bought for three-and-six at Shoolbred's, but both ladies sat on me at once.

We arrived at the Mansion House too early, which was rather fortunate, for I had an opportunity of speaking to his lordship, who graciously condescended to talk with me some minutes; but I must say I was disappointed to find he did not even know Mr. Perkupp, the principal.

I felt as if we had been invited to the Mansion House by one who did not know the Lord Mayor himself. Crowds arrived, and I shall never forget the grand sight. My humble pen can never describe it. I was a little annoyed with Carrie, who kept saying: 'Isn't it a pity we don't know anybody?'

Once she quite lost her head. I saw someone who looked like Franching, from Peckham, and was moving towards him when she seized me by the coat-tails, and said, quite loudly: 'Don't leave me,' which caused an elderly gentleman, in a court-suit, and a chain round him, and two ladies, to burst out laughing. There was an immense crowd in the supper-room, and, my stars! it was a splendid supper – any amount of champagne.

Carrie made a most hearty supper, for which I was pleased; for I sometimes think she is not strong. There was scarcely a dish she did not taste. I was so thirsty, I could not eat much. Receiving a sharp slap on the shoulder, I turned, and, to my amazement, saw Farmerson, our ironmonger. He said, in the most familiar way; 'This is better than Brickfield Terrace, eh?' I simply looked at him, and said coolly: 'I never expected to see you here.' He said, with a loud, coarse laugh: 'I like that – if *you*, why not *me*?' I replied: 'Certainly.' I wish I could have thought of something better to say. He said: 'Can I get your good lady anything?' Carrie said: 'No, I thank you,' for which I was pleased. I said, by way of reproof to him: 'You never sent to-day to paint the bath, as I requested.' Farmerson said: 'Pardon me, Mr. Pooter, no shop when we're in company, please.'

Before I could think of a reply, one of the sheriffs, in full Court costume, slapped Farmerson on the back and hailed him as an old friend, and asked him to dine with him at his lodge. I was astonished. For full five minutes they stood roaring with laughter, and stood digging each other in the ribs. They kept telling each other they didn't look a day older. They began embracing each other and drinking champagne.

To think that a man who mends our scraper should know any member of our aristocracy! I was just moving with Carrie, when Farmerson seized me rather roughly by the collar, and addressing the sheriff said: 'Let me introduce my neighbour, Pooter.'

'Mr Farmerson smokes all the way home in the cab',
illustration by Weedon Grossmith to *Diary of a Nobody*,
by George and Weedon Grossmith, 1892

He did not even say 'Mister.' The sheriff handed me a glass of champagne. I felt, after all, it was a great honour to drink a glass of wine with him, and I told him so. We stood chatting for some time, and at last I said: 'You must excuse me now if I join Mrs. Pooter.' When I approached her, she said: 'Don't let me take you away from friends. I am quite happy standing here alone in a crowd, knowing nobody!'

As it takes two to make a quarrel, and as it was neither the time nor the place for it, I gave my arm to Carrie, and said: 'I hope my darling little wife will dance with me, if only for the sake of saying we had danced at the Mansion House as guests of the Lord Mayor.' Finding the dancing after supper was less formal, and knowing how much Carrie used to admire my dancing in the days gone by, I put my arm round her waist and we commenced a waltz.

A most unfortunate accident occurred. I had got on a new pair of boots. Foolishly, I had omitted to take Carrie's advice; namely, to scratch the soles of them with the points of the scissors or to put a little wet on them. I had scarcely started when, like lightning, my left foot slipped away and I came down, the side of my head striking the floor with such violence that for a second or two I did not know what had happened. I need hardly say that Carrie fell with me with equal violence, breaking the comb in her hair and grazing her elbow.

There was a roar of laughter, which was immediately checked when people found that we had really hurt ourselves. A gentleman assisted Carrie to a seat, and I expressed myself pretty strongly on the danger of having a plain polished floor with no carpet or drugget to prevent people slipping. The gentleman, who said his name was Darwitts, insisted on escorting Carrie to have a glass of wine, an invitation which I was pleased to allow Carrie to accept.

I followed, and met Farmerson, who immediately said, in his loud voice: 'Oh, are you the one who went down?'

I answered with an indignant look.

With execrable taste, he said: 'Look here, old man, we are too old for this game. We must leave these capers to the youngsters. Come and have another glass, that is more in our line.'

Although I felt I was buying his silence by accepting, we followed the others into the supper-room.

Neither Carrie nor I, after our unfortunate mishap, felt inclined to stay longer. As we were departing, Farmerson said: 'Are you going? if so, you might give me a lift.'

I thought it better to consent, but wish I had first consulted Carrie.

'Mr Padge', illustration by Weedon Grossmith to *Diary of a Nobody*, by George and Weedon Grossmith, 1892

Readers new to this masterpiece must discover for themselves why Carrie was cross next day, how Gowing came and played the fool in a vulgar manner, and why Mr Pooter was annoyed with the *Blackfriars Bi-Weekly News*. They have only to explore further and meet the most laconic character in all English Literature – Mr Padge, who keeps turning up and taking the best armchair and never says anything but 'That's right'.

A strikingly different account of life in the 1890s can be discovered in the works of Arthur M. Binstead – *A Pink 'Un and a Pelican, Pitcher in Paradise, Gal's Gossip*, etc. Binstead was a renowned regular contributor to 'The Pink 'Un' *(The Sporting Times)* and was himself a sporting man-about-town type, whose large acquaintance included Bohemian journalists racing bloods and prominent bookies, theatrical people, and the fair acquiescent ladies to be found in the promenade at the Empire. Among his admirers were Belloc, Arnold Bennett, E. V. Lucas, Professor Raleigh, Lord Rosebery. I have read Binstead off and on for years, always with amusement – he can tell a funny story with great gusto and some art – he also dramatically reveals what is to us a lost world – but even so I feel that his devotees named above tend to force their enthusiasm. He is good, but not *that* good. His favourite adjectives for his friends – either 'poor' or 'good old' – make us feel uneasy. 'Poor' is applied to the cleverish, lively but foolish young men who stayed up until four in the morning, full of old brandy, and died before they reached their forties. The 'good old' are tougher survivors, not always really old and perhaps rarely very good. The eating and drinking – at ridiculous low prices that leave us gasping with envy – are mostly on a stupendous scale. One of their favourite restaurants was Romano's, whose proprietor was usually referred to as 'the Roman':

Although the wellworn growl at the Roman's prices has been swollen into a roar by hundreds of men who never paid a bill there, no doubt exists that his tariff was a bit steep at times. Indeed, I call to mind an occasion on which he and four or five others had been lunching together. It had been anybody's table, and, as was not infrequently the case, the question of the bill was ultimately submitted to the hazard of the gentle flutter. It was the Roman himself who proposed it, and in the heaven-ordained order of such things, it was the Roman who got it. Then he adjusted his pince-nez, glanced in awe at some of the items, and, completely forgetting himself, roared out:

'Foura-pound eight! For what? What aswindling prices! Whata hava we ahad for it, I like to aknow! Of all whatyoucall outa-rageous – '

At this point, however, a roar of unsympathetic laughter broke up the Roman's soliloquy and recalled his attention to the fact that he was still in his own restaurant.

However, most of Binstead's tales are longer, riper, juicier than that.

We might as well leave the century here, with Binstead and his friends hurrying back from a race meeting to change into 'white tie and tails', which they seem to have done every evening at about seven o'clock. The hansoms go click-clacking away towards Piccadilly, Leicester Square and the Strand. Their night will be just starting when Mr Pooter, after a game of dominoes with Gowing or Cummings, is wondering if it is not close to bedtime. One of their nights, too often ending at dawn, would put him to bed for a couple of days. Yet they are not among the immortals – and Mr Pooter is.

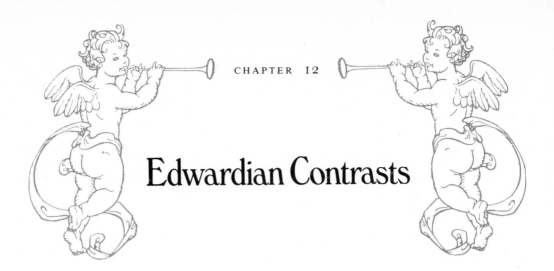

CHAPTER 12

Edwardian Contrasts

The most important writer, as a world figure, to appear in this chapter is H. G. Wells, so let us begin with him. He had an astonishingly large rich personality but it had to find room for and support too many conflicting characters. A great humorist cannot live long at ease with an impatient reformer and a thundering prophet. These two cannot afford to laugh at themselves, at least not openly in public. (Almost to the end Wells's innate humour spilled over into his twinkling talk, as I know because we often met during his later years.) I have been acquainted with a number of men who thought they were literary geniuses when they weren't: H.G. really was one, but was so bent on teaching and preaching that he swept aside any notion of being a literary genius. Except when he was at his worst, humour kept bubbling up in him, quite apart from his two comic classics, *Kipps* and *Mr. Polly*. But even here, among these treasures of humour, the real precious thing, the reformer and the prophet, both equally impatient, are trying to interfere. (Indeed, he found it hard to finish *Kipps*.) Here we have to ignore the world figure, the educator of remote nations, and keep to our subject, and when we do this we have to mourn the loss of a really great humorist, who might have given us book after book, arising out of a sense of reality, irony, and affection, all to be found in *Kipps* and *Mr. Polly*. When he wanted to be humorous he discovered by instinct the right breadth and depth and expansiveness. Though he would not have thanked you for saying so, he was already in the great tradition. Having once known them, who could forget the timid entrances of Kipps into local society, with Mr Coote as chaperone? Or the highly individual linguistics of Mr Polly, the saga of his conflict with Uncle Jim at the Potwell Inn, or his final encounter with Miriam? But though gleams of humour rarely fade out, where are the successors of these two masterworks? At his funeral service, which I had to conduct, I paid a heartfelt tribute to his value and fame as a world figure; but now, writing about English Humour, there is something I might not unreasonably add. Too much of his later work was spoilt by too much impatience and intolerance of all opposition, too much splenetic repetition, losing not winning his readers; and I have sometimes wondered if that was not the revenge of the great humorist in him that he silenced and tried to forget. But even so, I do not expect to meet anybody better than Kipps and Mr Polly along the way in this chapter.

Now I must do something I don't want to do – I must admit a disappointment. In the early 1920s I wrote a rather solemn appreciation of W. W. Jacobs and his tales. He had been one of my father's favourites, and I had grown up with his books around the house. I had never seen one of his sleepy decayed little ports, where his schooners landed and put ashore his comic sailors; but, thanks to Jacobs, I could imagine and enjoy them. (To give him his due – he did create a little world of his own.) But I wasn't simply trying to please my father, still alive then, when I wrote that appreciation. I was pleasing myself, still under the spell of Jacobs's atmosphere, neat little plots and sly humour. I hadn't read him again for many years – not even, I think, at odd moments – and I looked forward to bringing him into this book. To prepare myself, I read some of the longer tales, remembering that *The Skipper's Wooing*, dating from the 1890s, had been one of my first favourites; and I went through scores of his short stories, belonging to this century. And – alas, alas! – I moved uneasily between mild amusement and boredom. The old laughable magic had vanished. There are two possible explanations of this failure. (I refuse to believe I am now incapable of laughing at anything.) The first, which I am afraid will be generally accepted, is that Jacobs, so quiet and mild – in his humour, for he did write two or three good horror stories – withers in our later atmosphere, turning into an outdated, faded funny man. Out of an old loyalty, I prefer the second explanation, which is that long ago I sucked most of the juice and nourishment out of his tales and could not do it all over again. (This can happen to us with authors far more important than Jacobs – e.g. for me with writers as different as Swinburne and Whitman.) So, for the sake of readers who do not know this modest humorist at all, I include a fairly typical sample of his method and manner. Mr Gunnill, after a riotous night, is facing his indignant daughter, young females in Jacobs being either far too shy or quite ferocious:

'Bailed out,' said Miss Gunnill, in a deep and thrilling voice; 'bailed out at one o'clock in the morning, brought home singing loud enough for half a dozen, and then talking about flowers!'

Mr. Gunnill coughed again.

'I was dreaming,' pursued Miss Gunnill, plaintively, 'sleeping peacefully, when I was awoke by a horrible noise.'

'That couldn't ha' been me,' protested her father. 'I was only a bit cheerful. It was Benjamin Ely's birthday yesterday and after we left the Lion they started singing, and I just hummed to keep 'em company. It wasn't singing, mind you, only humming – when up comes that interfering Cooper and takes me off.'

Miss Gunnill shivered, and with her pretty cheek in her hand, sat by the window the very picture of despondency. 'Why didn't he take the others?' she inquired.

'*Ah!*' said Mr. Gunnill, with great emphasis, 'that's what a lot more of us would like to know. P'r'aps, if you'd been more polite to Mrs. Cooper, instead o' putting it about that she looked young enough to be his mother, it wouldn't have happened.'

His daughter shook her head impatiently and, on Mr. Gunnill making an allusion to breakfast, expressed surprise that he had got the heart to eat anything. Mr. Gunnill pressing the point, however, she arose and began to set the table, the undue care with which she smoothed out the creases of the tablecloth, and the mathematical exactness with which she placed the various articles, all being so many extra smarts in his wound. When she finally placed enough food for a dozen people he began to show signs of a little spirit.

'Ain't you going to have any?' he demanded, as Miss Gunnill resumed her seat by the window.

'*Me?*' said the girl, with a shudder. 'Breakfast? The disgrace is breakfast enough for me. I couldn't eat a morsel; it would choke me.'

Mr. Gunnill eyed her over the rim of his teacup. 'I come down an hour ago,' he said casually, as he helped himself to some bacon.

Miss Gunnill started despite herself. 'Oh!' she said, listlessly.

'And I see you making a very good breakfast all by yourself in the kitchen,' continued her father, in a voice not free from the taint of triumph.

The discomfited Selina rose and stood regarding him; Mr. Gunnill, after a vain attempt to meet her gaze, busied himself with his meal.

'The idea of watching every mouthful I eat!' said Miss Gunnill tragically; 'the idea of complaining because I have some breakfast! I'd never have believed it of you, never! it's shameful! Fancy grudging your own daughter the food she eats?'

Readers whose fancy is tickled by this extract – and I shall be with them in spirit – may rest assured that there is plenty of W. W. Jacobs waiting for them.

The next humorous man on my list offers the sharpest possible contrast to Jacobs, being huge, picturesque, flamboyant both in and out of his writing. And who could this be but G. K. Chesterton? He might be described as a poetical and polemical humorist. He did a great deal of 'thinking in fun while feeling in earnest'. At his best he could combine polemic and debate with genuine high spirits. Even if you suspected his reasoning – and he was very fond of false analogies – you enjoyed him. His fellow Catholics may deny this, but to my mind he is at his best, in the highest spirits, in his earliest work. (A very serious illness in 1914–15 slowed him down, and he never quite recovered the old zest and sparkle and cheerful impudence. When I met him occasionally after the War he was drinking ginger ale instead of wine, and it was as if the wine had been drained out of his work.) But his first prose books are astonishing, as if he started – bang! – at the top of his form, both brilliant and assured. To my mind he never offered us a better collection of essays than his *Tremendous Trifles* (1909), beginning, some happy readers may remember, with the account of how he went on the South Downs to draw with coloured chalks, found to his disgust that he had forgotten to bring any white chalk, only to discover that he was sitting on a whole hill of white chalk.

His book on Dickens, which can be read with excitement to this day, goes back to

1906. It is filled with fun, sound criticism, and an intuitive wisdom that ought to appeal to us here. The following is an example of it, when he is discussing the way in which we are attracted to notable comic characters:

> To every man alive, one must hope, it has in some manner happened that he has talked with his more fascinating friends round a table on some night when all the numerous personalities unfolded themselves like great tropical flowers. All fell into their parts as in some delightful impromptu play. Every man was more himself than he has ever been in this vale of tears. Every man was a beautiful caricature of himself. The man who has known such nights will understand the exaggerations of 'Pickwick'. The man who has not known such nights will not enjoy 'Pickwick' nor (I imagine) Heaven. . . .

Again take this enlargement of Mrs Nickleby:

> It is exquisitely characteristic of Dickens that the truly great achievement of the story is the person who delays the story. Mrs. Nickleby, with her beautiful mazes of memory, does her best to prevent the story of Nicholas Nickleby from being told. And she does well. There is no particular necessity that we should know what happens to Madeline Bray. There is a desperate and crying necessity that we should know Mrs. Nickleby once had a foot-boy who had a wart on his nose and a driver who had a green shade over his left eye. If Mrs. Nickleby is a fool, she is one of those fools who are wiser than the world. She stands for a great truth which we must not forget; the truth that experience is not in real life a saddening thing at all. The people who have had misfortunes are generally the people who love to talk about them. Experience is one of the gaieties of old age, one of its dissipations. Mere memory becomes a kind of debauch. Experience may be disheartening to those who are foolish enough to try to co-ordinate it and draw deductions from it. But to those happy souls, like Mrs. Nickleby, to whom relevancy is nothing, the whole of their past life is like an inexhaustible fairyland. Just as we take a rambling walk because we know that a whole district is beautiful, so they indulge a rambling mind because they know that a whole existence is interesting. A boy does not plunge into the future more romantically and at random, than they plunge into their past. . . .

Any reader who sees this simply as so many cheerfully impudent paradoxes has not thought about life and the people he has met in it.

Chesterton is not a creative humorist, not even in his fantastic tales like *The Napoleon of Notting Hill* or *The Man Who was Thursday*. (The *Father Brown* stories seem to me on a lower level of invention.) He is always working with ideas and polemic. But everything he did, especially in his earlier work, is steeped in humour and enriched by it. Even if he does not succeed in converting us – and I for one reject many of his deepest convictions – we ought to recognize him as a great fruity character whose sense of humour should appeal to our sense of it. The space he occupied at one time, a time when gifted writers were important, long before film stars and 'television personalities' took a greater hold on the public, encouraged a reaction against him. Now it appears that at last he is coming back into favour. This is a victory for humour in polemical writing.

Chesterton's friend and close ally, Hilaire Belloc, whom I met more often, cannot be described as a humorist. He had an enormous sense of fun, together with a sharp satirical wit, but he lacked the tolerance and indulgence of the humorous man. Though he looked almost like the John Bull of the cartoonists, he was, I fancy, both in heart and mind more French than English. (He had a French father and an English mother, and he was the kind of man to take more from his father than from his mother.) He was a whale of a character, but it was not a humorous whale.

'A pretty wit,' said *Pall Mall*, noticing Max Beerbohm's earliest work. Though a more substantial author, with many editions to his credit, than we generally imagine him to be, the 'pretty wit' aspect of his work, personality, and career still remains. Even after living for years in Rapallo, with the twentieth century rolling on through iron, blood and tears, he still seemed to emerge, a dainty cult figure, still from the Nineties, still wearing a top hat. He has of course plenty of humour of a rather detached fastidious kind, but I think he would have been shocked if anybody had

Ivor Novello in *The Happy Hypocrite*, by Max Beerbohm, His Majesty's, 1936

called him a humorist. And probably he would have been right. Though he made a name for himself, on radio in his last years, he rarely plunged into life, but kept writing – and writing superbly well – round the edge of literature. He could make a break, as in *The Happy Hypocrite*, that solemn lark, but most of his themes are literary; he was always writing about writers. (But, as his collected notices prove, he was a useful and sensible dramatic critic.) If I could keep only one book of his, my choice would be *A Christmas Garland*, the best assembly of parodies of this or any other century, keeping deliciously close to his victims in style, manner and matter. (They beat his drawings, in my estimation.) His most sustained effort, *Zuleika Dobson*, perhaps hovers rather uncertainly between absurdity and a convincing narrative, though it has its moments. For example, her talk with the Duke:

'You don't believe in the love that corrodes, the love that ruins?'
'No' laughed Zuleika.
'You have never dipped into the Greek pastoral poets, nor sampled the Elizabethan sonneteers?'
'No, never. You will think me lamentably crude: my experience of life has been drawn from life itself.'
'Yet often you talk as though you had read rather much. Your way of speech has what is called "the literary flavour".'
'Ah, that is an unfortunate trick which I caught from a writer, a Mr Beerbohm, who once sat next to me at dinner somewhere. I can't break myself of it. I assure you I hardly ever open a book. . . .'

I am particularly fond of the end of Zuleika's story, when, having exhausted the possibilities of Oxford, she decides (mistakenly, I think) to try Cambridge.

. . . And now she wheeled round and swiftly glided to that little table on which stood her two books. She snatched Bradshaw.
We always intervene between Bradshaw and any one whom we see consulting him. 'Mademoiselle will permit me to find that which she seeks?' asked Mélisande.
'Be quiet,' said Zuleika. We always repulse, at first, any one who intervenes between us and Bradshaw.
We always end by accepting the intervention. 'See if it is possible to go direct from here to Cambridge,' said Zuleika, handing the book on. 'If it isn't, then – well, see how one *does* get there.'
We never have any confidence in the intervener. Nor is the intervener, when it comes to the point, sanguine. With mistrust mounting to exasperation Zuleika sat watching the faint and frantic researches of her maid.
'Stop!' she said suddenly. 'I have a much better idea. Go down very early to the station. See the station-master. Order me a special train. For ten o'clock, say.'
Rising, she stretched her arms above her head. Her lips parted in a yawn, met in a

smile. With both hands she pushed back her hair from her shoulders, and twisted it into a loose knot. Very lightly she slipped up into bed, and very soon she was asleep.

Yes – a very pretty wit.

We must salute along the way, with nods of recognition and grateful smiles, various men who have entertained us generously. I am thinking, for example, of 'Q' (Quiller-Couch) and his Cornish tales; of Arnold Bennett (especially for *The Card*); of the sardonic E. F. Benson and his chief victim, Lucia – and certainly *Lucia in London*; of those renowned *Punch* men, A. A. Milne and A. P. Herbert, though both of them did their best work outside the paper. Nevertheless, I propose to single out for special attention a man who must have had fewer readers than any of the above, if only because he is the most rewarding example I know of a not unfamiliar type, namely, the Humorist in Disguise.

His name was Ernest Bramah Smith, but as an author he left out the 'Smith'. After trying to make farming pay, he passed some years in China, and it is from there he borrowed his disguise, relating the adventures of one Kai Lung, a wandering story-teller, unrolling his mat in a hundred market places. All is written in a solemn mock-Oriental manner and style, the launching pad for innumerable shafts of wit and humour. Either you find this a joy for ever – and Bramah has always had his faithful devotees, of whom I am one; or you don't care for this kind of elaborate fooling. (I have yet to meet a feminine Bramah enthusiast.) I feel I must have here a large number of readers who neither accept (with joy) Kai Lung nor reject him, not having encountered him at all. With these in mind, I could either allow Kai Lung to introduce himself or extract various shining nuggets of wit, like this tribute to a Beauty: 'After secretly observing the unstudied grace of her movements, the most celebrated picture-maker of the province burned the implements of his craft, and began life anew as a trainer of performing elephants.' But – as they say here – however entrancing it is to wander unchecked through a garden of bright images, I had better allow Kai Lung to introduce himself:

Across the glade two maidens stood in poised expectancy within the shadow of a wild fig-tree, both their gaze and their attitude denoting a fixed intention to be prepared for any emergency. Not being desirous that this should tend towards their abrupt departure, Kai Lung rose guardedly to his feet, with many gestures of polite reassurance, and having bowed several times to indicate his pacific nature, he stood in an attitude of deferential admiration. At this display the elder and less attractive of the maidens fled, uttering loud and continous cries of apprehension in order to conceal the direction of her flight. The other remained, however, and even moved a few steps nearer to Kai Lung, as though encouraged by his appearance, so that he was able to regard her varying details more appreciably. As she advanced she plucked a red blossom from a thorny bush, and from time to time she shortened the broken stalk between her jade teeth.

'Courteous loiterer,' she said, in a very pearl-like voice, when they had thus regarded one another for a few beats of time, 'what is your honourable name, and who are you who tarry here, journeying neither to the east nor to the west?'

'The answer is necessarily commonplace and unworthy to your polite interest,' was the diffident reply. 'My unbecoming name is Kai, to which has been added that of Lung. By profession I am an incapable relater of imagined tales, and to this end I spread my mat wherever my uplifted voice can entice together a company to listen. Should my feeble efforts be deemed worthy of reward, those who stand around may perchance contribute to my scanty store, but sometimes this is judged superfluous. For this cause I now turn my expectant feet from Loo-chow towards the untried city of Yu-ping, but the undiminished li stretching relentlessly before me, I sought beneath these trees a refuge from the noontide sun.'

'The occupation is a dignified one, being to no great degree removed from that of the Sages who compiled The Books,' remarked the maiden, with an encouraging smile. 'Are there many stories known to your retentive mind?'

'In one form or another, all that exist are within my mental grasp,' admitted Kai Lung modestly. 'Thus equipped there is no arising emergency for which I am unprepared.'

'There are other things that I would learn of your craft. What kind of story is the most favourably received, and the one whereby your collecting bowl is the least ignored?'

'That depends on the nature and condition of those who stand around, and therein lies much that is essential to the art,' replied Kai Lung, not without an element of pride. 'Should the company be chiefly formed of the illiterate and the immature of both sexes, stories depicting the embarrassment of unnaturally round-bodied mandarins, the unpremeditated flight of eccentrically-garbed passers-by into vats of powdered rice, the despair of guardians of the street when assailed by showers of eggs and overripe loquats, or any other variety of humiliating pain inflicted upon the innocent and unwary, never fail to win approval. The prosperous and substantial find contentment in hearing of the unassuming virtues and frugal lives of the poor and unsuccessful. Those of humble origin, especially teahouse maidens and the like, are only really at home among stories of the exalted and quick-moving, the profusion of their robes, the magnificence of their palaces, and the general high-minded depravity of their lives. Ordinary persons require stories dealing lavishly with all the emotions, so that they may thereby have a feeling of sufficiency when contributing to the collecting bowl.'

Now either you have a taste for this grave ironic drollery or you have not. If you have – and there are three volumes waiting for you – then I can assure you that you will have joined some of the wisest and choicest spirits of this age, a kind of noble Kai Lung conspiracy.

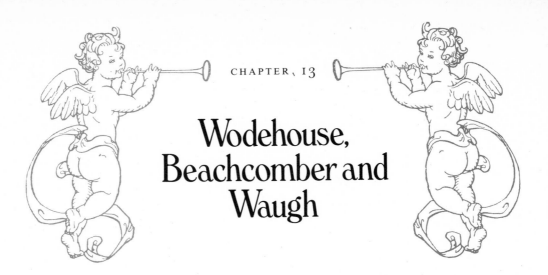

Wodehouse, Beachcomber and Waugh

I am now about to run into trouble. And there is no help for it: a man must stand by his beliefs. It is ironical too that, after dipping into several Wodehouses this afternoon, I began at the tea hour *Uncle Fred in the Springtime*, with its full cast of aristocratic eccentrics and imbeciles, and very, very reluctantly indeed I pulled myself away from it to begin this piece of writing. Yes, we are about to discuss P. G. Wodehouse. *Everyman's Dictionary of Literary Biography*, which I frequently consult, calls Wodehouse 'the greatest humorous novelist' of our time. Now if the *Dictionary* is saying in effect that Wodehouse was a great humorist, then I have no option but to declare it is quite wrong. In my book – this one, in fact – he is not a great humorist at all. He cannot be squeezed into the company of great humorists, alongside Fielding, Sterne, Lamb, Dickens. He is simply not the same *kind* of writer. He has not their irony, their affection, their contact with reality. He does not begin to make us think about life or feel deeply about it. If humour once again is 'thinking in fun while feeling in earnest', he is not a humorist at all, let alone a great one. Compare, for instance, any book by Wodehouse with *The Diary of a Nobody*, and the essential difference should be apparent at once.

This is not an attack on Wodehouse but an attempt, quite sympathetic, to explain him. His huge success has been well deserved. He has probably been the king of our funny men in fiction. Over an astonishingly long period of time he has entertained, 'taken out of themselves', as people like to say, readers of all ages, shapes and sizes. He has made us laugh when often we never feel like laughing. Even when his invention has not been fruitful, when we have met the same sort of characters in the same kind of situations, his narrative, studded with ludicrous metaphors all in good crisp prose, has kept us merrily attentive. But while I have praised him, I have not yet explained him. Risking all on one throw, I will now come to that.

I believe this man, who lived so long, wrote so much, earned several fortunes, was really a schoolboy. He was of course no ordinary schoolboy but a brilliant super-de-luxe schoolboy. This explains what he wrote, how he behaved, why he succeeded. His 'eggs, beans, and crumpets' give us a schoolboy's notion of Edwardian young men-about-town. His sexless young women, running round breaking off their engagements, and his formidable bullying aunts, all belong to a schoolboy's world. So do his eccentric or quite dotty dukes and earls. His behaviour was mostly that of an elderly schoolboy: those letters anxiously inquiring about the School Second Eleven; his helpless dependence on his womenfolk to decide for him where he lived; his idiotic capture by the Nazis in the Second World War; there is no sign of a mature man here. Together with his talent for the absurd, this explains his success. Most of us who enjoy him still have a schoolboy somewhere in us, and to reach that schoolboy (aged about fifteen or sixteen), to let him enjoy himself, is a perfect escape from our adult problems and trials. When Oxford gave him an honorary doctorate, the senior dons there, guffawing and giggling away, had let loose the schoolboys in themselves. Wodehouse did very well as he was, but to become one of our 'great humorists' he would have had to grow up. And after that parting shot, I can happily return to *Uncle Fred in the Springtime*. 'Mustard' Pott is refusing to kidnap that noble animal, the Empress of Blandings:

> 'Well, between you and me, Lord I,' said Claude Pott, discarding loftiness and coming clean, 'there's another reason. I was once bitten by a pig.'
> 'Not really?'
> 'Yes, sir. And ever since then I've had a horror of the animals.'
> Lord Emsworth hastened to point out that the present was a special case. 'You can't be bitten by the Empress.'
> 'Oh, no? Who made that rule?'
> 'She's as gentle as a lamb.'
> 'I was once bitten by a lamb.'

No more work this afternoon!

So – to Beachcomber: my friend, in days long gone, J. B. Morton. Here I must be allowed to be personal; indeed to be personal for both of us, Mr Morton, even with serious work to hand, disdaining all forms of publicity. He and I must be the very last survivors of a band of talkative thirsty writers who met regularly, during the earlier 1920s, in certain Fleet Street pubs, almost always forgetting to eat any lunch. It was about then that he took over Beachcomber from his friend, D. B. Wyndham Lewis, a witty columnist himself (later as Timothy Shy) though never reaching the rich and riotous high spirits of Johnny Morton, as he was known to us then. I can see him now – though it is all of half a century ago – small and roundish, with a bark of a laugh, and nearly always red in the face through indignation, something infuriating having happened on his way to the pub. What of course I didn't know was that he was to become one of the best-known and most-loved humorous writers of our time, keeping up those high spirits during about forty years of daily journalism. I have read him with joy, but though we have both been around for so long, by some sad freak of chance we have never met since those early Fleet Street pub days. I was never avoiding him and I can only hope he was not carefully keeping out of my way. Anyhow, I have him pinned down here.

But I am too old and lazy to find my way through – what is it? – eighteen volumes of collected Beachcomber. So I am depending partly on my memory but mostly on *The Best of Beachcomber*, selected and introduced by Michael Frayn – himself a keen bright spirit, who seems to me to be broadening and deepening all the time, moving from sharp wit into humour. The only thing I missed in this volume was the reply to Roland Milk, the poet, when he wanted to do something Big and Clean: 'Go wash an elephant, Mr. Milk.' Otherwise, the best of those rich and riotous high spirits seem to be here. Beachcomber's early master was undoubtedly Rabelais, but it did not take him long to dart and flash around in a world of his own, making full use of his genius at finding ridiculous but highly suitable names for his characters. So here we begin again the tormented epic of Mr Justice Cocklecarrot and the twelve red-bearded dwarfs:

> Mr Justice Cocklecarrot began the hearing of a very curious case yesterday. A Mrs. Tasker is accused of ringing the doorbell of a Mrs. Renton, and then, when the door is opened, pushing a dozen red-bearded dwarfs into the hall and leaving them there.
>
> For some weeks Mrs. Renton had protested by letter and by telephone to Mrs. Tasker but one day she waited in the hall and caught Mrs. Tasker in the act of pushing the dwarfs into the hall. Mrs. Renton questioned them, and their leader said, 'We know nothing about it. It's just that this Mrs. Tasker pays us a shilling each every time she pushes us into your hall.'
>
> 'But why does she do it?' asked Mrs. Renton.
>
> 'That's what we don't know,' said the spokesman of the little men.

And from then on – as we all ought to know – the Cocklecarrot court was a shambles.

There also begins the unsavoury saga of Captain Foulenough:

News has just come in of the appearance of Captain Foulenough at Lady Drain's cocktail-party. He is said to have entered by the tradesman's entrance. Suspicions were aroused when he seized the arm of Aurora Bagstone, and holding it to his lips, in the manner of a flute-player, kissed it up and down the scale, from wrist to elbow. Aurora remarked afterwards, 'One does like to know who is kissing one, after all.'

Meanwhile Mr. Cowparsleigh had been flung down the steps of Mrs. Woodle's house in Crabapple Mews, and has threatened to make his uncle call in her overdraft.

For the benefit of the uninitiated I must explain that poor Augustus Cowparsleigh is unlucky because he is almost the exact double of the dreadful Captain Foulenough, with frequent humiliating consequences.

Under the heading 'Scenes at Bournemouth', we meet one of Beachcomber's steady favourites:

Dr Strabismus (Whom God Preserve) of Utrecht addressing the Premature Urn Burial Society at Bournemouth, confined himself to booing and hissing the audience. The moment the chairman began to introduce him the Doctor threw an egg at him, which, at such close range, spattered two ladies who were also on the platform. The Doctor then heckled the audience whenever any one of them tried to ask why he did not begin. Finally, he was removed by the police for creating a disturbance. He said afterwards, I seem to have got things the wrong way round.

There is a topical hint here for some lecturers visiting our universities.

'Dr Strabismus',
illustration by Nicolas Bentley to
Beachcomber (alias J. B. Morton)

We cannot overlook the strange sub-plot involving the Huntingdonshire Cabmen, now to be on film:

A camera unit is on its way to Corfu to select scenes for the *List of Huntingdonshire Cabmen*. It was thought, at first, that the film would have a Huntingdon background.

But, as it is a question of earning dollars, the glamour of Huntingdon is not thought powerful enough to excite American audiences.

Whether the Americans will be interested in the names of these cabmen is another matter. 'The whole idea is extremely daring, and the ballet amid the ruins of Luxor suggests that the approach to the task is an imaginative one.' So writes one of the most exasperatingly foolish of the critics.

I don't want to force myself into the role of Prodnose, but I must risk the suggestion that the above item would be better without its final sentence. The imbecility of the project reveals itself.

Where Beachcomber is at his best – and his best is enormous – he is not a direct satirist but is the inspired creator of glorious and instantly laughable nonsense that just has some seasoning of satire, a little pepper in the dish. Reading the specimens I have quoted, a lively young writer, not without talent, might tell himself he had only to let rip and bring out similar stuff by the yard. Well, no doubt he could do it for two or three days, though even then the quality might not be the same, but after a week or two he would be feeling exhausted and in need of a holiday somewhere. Fastened into the column for a couple of months, he would be going out of his mind. Beachcomber kept it up, going both into his mind and cheerfully out of it, for over fifty years. And this is not simply a journalistic feat. It represents a wonderful lovingly remembered contribution to English Humour. Johnny, the only other survivor of that Fleet Street gang which drank its lunches together now salutes you!

I now move to what might be called, if we were in the mystery-story department, *The Strange Case of Evelyn Waugh*. But I will explain that later. Here I recall the appearance, in September 1928, of his *Decline and Fall*. To my relief, it still holds up very well indeed, revealing all over again a new and original humorist with a very cool, impudent, deadpan manner, together with some excellent prose. The young author, only in his middle twenties, seemed to be working in the great tradition of comic story-telling. So, for example, he had his chief characters turning up over and over again in wildly different circumstances, and for one of them, the superb Captain Grimes – for ever in or out of 'the soup' – he was claiming a kind of immortality. This excited my admiration long ago, and did it all over again only the other day.

However, as I remembered how Waugh developed, certain things surprised me. A few quotations will help me to make my point. Here is that old fraud Dr Fagan, proprietor of Llanabba School:

'. . . Many of the boys come from the very best families. Little Lord Tangent has come to us this term, the Earl of Circumference's son, you know. Such a nice little chap, erratic, of course, like all his family, but he has *tone*.' Dr. Fagan gave a long sigh. 'I wish I could say the same for my staff. Between ourselves, Pennyfeather, I think I shall have to get rid of Grimes fairly soon. He is *not* out of the top drawer, and boys notice these things. . . .'

Now for Captain Grimes, who may not be 'out of the top drawer' but is a public-school man:

'. . . I've got a false leg, but that's different. Boys respect that. Think I lost it in the war. Actually,' said the Captain, 'and strictly between ourselves, mind, I was run over by a tram in Stoke-on-Trent when I was one-over-the-eight. . . . This looks like being the first end of term I've seen for two years,' he said dreamily. 'Funny thing, I can always get on all right for about six weeks, and then I land in the soup. I don't believe I was ever meant by Nature to be a schoolmaster. Temperament,' said Grimes, with a far-away look in his eyes – 'that's been my trouble, temperament and sex.'
   'Is it quite easy to get another job after – after you've been in the soup?' asked Paul.
   'Not at first, it isn't, but there're ways. Besides, you see, I'm a public-school man. That means everything. There's a blessed equity in the English social system,' said Grimes, 'that ensures the public-school man against starvation. One goes through four or five years of perfect hell at an age when life is bound to be hell anyway, and after that the social system never lets one down. . . .'

Now we jump forward to the trial that sends Paul to prison for shipping girls from Marseilles to South America, all to oblige his beautiful fiancée, Margot:

Margot Best-Chetwynd's name was not mentioned, though the judge in passing sentence remarked that 'No one could be ignorant of the callous insolence with which, on the very eve of arrest for this most infamous of crimes, the accused had been preparing to join his name with one honoured in his country's history, and to drag down to his own pitiable depths of depravity a lady of beauty, rank and stainless reputation. . . .'

All this when we already know that this same lady has been making a fortune out of the White Slave traffic.
   So what have we got here? We have a young writer, employing his own cool deadpan sort of humour but already going to work in the great tradition of comic story-telling. We have also a satirist with a radical outlook, sharply dismissing the social cant and nonsense of the 1920s. So far, so good. I then went on to re-read, again after many years, *Vile Bodies*, published in 1930. I found it a sad disappointment, lacking the shape and quality of *Decline and Fall*. It is broadly satirical; the Bright Young People and the titled gossip columnists are thoroughly roasted, but the process seemed tedious. Only the antics in Lottie Crump's hotel and the eccentricities of Colonel Blount made good comic reading. Mrs Ape and her Angels were a bore. The ubiquitious and omniscient Jesuit Father in this rambling tale reminded me that it was in 1930 that Waugh joined the Roman Catholic Church, becoming one of its most determined converts. ('Remember that I too am a Catholic, Mr. Waugh', said the Pope – or so the legend runs.) What seemed certain, after reading *Vile Bodies*, was that both the comic traditionalist and the lively radical of two or

three years before had somehow lost heart. Waugh was changing.

In the Prelude to *Decline and Fall* we read:

> A shriller note could now be heard rising from Sir Alastair's rooms; any who have heard
> that sound will shrink at the recollection of it; it is the sound of the English county
> families baying for broken glass. Soon they would all be tumbling out into the quad,
> crimson and roaring in their bottle-green evening coats, for the real romp of the
> evening.

Among their victims is innocent middle-class Paul Pennyfeather, who is 'debagged',
compelled to run round the quad without his trousers, and is finally sent down for
indecent behaviour. But soon, in the 1930s, Waugh moved away from the Paul
Pennyfeathers and began to identify himself with the Sir Alastairs and the roaring
bloods. From *the point of view of this book*, which is not dealing with literature in
general, Waugh took a wrong turning. Most of the gifts remained, notably the sharp
observation and the fine prose, at once precise and harmonious. But the humour did
not broaden and deepen. A new social arrogance emerged. The last trace of
affection, which could accept a Captain Grimes, now vanished, certainly as far as
the lower orders were concerned. On the other hand, the nobility, especially if it
were Catholic, began to be seen through a rather sentimental haze. I am not arguing
now that Waugh did not fulfil his literary promise. What I am suggesting is that if he
had not taken this wrong turning, if he had gone straight on from his beginning, he
might have become one of our great humorists. And I cannot help fancying that this
forsaken humorist finally had his revenge, for though Waugh in his later years had a
good family life and some devoted friends, he appears to have been confused and
unhappy, perhaps haunted by the ghost of the great humorist he might have been.

We have now arrived in our own time. I realise it will be impossible to finish this
chapter adequately – or evenly tidily. Books are piling up all round us. For all I
know, one of the batch of new novels, to which a reviewer has given two hundred
words each in last Sunday's paper, may be a masterpiece of humour. There is, of
course, plenty of facetiousness about, together with occasional explosions of savage
wit (with sex very often its subject); but we are looking for something else. Certainly,
real humour, not devoid of affection, can be found in Angus Wilson; Kingsley Amis
can be sharply droll, though brutality and a desire to shock get in his way as a
humorist; and Malcolm Bradbury is pulling genuine comedy out of his novels of
academic life. But I have a notion that life in England at the present time is not
favourable to humour. Just as envy has come into politics, so self-pity clouds our
cultural life. (Pop music seems to deafen us with it.) To begin with, there is this
notorious 'stress' about which we hear so much, a condition arriving out of noise,
traffic, worry about jobs and money, and a dark undercurrent of foreboding. And in
more intellectual circles there is now a snobbery of pessimism: your comedy is black
but this new man's is even blacker. But while the humorist should laugh at himself, it
is no use his crying at himself.

CHAPTER 14

Feminine Humour

This chapter, I feel, demands a longish introduction and a stout heart. I say this because there now appears to be a law against any discrimination between the sexes. I am too old and have been discriminating too long to obey this law, whatever penalties I risk. If necessary, ready to plead an enfeebled mind, I must declare that I still perceive some differences between men and women. I admit that some men seem rather like women, some women rather like men; but in the main, taking most men and most women, their attitudes of mind and their behaviour are not exactly the same. Nor will I admit, no matter how the daughters of liberation rage at me, that this separate feminine chapter is only another insult to womanhood, one more device of the chauvinistic male. I need a place in which I can do justice to women, even in terms of this book, admiring them and praising them – yes, for their humour.

Humourless women exist; I have met them on various public occasions, which seem to entice them. But I think they are far outnumbered by humourless men, solemn pompous fellows, capable of guffawing at an obvious bad joke but always taking themselves and their affairs with a heavy seriousness, as several million wives know only too well. (They may have to work a marriage like working a farm with oxen.) I have noticed time and again, when women are in feminine company that they enjoy, that while there are very few of those funny stories which most women I know dislike, there seems to be a plentiful supply of light satirical wit, much candid sharp humour, and fine eyes lighting up with laughter. They make a much better job of these little intimate meetings than we men do; have much more command of their own kind of humour; give themselves more freely to it. I am describing life not literature; though it is worth remembering that highly creative humorists owe a great deal to the feminine element deep in their being.

The term *sharp* is important here. Women on the whole have sharper eyes and ears, and when not in the grip of strong emotions have sharper minds, quick to notice pretensions, dubious motives, and all manner of social absurdities. They live closer to life, the actual living tissue of it, than we men do, half lost as we are in doubtful abstractions and vanity, so often lacking in self-knowledge.

Except in an intimate circle and where young children are involved, feminine humour is less indulgent than masculine humour. It uses irony; it is in close contact with reality; but more often than not it lacks the third element – affection. I am not saying that women lack affection; I am not an idiot; what I am saying is that outside the exceptional circumstances noted above, feminine humour in general is not affectionate. While relishing absurdity, it also points an accusing finger. Largely lacking affection *as humour* – affection arriving elsewhere – it is not indulgent nor of course self-indulgent, as comic male writers so often are. Most women novelists, I suggest, use humour briefly then pass on to more serious matters. Humour of a sharper sort is there in their work, enlivening it, glinting away, but they are not keeping at their desks, month after month, to make us laugh. With a few, a very few, exceptions, to which we shall come, they are not offering themselves as humorists, just because they have a sense of humour. And here I have in mind only the sort of work that is worth reading. The men have no monopoly of idly facetious stuff, with anything for a giggle; women can exploit that market too, perhaps more today than yesterday; but here we can leave them alone.

I cannot begin to go through scores and scores of feminine novels to prove that women writers make effective use of their own kind of humour. I need to examine here, at reasonable length, one or two prominent women writers who have made exceptional use of their humour or those who, unlike all their feminine colleagues, have frankly offered themselves to us as humorists. The company may be sparse, but it will be good.

Sweeping aside her predecessors, from coarse Aphra Behn to prim Fanny Burney, I shall begin with no less a person than Jane Austen. This is not because her reputation has lasted longest and has remained firmly at the top. After all, I am not engaged in a critical study of the feminine novel. My business here remains with humour in all its forms, which must not exclude – for reasons already stated – satirical comment and wit.

Jane Austen seems to me all-important because there can be found in her a greater variety of feminine humour than anybody else can show. Moreover, she is capable of ignoring what I have already said about feminine humour. For example, I suggested earlier that women novelists use humour briefly then pass on to more serious matters. Jane Austen can do this of course, but she can also deliberately refuse to do it. I have also said that, unlike male humorists, women hardly ever *indulge* their comic characters, clearing a space for them, stopping everything else to show them off. But not only can Jane Austen do this, *she can overdo it.*

I propose to devote most attention to *Pride and Prejudice* because it is unlike the others in one important particular. It offers us a double attack upon pretence, affectation, hypocrisy, stupidity, sheer silliness. One comes from Jane herself, the other comes from her heroine, the delectable, sharply observant and free-spoken Elizabeth Bennet. We have here, you may say, two feminine humorists at work, as we have not, for example, in *Emma*, a spoilt miss far removed from Elizabeth Bennet. Until we come to the visit to Pemberley and then the terrible disaster of Lydia's elopement (which would mean nothing now, so far and so fast have we travelled), this novel almost makes us feel we are witnessing a sparkling comedy. This could include Mr Collins if his character and appearance were scaled down. That delicious little scene at the beginning of Mr Collins's visit will enable me to make two points.

. . . 'I am happy on every occasion to offer those little delicate compliments which are always acceptable to ladies. I have more than once observed to Lady Catherine, that her charming daughter seemed born to be a duchess, and that the most elevated rank, instead of giving her consequence, would be adorned by her. – These are the kind of little things which please her ladyship, and it is a sort of attention which I feel myself peculiarly bound to pay.'

'You judge very properly,' said Mr. Bennet, 'and it is happy for you that you possess the talent of flattering with delicacy. May I ask whether these pleasing attentions proceed from the impulse of the moment, or are the result of previous study?'

'They arise chiefly from what is passing at the time, and though I amuse myself with suggesting and arranging such little elegant compliments as may be adapted to ordinary occasions, I always wish to give them as unstudied an air as possible.'

Mr. Bennet's expectations were fully answered. His cousin was as absurd as he had hoped, and he listened to him with the keenest enjoyment, maintaining at the same time the most resolute composure of countenance, and except in an occasional glance at Elizabeth, requiring no partner in his pleasure.

By tea-time, however, the dose had been enough, and Mr. Bennet was glad to take his guest into the drawing-room again, and, when tea was over, glad to invite him to read aloud to the ladies. . . .

The two points are these. From now on, Mr Collins is to be overexposed. Mr Bennet is to be underexposed; there is, to my mind, not enough of him. Certainly the fool can be expanded and expanded, whereas the sarcastic and ironical character will not stand such expansion; but even so, I could take more of Mr Bennet, who is merely allowed to drop a few gems, and much less of Mr Collins, who is recklessly indulged.

I did not think so once. Fifty years ago, when I included Mr Collins in my *English Comic Characters*, I could describe him in this fashion:

This simple and by no means entirely prosaic soul, having taken possession so early of his heart's desire, is so happy, so lost in wonder at his own good fortune, that he is a man apart and the happiest creature in the book, for all his solemn airs. He may bore other people, but nothing bores him. He comes into Hertfordshire, to visit the Bennets, as if he were entering fairyland. He admires the furniture, the pictures, the cooking, and his five fair cousins; everywhere he goes, he finds something to admire and to wonder at; he cannot dance at all well, but he is willing to·try; he does not know how to play whist, but sits down to it with pleasure and declares he will be glad to improve himself; if one young lady is not eligible, he immediately transfers his affections to the next; nothing comes amiss. How should it when he is still the vicar of Hunsford and still under the kindly patronage ·of no less a person than Lady Catherine?. . . Mr. Collins, secretly dazed and moonstruck under his elaborate show of formality, has allowed the little imagination he has to be entirely dominated by the wonder of it all; he is so delighted at being in his own place that you cannot expect him to be able to put himself in anybody else's place. . . . He is not only the happiest creature in the book, he is also the least sophisticated. . . .

I then pointed out that Mrs Bennet is silly and shallow enough, all her designs transparent, but compared with Mr Collins she is almost deep. We discover this in that delicious snatch of dialogue between them when Elizabeth, much to her mother's disgust, has refused Mr Collins:

'But depend upon it, Mr. Collins,' she added, 'that Lizzie shall be brought to reason. I will speak to her about it myself directly. She is a very headstrong, foolish girl, and does not know her own interest; but I will *make* her know it.'

'Pardon me for interrupting you, madam,' cried Mr. Collins; 'but if she is really headstrong and foolish, I know not whether she would altogether be a very desirable wife to a man in my situation, who naturally looks for happiness in the marriage state. If, therefore, she actually persists in rejecting my suit, perhaps it were better not to force her into accepting me, because if liable to such defects of temper, she could not contribute much to my felicity. . . .'

Mr Collins's proposal to Elizabeth Bennet. Illustration by Hugh Thomson to *Pride and Prejudice*, by Jane Austen, 1894 edition

This wonder-struck, poetical Mr Collins belongs to the paradoxical eloquence of 1925. In 1975 I am less eloquent but more sensible. I think Jane Austen over-indulges this character, good as he is. There comes a point when we want to say to Mr Collins what Mr Bennet said to his daughter after she had been singing too much: 'You have delighted us long enough.' Even so, his proposal to Elizabeth is a masterpiece of heavy male tactlessness, with every remark he makes calculated to feed her contempt or anger. As he brings up his reasons, he sinks deeper and deeper into the morass:

'My reasons for marrying are, first, that I think it a right thing for every clergyman in easy circumstances (like myself) to set the example of matrimony in his parish; secondly, that I am convinced it will add very greatly to my happiness; and thirdly, which perhaps I ought to have mentioned earlier, that it is the particular advice and recommendation of the very noble lady whom I have the honour of calling patroness. Twice has she condescended to give me her opinion (unasked too!) on this subject; and it was the very Saturday night before I left Hunsford – between our pools at quadrille, while Mrs. Jenkinson was arranging Miss de Bourgh's footstool, that she said, "Mr. Collins, you must marry. A clergyman like you must marry. – Chuse properly, chuse a gentlewoman for *my* sake; and for your *own*, let her be an active, useful sort of person, not brought up high, but able to make a small income go a good way. This is my advice. Find such a woman as soon as you can, bring her to Hunsford, and I will visit her".'

On this high level of absurdity, we cannot have too much of Mr Collins; but the fact remains that Jane Austen did overindulge him later, when he is our host at Hunsford. Her successors in the feminine novel would have pointed a finger of ridicule and scorn, and then moved on. But could they have created a Mr Collins?

Now I take leave to introduce another and longer quotation, involving Mr Collins, because it brings us to another – and more familiar – level of feminine humour:

The Bennets were engaged to dine with the Lucases, and again during the chief of the day was Miss Lucas so kind as to listen to Mr. Collins. Elizabeth took an opportunity of thanking her. 'It keeps him in good humour,' said she, 'and I am more obliged to you than I can express.' Charlotte assured her friend of her satisfaction in being useful, and that it amply repaid her for the little Charlotte's kindness extended farther than Elizabeth had any conception of; – its object was nothing else than to secure her from any return of Mr. Collins's addresses, by engaging them towards herself. Such was Miss Lucas's scheme; and appearances were so favourable, that when they parted at night, she would have felt almost sure of success if he had not been to leave Hertfordshire so very soon. But here she did injustice to the fire and independence of his character, for it led him to escape out of Longbourn House the next morning with admirable slyness, and hasten to Lucas Lodge to throw himself at her feet. He was anxious to avoid the notice of his cousins from a conviction that if they saw him depart, they could not fail to conjecture his design, and he was not willing to have the attempt known till its success

could be known likewise; for though feeling almost secure, and with reason, for Charlotte had been tolerably encouraging, he was comparatively diffident since the adventure of Wednesday. His reception, however, was of the most flattering kind. Miss Lucas perceived him from the upper window as he walked towards the house, and instantly set out to meet him accidentally in the lane. But little had she dared to hope that so much love and eloquence awaited her there.

In as short a time as Mr. Collins's long speeches would allow, everything was settled between them to the satisfaction of both; and as they entered the house he earnestly entreated her to name the day that was to make him the happiest of men; and though such a solicitation must be waived for the present, the lady felt no inclination to trifle with his happiness. The stupidity with which he was favoured by nature must guard his courtship from any charm that could make a woman wish for its continuance; and Miss Lucas, who accepted him solely from the pure and disinterested desire of an establishment, cared not how soon that establishment were gained.

This might be described, in tobacco terms, as *medium flavour* as against the *full rich flavour* of solo performances by Mr Collins. But it is fairly sharp too.

We must remember that Charlotte Lucas was a sensible girl and one of Elizabeth's very few friends. How great then was her anxiety to be married and have 'an establishment' when she was ready to live with Mr Collins, all in the shadow of Lady Catherine de Bourgh! Reading *Pride and Prejudice* again after some years, I am struck by its comparative severity, its hard critical choice of characters, probably designed to bring Elizabeth herself into high relief. Consider the Bennet family itself. Mr Bennet is far from being a fool, yet he behaves towards his family foolishly and indolently. (Elizabeth is his favourite, so far as he has one, but they are not close.) Jane is beautiful and sweet-tempered but lacks character. Even making some allowance for their age, the three younger girls are silly, with Lydia wild as well, and Mrs Bennet is a gabbling idiot. Bingley is weak and easily deceived, and his sisters are scheming liars. Until he falls in love, Darcy is insufferable. His aunt, Lady Catherine, is a dictatorial self-satisfied monster, and her daughter a sickly nothing. Wickham is a smooth conniving spendthrift. What a cast! It cannot be a coincidence that Elizabeth's Uncle and Aunt Gardiner, a sensible and kind pair, very helpful to the development of the tale, are felt to be a threat to the 'consequence' of the Bennet family because they live in London and he earns a living instead of yawning on an estate somewhere. Was there some division in Jane Austen herself here? Was there a touch of the social rebel in the young Jane who first began the novel or in the older Jane who revised it?

I wonder too about 'female delicacy'. Sometimes it is straight, sometimes ironical. It can well be ironical if we consider what these delicate creatures are really like

(*opposite*) Mr Collins's proposal to Charlotte Lucas. Illustration by Hugh Thomson
to *Pride and Prejudice*, by Jane Austen, 1894 edition

behind their parasols, fans and simpers. Too many of them, mothers and daughters, are ruthless predators, greedy for money and social 'consequence', scheming and deceitful, determined to trap and then tame some patronising male, who does not understand what is happening to him. Jane Austen's own genuine delicacy concentrates on the psychological snares, ignoring all but the most innocent of the physical traps, but I cannot help remembering, from researches into Regency social life, that one of the best markets for pornography then was to be found in superior girls' boarding schools. But I don't regret Jane Austen's comparative ignorance and innocence. She knew all she needed to know. Her chosen field was deliberately kept small, but she knew every flower and weed in it.

We jump now to a little scene almost at the end of the novel. Darcy, a changed man now that he loves and is beloved, makes his confession: 'I have been a selfish being all my life, in practice, though not in principle.' He was spoilt as a child, given good principles but left to follow them in pride and concern; so on and so forth. (Incidentally, even now, when we are regularly dosed with the castor oil of envy and egalitarianism, a very handsome young man of a rich family can easily have been spoilt to the point of ruin, as we can read in our newspapers.) Then after some frank talk between the lovers, Bingley is mentioned, and Darcy is still rather complacent about his domination over him. Now comes the lightning stroke of humour, in its way the key to the whole book. Elizabeth is contemplating Darcy with her bright sharp eyes:

> Elizabeth longed to observe that Mr. Bingley had been a most delightful friend – so easily guided, that his worth was invaluable; but she checked herself. She remembered that he [Darcy] had yet to learn to be laughed at, and it was rather too early to begin. . . .

There it is. She loves him, sincerely, deeply, but even so will soon begin to laugh at him – for his own good and her pleasure. Perhaps *it was rather too early to begin* ought to have ended *Pride and Prejudice*.

I have been re-reading *Emma*, my next favourite, with less enthusiasm. But then I am devoted to Elizabeth Bennet, and compared with this pet Emma is rather a tiresome girl. The story is, of course, cunningly constructed but you have to be fonder than I am now of Highbury and its tittle-tattle not to be impatient with its slow progress. (Middle age brings patience. Old age begins to remove it.) To my mind it never achieves the sparkling comedy effect that the earlier novel does, but then, of course, its author has a different aim in view – a leisurely chronicle – spiced with irony as soon as we realise early on that Emma is unconsciously in love with Knightley. It has plenty of very gentle humour along the way but is no firework display of comic characters.

However, Mr Woodhouse is the best valetudinarian in English literature. I would hate an evening of him but can read about him with delight. Our introduction to him, at a supper party at his house, is perfect:

Upon such occasions poor Mr. Woodhouse's feelings were in sad warfare. He loved to have the cloth laid, because it had been the fashion of his youth, but his conviction of suppers being very unwholesome made him rather sorry to see anything put on it; and while his hospitality would have welcomed his visitors to everything, his care for their health made him grieve that they would eat.

Such another small basin of thin gruel as his own was all that he could, with thorough self-approbation, recommend; though he might constrain himself, while the ladies were comfortably clearing the nicer things, to say – 'Mrs. Bates, let me propose your venturing on one of these eggs. An egg boiled very soft is not unwholesome. Serle understands the boiling of an egg better than anybody. I would not recommend an egg boiled by anybody else – but you need not be afraid, they are very small, you see – one of our small eggs will not hurt you. Miss Bates, let Emma help you to a *little* bit of tart – a *very* little bit. Ours are all apple-tarts. You need not be afraid of unwholesome preserves here. I do not advise the custard. Mrs. Goddard, what say you to *half* a glass of wine? A *small* half-glass, put into a tumbler of water? I do not think it could disagree with you.'

That speech is a tiny masterpiece. And having brought him so beautifully to life, she does not overindulge him, as she did Mr Collins. And indeed, though he keeps turning up, I could do with more of him, especially playing host at a supper party.

What about Miss Bates, though? First, here is either a reminder or a tasting sample – Miss Bates is attending a party:

'So very obliging of you! No rain at all. Nothing to signify. I do not care for myself. Quite thick shoes. And Jane declares – Well!' (as soon as she was within the door) 'well! This is brilliant indeed! This is admirable! Excellently contrived, upon my word. Nothing wanting. Could not have imagined it. So well lighted up! Jane, Jane, look! did you ever see anything – ? Oh! Mr. Weston, you really must have had Aladdin's lamp. Good Mrs. Stokes would not know her own room again. I saw her as I came in; she was standing in the entrance. "Oh! Mrs. Stokes," said I – but I had not time for more.' She was now met by Mrs. Weston. 'Very well. I thank you, ma'am. I hope you are quite well. Very happy to hear it. So afraid you might have a headache! seeing you pass by so often, and knowing how much trouble you must have. Delighted to hear it indeed! – Ah! dear Mrs. Elton, so obliged to you for the carriage; excellent time; Jane and I quite ready. Did not keep the horses a moment. Most comfortable carriage. Oh! and I am sure our thanks are due to you, Mrs. Weston, on that score. Mrs. Elton had most kindly sent Jane a note, or we should have been. But two such offers in one day! Never were such neighbours. I said to my mother, "Upon my word, ma'am – " Thank you, my mother is remarkably well. Gone to Mr. Woodhouse's. I made her take her shawl – for the evenings are not warm – her large new shawl, Mrs. Dixon's wedding present. So kind of her to think of my mother! Bought at Weymouth, you know; Mr. Dixon's choice. There were three others, Jane says, which they hesitated about some time. Colonel Campbell rather preferred an olive. – My dear Jane, are you sure you did not wet your feet? It was but a drop or two, but I am so afraid; but Mr. Frank Churchill was so extremely – and there was a mat to step upon. I shall never forget his extreme politeness. Oh! Mr. Frank Churchill, I must tell you my mother's spectacles have never been in fault since; the rivet never came out again. My mother often talks of your good-nature; does not she, Jane? Do not we often talk of Mr. Frank Churchill? Ah! here's Miss Woodhouse, how do you do? Very well, I thank you, quite well. This is meeting quite in fairy-land. Such a transformation!'

And readers new to *Emma* may be assured that this is a mere slice off a joint.

If I were transformed into my 1925 self, I might well write a very eloquent piece on Miss Bates. It would declare that Miss Bates was a middle-aged spinster, scraping along on a tiny income and having to care for an invalid old mother, no doubt secretly laughed at or despised, nevertheless secure in her discovery that happiness (which most of the other characters are busy seeking) is all in the mind. And I would overdo it, just as Jane Austen, to my taste now, overdoes Miss Bates. Make no mistake, her breathless monologues are superbly written – and some clever actress ought to entertain us with them – but many of us, including myself, are now too impatient to enjoy them. Our whole era, we might say, has speeded us up past the point where we can relish the whole of Miss Bates. There is a time element in this enjoyment of humour.

We now come down from the high peaks. There are of course glints and thrusts of humour in *Mansfield Park*, but a certain religiosity creeps in not favourable to it; and Fanny Price cannot rival Elizabeth Bennet's satirical sharp observation or Emma Woodhouse's bubbling self-confidence. *Sense and Sensibility* is all very well, but from a humorous point of view it suffers from the fact that its finest scene comes too early. This is the scene in which John Dashwood and his wife solemnly and gradually whittle down their obligations to their impoverished relatives, one of Jane's master-pieces of satire. And even *Persuasion*, with its tender fading light, is not without its moments of satirical humour. For family reasons the Navy was close to Jane's heart; so now we have that self-important snob-de-luxe, Sir Walter Elliot, condemning the service and equally busy condemning himself. Sir Walter begins:

'The profession has its utility, but I should be sorry to see any friend of mine belonging to it.'

'Indeed!' was the reply, and with a look of surprise.

'Yes; it is in two points offensive to me; I have but two strong grounds of objection to it. First, as being the means of bringing persons of obscure birth into undue distinction, and raising men to honours which their fathers and grandfathers never dreamt of; and, secondly, as it cuts up a man's youth and vigour most horribly; a sailor grows old sooner than any other man; I have observed it all my life. A man is in greater danger in the navy of being insulted by the rise of one whose father his father might have disdained to speak to, and of becoming prematurely an object of disgust himself, than in any other line. . . .'

So much for Sir Walter, secure behind the protection of those weather-beaten ships and men.

Jane Austen's humour outside her novels can be well illustrated by her exchange of letters with one James Stanier Clarke (a kind of Mr Collins on high) in 1816, after she had sent a copy of *Emma* to the Prince Regent, about to marry his daughter to Prince Leopold of Coburg. After conveying the Regent's thanks, Mr Clarke goes on:

> . . . The Prince Regent has just left us for London; and having been pleased to appoint me Chaplain and Private English Secretary to the Prince of Coburg, I remain here with His Serene Highness and a select party until the marriage. Perhaps when you again appear in print you may chuse to dedicate your volumes to Prince Leopold: any historical romance, illustrative of the history of the august House of Coburg, would just now be very interesting. . . .

In her reply, Jane tried fairly hard not to laugh at him:

> . . . I am fully sensible that an historical romance, founded on the House of Saxe Coburg, might be much more to the purpose of profit or popularity than such pictures of domestic life in country villages as I deal in. But I could no more write a romance than an epic poem. I could not sit seriously down to write a serious romance under any other motive than to save my life; and if it were indispensable for me to keep it up and never relax into laughing at myself or other people, I am sure I would be hung before I had finished the first chapter. No, I must keep to my own style and go on in my own way. . . .

It was the way of an enchanting woman.

I have just read Mrs Gaskell's *Cranford* again, and after such a long time that I brought nothing to it except a vague recollection of one 'Miss Matty' and a man or men called Brown. I knew that it was an idyllic version of its author's girlhood memories of Knutsford. I knew about Mrs Gaskell herself, of course; how she was beautiful, sweet-tempered, sensible and humorous, but capable of writing, with as much truth and sincerity as the taste of the time would allow, on strong subjects; a splendid all-round woman, whose large heart failed her, so that she died in her middle fifties. I did not know, but soon discovered, that *Cranford* was published in 1853, after being serialised by Dickens, an admiring friend. But was I wasting my time, reading such a book all over again? Would so much faded lavender, chapters probably reduced now to selected reading for rather old-fashioned girls' schools, be worth more than a mere mention in a book on English Humour? Time was precious – not mine to me so much, but publishers are impatient – but I had to find out for myself what the thing was worth. This is what I have done. And my conclusion is that no book on English Humour, addressed to readers of our own day, aware of the spirit of our own age, can afford to shrug away *Cranford*. It represents, as we shall see, a particular form of humour that is now neglected and that we cannot now afford to neglect. We need it.

If Jane Austen frequently attends to what any man feels are feminine small potatoes, Mrs Gaskell here is chiefly concerned with even smaller potatoes, almost invisible to the masculine eye. She lets us know what we are in for in her opening paragraph:

In the first place, Cranford is in possession of the Amazons; all the holders of houses above a certain rent are women. If a married couple come to settle in the town, somehow the gentleman disappears; he is either fairly frightened to death by being the only man in the Cranford evening parties, or he is accounted for by being with his regiment, his ship, or closely engaged in business all the week in the great neighbouring commercial town of Drumble, distant only twenty miles on a railroad. In short, whatever does become of the gentlemen, they are not at Cranford. . . .

. . after tea. . . . 'Hush, ladies! if you please, hush!', illustration by Hugh Thomson to *Cranford*, by Mrs Gaskell, 1891 edition

After making an exception of the surgeon, and pointing to their responsibility for the gardens, she goes on:

. . . For deciding all questions of literature and politics without troubling themselves with unnecessary reasons or arguments; for obtaining clear and correct knowledge of everybody's affairs in the parish; for keeping their neat maid-servants in admirable order; for kindness (somewhat dictatorial) to the poor, and real tender good offices to each other whenever they are in distress, the ladies of Cranford are quite sufficient. 'A man,' as one of them observed to me once, 'is *so* in the way in a house!' Although the ladies of Cranford know all each other's proceedings, they are exceedingly indifferent to each other's opinions. Indeed, as each has her own individuality, not to say eccentricity, pretty strongly developed, nothing is so easy as verbal retaliation; but, somehow, goodwill reigns among them to a considerable degree.

So, I repeat, the male reader knows what he is in for; many measures indeed of very small beer. The sex that notices everything in the immediate foreground is really hard at work noticing the tiniest details here, in this ladylike society of spinsters and widows. It is true there are a few desperate incidents, like Captain Brown's fatal accident on the railway, the disappearance of poor Peter Jenkyns after being flogged by his father, the failure of the bank that leaves Miss Matty almost penniless. But, for the most part, almost anything creates an event in the lives of these ladies. A new cap or bonnet is an event and the arrival of a new silk gown – very rare indeed, most of these ladies living carefully on small incomes – is equal to a conflagration as news. A party – usually a game of cards, tea, thin bread-and-butter and biscuits – is a triple event: excited speculation beforehand; the occasion itself; then calls all round to discuss it. Class distinctions are elaborate and supremely important. Should Miss Betty Barker, having now retired from her superior millinery establishment, be promoted into being accepted as a hostess? She was, even by the Honourable Mrs Jamieson, who ruled the roost socially; and now she gave her first party:

. . . Miss Betty Barker was a proud and happy woman. She stirred the fire, and shut the door, and sat as near to it as she could, quite on the edge of her chair. When Peggy [the maid] came in tottering under the weight of the tea-tray, I noticed that Miss Barker was sadly afraid lest Peggy should not keep her distance sufficiently. She and her mistress were on very familiar terms in their everyday intercourse, and Peggy wanted now to make several little confidences to her, which Miss Barker was on thorns to hear, but which she thought it her duty, as a lady, to repress. So she turned away from all Peggy's asides and signs; but she made one or two very malapropos answers to what was said; and at last, seized with a bright idea, she exclaimed: 'Poor, sweet Carlo! I'm forgetting him. Come downstairs with me, poor ittie doggie, and it shall have its tea, it shall!'

In a few minutes she returned, bland and benignant as before; but I thought she had forgotten to give the 'poor ittie doggie' anything to eat, judging by the avidity with which he swallowed down chance pieces of cake. The tea-tray was abundantly loaded – I was pleased to see it, I was so hungry; but I was afraid the ladies present might think it vulgarly heaped up. I know they would have done at their own houses; but somehow the heaps disappeared here. I saw Mrs. Jamieson eating seed-cake, slowly and considerately, as she did everything; and I was rather surprised, for I knew she had told us, on the occasion of her last party, that she never had it in her house, it reminded her so much of scented soap. She always gave us Savoy biscuits. However, Mrs. Jamieson was kindly indulgent to Miss Barker's want of knowledge of the customs of high life; and to spare her feelings, ate three large pieces of seed-cake, with a placid, ruminating expression of countenance, not unlike a cow's.

And this is nothing to what followed, after games had been played, for with supper came scalloped oysters, potted lobsters, and various sweet dainties; and the ladies, submitting to the whims of one lately in trade, are even persuaded to try a little cherry brandy.

When Martha, the maid who came from a farm, was asked to 'Listen to reason', she replied, 'I'll not listen to reason. Reason always means what someone else has got to say.' What someone else, an average male reader, has probably got to say, at this point, is that he doesn't understand why I am bothering my head or his with this old-fashioned, tittle-tattle feminine stuff, holding up my account of humour. To which I can only reply that we have here in *Cranford* a kind of humour we have not stumbled upon before; and that, after giving the subject some thought, I believe it is a kind of humour we have been wrong to neglect and ignore. (I will risk a personal comment here. In my own creative work I have dealt largely in humour, writing two very long comic novels and several shorter ones, but, except possibly in brief passages in two or three plays, I have never come near to this kind of humour – and *now I am sorry!*) Clearly I must do my best to describe this humour.

To begin with, it is the opposite of what we find almost everywhere now in popular comic programmes: on television; in clubs worked by stand-up comedians; in the theatre of farce. Their audiences are attacked, to be shaken into big belly-laughs, by humour that is aggressive, coarse in grain, predominantly masculine. (Women join in the laughs because women are great joiners-in, especially if taken out for the evening.) This humour does not ask for heart and imagination. Little thought and not much feeling are required from its audience. It sets out to blitz a comparatively small part of the personality. This is why when we are suddenly shown its captive and uproarious audience – let us say, a TV glimpse of a stand-up comic mowing them down at a club – most of us are apt to feel embarrassed and would prefer to look at something else. This is not an attack on popular comic programmes – some of its humour can be very good of its sort – but an account of it helps us to understand a very different kind of humour.

A brief last quotation from *Cranford* might help too:

The next morning news came, both official and otherwise, that the Town and Country Bank had stopped payment. Miss Matty was ruined.

She tried to speak quietly to me; but when she came to the actual fact that she would have but about five shillings a week to live upon, she could not restrain a few tears.

'I am not crying for myself, dear,' said she, wiping them away; 'I believe I am crying for the very silly thought of how my mother would grieve if she could know; she always cared for us so much more than for herself. But many a poor person has less, and I am not very extravagant, and, thank God, when the neck of mutton, and Martha's wages, and the rent are paid, I have not a farthing owing. Poor Martha! I think she'll be sorry to leave me.'

Miss Matty smiled at me through her tears, and she would fain have had me see only the smile, not the tears.

Miss Matty, illustration by Hugh Thomson to *Cranford*, by Mrs Gaskell, 1891 edition

We could call this *tender humour*. With it the soft laughter and the smiles soon dissolve into tears. While it is essentially feminine in spirit, any man not armoured in *machismo*, too stiffly male, might create it. And, I repeat, it is a kind of humour we have been wrong to neglect or ignore. We need it, and indeed have never needed it more than we do now. Tears? Yes, tears if they come easily and naturally. If we occasionally wept together, we might stop sneering and snarling at one another. Our forefathers – and the bravest and most resolute of them – were not ashamed of tears. (In the summer of 1940 I saw and heard Winston Churchill making a speech in the House of Commons. The tears were rolling down his cheeks, because the subject moved him deeply.) I suspect we are too dry-eyed and dry-hearted. It would do us no harm – probably much good – if we occasionally came out of a theatre, temporarily free from a non-stop giggle, with damp cheeks, with our sympathies broadened instead of being even further constricted. Women hurry upstairs to weep, but are we men going to pretend that we are braver, more patient, more enduring and hopeful than they are? I am not asking for more *Cranfords* – after all, a Mid-Victorian idyllic account of Early Victorian life – but for more of that particular humour which Mrs Gaskell distilled from her memories. I am not asking for it all the time. I am asking for it some of the time, just as I might wish for a little rain in a long dry season.

We must now rush past a hundred women's novels in which, as I suggested earlier, there are admirable glints and flickers of essentially feminine humour, born of sharp eyes and ears and critical minds, but never indulged to hold up the tale that must be told. This brings us to two clever women of our own time sufficiently unusual, brave enough, we might say, to come before us as humorists. Both produced other kinds of work, admirable of their sort, but these are outside our province here. The first of these courageous ladies is E. M. Delafield; the books in question being *Diary of a Provincial Lady* (1930) and *The Provincial Lady in War-Time* (1940). (There were two other Provincial Lady diaries between these.) They are now so far removed in time that they have acquired a social-historical interest, but they still succeed, it seems to me – and I have just re-read them – as humour. I must admit they are spiced with irony that other readers may miss, simply because I knew E. M. Delafield fairly well as a firm strongish character, whereas her Provincial Lady is presented in terms of very feminine inadequacies, a frequent sense of inferiority, all manner of doubts and dubieties. Here, in 1930, she is at the bank hoping for an overdraft:

> Am never much exhilarated at this prospect, and do not in the least find that it becomes less unpleasant with repetition, but rather the contrary. Experience customary difficulty in getting to the point, and Bank Manager and I discuss weather, political situation, and probable starters for the Grand National with passionate suavity for some time. Inevitable pause occurs, and we look at one another across immense expanse of pink blotting-paper. Irrelevant impulse rises in me to ask if he has other supply, for use, in writing-table drawer, or if fresh pad is brought in whenever a client calls. (Strange divagations of the human brain under the stress of extreme nervousness presents itself here as interesting topic for speculation. Should like to hear opinion of Professor met last night on this point. Subject far preferable to Molecules.)
>
> . . . Bank Manager reduces me to spiritual pulp by suggesting that we should see how the Account Stands at the Moment. Am naturally compelled to agree to this with air of well-bred and detached amusement, but am in reality well aware that the Account Stands – or, more accurately totters – on a Debit Balance of Thirteen Pounds, two shillings and tenpence. Large sheet of paper, bearing this impressive statement, is presently brought in and laid before us.
>
> Negotiations resumed.
>
> Eventually emerge into the street with purpose accomplished, but feeling completely unstrung for the day. Rose is kindness personified, produces Bovril and an excellent lunch, and agrees with me that it is All Nonsense to say that Wealth wouldn't mean Happiness, because we know quite well that it *would*.

Another and very different scene, also genuinely chosen at random:

> Barbara calls. Can she, she says, speak to me in *confidence*. Sit, seething with excitement, in the hope that I am at least going to be told that Barbara is engaged. Try to keep this out of sight, and to maintain expression of earnest and sympathetic attention only, whilst Barbara says that it is sometimes difficult to know which way Duty lies, that

she has always thought a true woman's highest vocation is home-making, and that the love of a Good Man is the crown of life. I say Yes, Yes, to all of this. (Discover, on thinking it over, that I do not agree with any of it, and am shocked at my own extraordinary duplicity.)

Barbara at length admits that Crosbie has asked her to marry him – he did it, she says, at the Zoo – and go out with him as his wife to the Himalayas. This, says Barbara, is where all becomes difficult. She may be old-fashioned – no doubt she is – but can she leave her mother alone? No, she cannot. Can she, on the other hand, give up dear Crosbie, who has never loved a girl before, and says that he never will again? No, she cannot.

Barbara weeps. I kiss her. (Tea is brought in.) I sit down in confusion and begin to talk about the Vicarage daffodils being earlier than ours. . . . Atmosphere ruined, and destruction completed by my own necessary enquiries as to Barbara's wishes in the matter of milk, sugar, bread-and-butter, and so on. (*Mem:* Must speak to Cook about sending in minute segment of sponge-cake, remains of one which, to my certain recollection, made its first appearance more than ten days ago. Also, why perpetual and unappetising procession of small rock-cakes?)

Robert [husband] comes in, he talks of swine-fever, all further confidence becomes impossible. Barbara takes her leave immediately after tea, only asking if I could look in on her mother and have a Little Talk? I reluctantly agree to do so, and she mounts her bicycle and rides off. Robert says, That girl holds herself well, but it's a pity she has those ankles.

Its successor, ten years later, *The Provincial Lady in War-Time*, is not so funny on a personal level, but it offers us a bright satirical picture of the Phoney War period. These were the months when the lucky few Got Into Something and then found they had little or nothing to do, except wear a uniform or a badge, while so many others, especially the middle class, were running round trying to Get Into Something. Now established as a writer, the Provincial Lady penetrates at last the Ministry of Information, arriving at a Mr M. and a young man with a beard. Can she do anything?

All of us can do something, replies Mr. M. There are, for instance, a number of quite false rumours going about. These can be tracked to the source – (how?) – descredited and contradicted.

The man with the beard breaks in, to tell me that in the last War there were innumerable alarms concerning spies in our midst.

(As it is quite evident, notwithstanding the beard, that he was still in his cradle at the time of the last war, whilst I had left mine some twenty years earlier, this information would really come better from me to him.)

The Government wishes to sift these rumours, one and all – (they will have their hands full if they undertake anything of the kind) – and it is possible to assist them in this respect.

Could I, for instance, tell him what is being said in the extreme North of England where I live?

Actually, it is the extreme *West* that I live. Of course, of course. . . . What exactly then, is being said in the extreme West?

Complete blank comes over me. Can remember nothing but that we have told ourselves that even if butter *is* rationed we can get plenty of clotted cream, and that we really needn't bother to take our gas-masks wherever we go. . . . Can see that my chances of getting a job – never very good – are now practically moribund. . . . Mr. M. tells me – evidently in order to get rid of me – that I had better see Captain Skein-Tring. He is – or *was*, two days ago – in Room 4978, on the fourth floor, in the other building. . . .

However, Mr M. takes pity on her and offers to escort her himself:

. . . We meet with a pallid young man carrying hundreds of files, to whom Mr. M. says compassionately, Hallo, Basil, moving again?

Basil says Yes, wearily, and toils on, and Mr. M. explains that Poor Basil has been moved three times within the last ten days.

Just as he disappears from view Mr. M. recalls him, to ask if he knows whether Capt. Skein-Tring is still in Propaganda, 4978. Basil looks utterly bewildered and replies that he has never heard of anybody called Skein-Tring. Anyhow, the Propaganda people have all been transferred now, and the department has been taken over by the people from National Economy.

Mr. M. groans, but pushes valiantly on, and this bulldog spirit is rewarded by totally unexpected appearance – evidently the very last thing he has expected – of Captain S.-T.'s name on the door of Room 4978. He accordingly takes me in and introduces me, says that I shall be absolutely all right with Jerry, hopes – I think untruthfully – that we may meet again, and goes.

(left to right) Mademoiselle, the Rector, 'Very, very distinguished novelist', and Cissie Crabbe. all illustrations by Arthur Watts to *Diary of a Provincial Lady*, by E. M. Delafield, 1930

As soon as Jerry understands that she is a writer, he tells her that 'All You People' must go on *exactly as usual*, but keep away from war topics. Not a word about the war:

> I feel obliged to point out to Jerry that the present international situation is what most people, at the moment, wish to know about. Jerry taps on his writing-desk very imperatively indeed and tells me that All You People are the same. All anxious to do something about the war. Well, we mustn't. We must keep right out of it. Forget about it. Go on writing just as though it didn't exist. . . . Authors, poets, artists – (can see that the word he really has in mind is riffraff) – and All You People must really come into line and be content to carry on exactly as usual. Otherwise, simply doing more harm than good. . . .

As I never happened to visit the Ministry of Information looking for a job, I cannot vouch for the truth of this account of it, but I suspect that satire here has not left truth far behind. Meanwhile, the Provincial Lady, just to be Doing Something, has volunteered to take night duty at a large canteen, where various kinds of war-workers, though probably doing nothing all day, have to keep late hours. Here is one out of many glimpses of her there:

> Serena is not on duty when I arrive, and telephone-call to her flat has only produced very long and painstaking reply in indifferent English from one of her refugees, of which I understand scarcely a word, except that Serena is The Angel of Hampstead, is it not? Agree that it is, and exchange cordial farewells with the Refugee who says something that I think refers to the goodness of my heart. (Undeserved.)
>
> Canteen gramophone has altered its repertoire – this a distinct relief – and now we have 'Love Never Grows Old' and 'Run, rabbit, run'. Final chorus to the latter – Run, Hitler, run – I think a great mistake and quote to myself Dr. Dunstan from *The Human Boy*: 'It ill becomes us, sir, to jest at a fallen potentate – and still less before he has fallen.'
>
> Helpers behind the counter now number two very young and rather pretty sisters, who say that they wish to be called Patricia and Juanita. Tendency on the part of all the male *clientèle*, to be served by them and nobody else, and they hold immense conversations, in undertones, with youths in leather jackets and brightly-coloured ties.
>
> This leaves Red Cross workers, female ambulance drivers, elderly special constables and stretcher-bearers, to me.
>
> One of these – grey-headed man in spectacles – comes up and scrutinises the menu at great length and then enquires What there is to-night? Suppose his sight has been dimmed by time, and offer to read him the list. He looks offended and says No, no, he has read it. Retrieve this error by asserting that I only made the suggestion because the menu seemed to be so illegibly written.
>
> Instant judgment follows, as Scottish lady leans down from elevation beside the urns and says severely that *she* wrote out those cards and took particular pains to see that they were not illegible.

Decide to abandon the whole question without attempting any explanations whatever.

Social historians, wanting to examine some of the most foolish months in English history, may find some good material in this book. And even if they don't they can enjoy its humour. Finally, as irony is never far away from humour, I offer a last melancholy point. I knew E. M. Delafield (her real maiden name was de la Pasture – a kind of joke here too) for many years, and though I fully recognized and much relished her humorous gifts, she always seemed to me a tragic figure. She died, too soon, in 1943.

Something not dissimilar might be said of Nancy Mitford, a gallant, laughter-loving spirit, condemned to a long painful illness, during which, we are told, she begged her correspondents and visitors to tell her 'something funny'. They cannot have found this very easy, but let us hope they did find a funny something for her. Long before, she had found something very funny for them – and us. Here I refer particularly to *The Pursuit of Love*, the first (1945) of her three very successful novels. It is also the best of them, that is, if we are considering her as a feminine humorist. If this appears to impose a severe limit on her, then I am sorry, but I am judging her from the point of view of her own highest standard, though of course I may not be free from personal prejudice. But I must add that I admire her as a writer and liked her as a person, a 'Non-U' looking at a 'U' – though I do say 'writing paper' and not 'notepaper'.

Let it be said at once that the two later novels have their share of wit, sharp observation and flashes of humour. As for example, the subject here being sex:

. . . Jassy and Victoria made me laugh so much and I loved them so much, that it was impossible for me to wish them very different from what they were. Hardly had I arrived in the house than I was lugged off to their secret meeting-place, the Hons' cupboard, to be asked what IT was like.

'Linda says it's not all it's cracked up to be,' said Jassy, 'and we don't wonder when we think of Tony.'

'But Louisa says, once you get used to it, it's utter utter blissikins,' said Victoria, 'and we do wonder, when we think of John.'

'What's wrong with poor Tony and John?' 'Dull and old. Come on then Fanny – tell.'

I said I agreed with Louisa, but refused to enter into details.

'It is unfair, nobody ever tells. Sadie doesn't even know, that's quite obvious, and Louisa is an old prig, but we did think we could count on Linda and you. Very well then, we shall go to our marriage beds in ignorance, like Victorian ladies, and in the morning we shall be found stark staring mad with horror, and live sixty more years in an expensive bin, and then perhaps you'll wish you had been more helpful.'

'Weighted down with jewels and Valenciennes costing thousands,' said Victoria. 'The Lecturer was here last week and he was telling Sadie some very nice sexy stories about that kind of thing – of course, we weren't meant to hear but you can just guess what happened. Sadie didn't listen and we did.'

'I should ask the Lecturer for information,' I said. 'He'd tell.'

'He'd show. No thank you very much.'

The whole thing is a neatly constructed but rather slow-moving comedy, with the beautiful bored Polly suddenly going off like an idiot to marry Boy, the Lecturer, more than twice her age and completely unsuitable. But then Lady Montdore is plucked out of her despair by Cedric, the heir from Nova Scotia (via Paris), the pansy-aesthete narcissus, who rejuvenates her. (Remember, he always refers to himself as One.) There is a bit too much Cedric, though he is beautifully captured; but I like this encounter:

> The country however, hummed and buzzed with Cedric, and little else was talked of.
> I need hardly say that Uncle Matthew, after one look, found that the word sewer had
> become obsolete and inadequate. Scowling, growling, flashing of eyes and grinding of
> teeth, to a degree hitherto reserved for Boy Dougdale, were intensified a hundredfold at
> the mere thought of Cedric, and accompanied by swelling veins and apoplectic noises.
> The drawers at Alconleigh were emptied of the yellowing slips of paper on which my
> uncle's hates had mouldered all these years, and each now contained a clean new slip
> with the name, carefully printed in black ink, Cedric Hampton. There was a terrible
> scene on Oxford platform one day. Cedric went to the bookstall to buy *Vogue*, having
> mislaid his own copy. Uncle Matthew, who was waiting there for a train, happened to
> notice that the seams of his coat were piped in a contrasting shade. This was too much
> for his self-control. He fell upon Cedric and began to shake him like a rat; just then, very
> fortunately, the train came in, whereupon my uncle, who suffered terribly from train
> fever, dropped Cedric and rushed to catch it. 'You'd never think,' as Cedric said
> afterwards, 'that buying *Vogue Magazine* could be so dangerous. It was well worth it
> though, lovely Spring modes.'

That last remark, both in sense and rhythm, is superb.

The Blessing has been called Nancy Mitford's best book. This seems to me a curious judgment. It is not in the same league as *The Pursuit of Love*. Even on its own level I don't see it as a satisfactory novel. To begin with, long before that little monster, Sigi, has received in the final paragraph of the story 'a tremendous box on the ears', I have been hoping over and over again that somebody would clout him. We have to suffer too much of this malicious imp. A further weakness is that this novel is written almost entirely out of Nancy's love affair with France – or certainly with Paris. I know nothing about aristocratic circles in that city – or in any other, for that matter – but in *The Blessing* I find them silly rather than delicious and amusing. And when Nancy tries some bold invention, to help round off the tale, she hardly succeeds: so, for example, we can't believe that that dull American is really a Russian agent. On the other hand, the brilliant Albertine's account of another

American does give us a welcome splash of impudent humour:

'I wish I understood Americans,' said Charles-Eduard. 'They are very strange. So good and yet so dull.'

'What makes you think they are so good?'

'You can see it, shining in their eyes.'

'That's not goodness, that's contact lenses – a kind of spectacle they wear next the eyeball. I had an American lover after the liberation and I used to tap his eye with my nail file. He was a very curious man. Imagine, his huge, healthy-looking body hardly functioned at all by itself. He couldn't walk a yard; I took him to Versailles, and half-way across the Galerie des Glaces he lay on the floor and cried for his mother. He couldn't do you know what without his *lavages*, he could only digest yoghourt and raw carrots, he couldn't sleep without a sleeping draught or wake up without benzedrine, and he had to have a good strong blood transfusion every morning before he could face the day. It was like having another automaton in the house.'

'You had him in the house?'

Albertine, who hated too much intimacy, had never done this with any of her lovers.

'For the central heating, dearest,' she said apologetically. 'It was that very cold winter. Americans have no circulation of their own – even their motors are artificially heated in winter and cooled in summer. . . .'

But back, I say, to Alconleigh, to those urgent or shrieking discussions in the Hons' cupboard, to Uncle Matthew in his blood-thirsty glory and his gramophone turned on at full blast in the early morning, to the girls tearful over the smallest creature and madly speculating about love and sex:

Alconleigh was a large, ugly, north-facing, Georgian house, built with only one intention, that of sheltering, when the weather was too bad to be out of doors, a succession of bucolic squires, their wives, their enormous families, their dogs, their horses, their father's relict, and their unmarried sisters. There was no attempt at decoration, at softening the lines, no apology for a façade, it was all as grim and as bare as a barracks, stuck upon the high hillside. Within the keynote, the theme, was death. Not death of maidens, not death romantically accoutred with urns and weeping willows, cypresses and valedictory odes, but the death of warriors and of animals, stark, real. On the walls halberds and pikes and ancient muskets were arranged in crude patterns with the heads of beasts slaughtered in many lands, with the flags and uniforms of bygone Radletts. Glass-topped cases contained, not miniatures of ladies, but minia-tures of the medals of their lords, badges, penholders made of tiger's teeth, the hoof of a favourite horse, telegrams announcing casualties in battle, and commissions written out in parchment scrolls, all lying together in a timeless jumble.

And the irony here is that this fortress of the masculine principle should not be filled with bristling males – only represented by one, though a ripe specimen, Uncle

Matthew – but has to be the cosy nest of wondering, fearful, protesting, tender females of various ages.

Nancy Mitford has admitted that these Alconleigh chapters, whenever they appear, come from memories of her childhood and youth, and in fact are autobiographical. But appreciative readers must not be deceived by this confession. It is one thing to remember; it is quite another thing to order and arrange, to relate and cunningly present such memories, creating a clear and satisfying picture out of a mere hotchpotch of recollections. And this, Nancy Mitford did with superb humorous skill, giving her a high rank indeed among deeply feminine humorists. Moreover, there emerges from these chapters, in the shape of Uncle Matthew, a memorable and rich comic character, always a triumph for any humorist. (Had I known him at the time, over fifty years ago, I would certainly have included him in my gallery, *The English Comic Characters*.) Who can forget his grinding dentures, the blue glare of his eyes, his early-morning gramophone recitals or cracking of stock whips; his dislike of all foreigners or various 'sewers' in local society; his hatred of dining out ('Plenty of good food at home'); his horror of sending money abroad or of doing anything to leave his own country in the lurch, something done now by better-educated professional men without a qualm? If we must have a last glimpse of him, let us try him with Shakespeare:

> Uncle Matthew went with Aunt Sadie and Linda on one occasion to a Shakespeare play, *Romeo and Juliet*. It was not a success. He cried copiously, and went into a furious rage because it ended badly. 'All the fault of that damned padre,' he kept saying on the way home, still wiping his eyes. 'That fella what's 'is name, Romeo, might have known a blasted papist would mess up the whole thing. Silly old fool of a nurse too, I bet she was an R.C., dismal old bitch.'

There is more than memory here, there is *creation*. Nancy Mitford, I feel, at her best is a feminine humorist of a high order.

There is plenty of feminine humour about, even though many younger women novelists appear to be too intense to aim at laughter. (Moreover, a fairly settled society is more favourable to humour.) The movement generally called 'Women's Lib' does not seem likely to produce more and better feminine humour. If it should succeed, what it will probably offer us is a number of women who have been turned into second-rate men, and we do not need any more second-rate men. What my sex needs is an ample supply of first-rate women, who can look at us and listen to us not without sympathy but are always prepared to laugh at us, knowing full well they have more sense than we have, so many thick-skinned pompous chaps. We live in a world that appears to be breeding more and more fanatics and lawless imbeciles. It cries out for Woman to assert her instinctive feeling for unity and harmony. And also, as a bonus, her natural humour.

CHAPTER 15

Clowns and
the Comic Stage

Advising the players, Hamlet is made to say, 'Let those that play your clowns speak no more than is set down for them.' I don't know if this injunction was necessary in Elsinore – not, I imagine, a good date for clowns – but any Elizabethan dramatist knew what Hamlet had in mind. The truth was, any ordinary English audience loved clowning. The people wanted to laugh. They had wanted this from the first, so that the Mystery plays, the Moralities and Interludes, had had their share – and perhaps more than their share – of rough comic stuff, turning even devils and demons into droll fellows. And when the professional Theatre finally arrived, the clowns could not be banished but were more important than ever. The best of them, men like Will Summer, Richard Tarlton, Will Kemp, not only played parts but were allowed to do what we should call now individual 'turns', exploiting their humorous personalities. Solemn young men from the Universities insisted that English drama should model itself on Latin tragedy; but this was all in vain. The

Will Kemp who in nine days danced from London to Norwich
in 1600 – a contemporary woodcut

Richard Tarlton –
a contemporary illustration

people who crowded into the cheaper parts of the London Theatre did not object to
some tragic action, so long as it was exciting, but there had to be clowning too. Listen
to Simon the Tanner, Mayor of Quinborough, in Middleton's comedy:

> O, the clowns that I have seen in my time! The very peeping out of one of them would
> have made a young heir laugh, though his father lay-a-dying; a man undone by law
> (the saddest case that can be) might for his twopence have burst himself with laughing,
> and ended all his miseries. Here was a merry world, my masters!

There was something here that could not be ignored, and the best dramatists did all
they could to meet this demand without making a hotchpotch out of their plays.
Here, as elsewhere, Shakespeare took the lead, bringing a breadth and depth of
humanity to his comic scenes.

However, the Jacobean playwrights substituted genteel wit for broad humour,
and the clowns disappeared, giving place to comic character actors, often playing
intriguing servants, foreign valets and the like. But all were swept away by the
Puritans, who closed the theatres. Most of the ordinary people, those who had loved

the clowns in the old days, were not Puritans and saw nothing sinful in entertainment and laughter. For their sake there came a 'Black Market' in touring troupes. Because there had to be no play-acting, groups of strolling players pretended to offer nothing more sinful than exhibitions of rope dancing and similar exercises, but in fact they contrived to introduce various well-known comic scenes, including, we are told, some of Falstaff's. (We know that one Robert Cox – all honour to him! – organised many of these troupes.) Even after the Restoration, when theatres to please the Court and nobility were opened, these so-called 'Humours' and 'Drolleries' must have been seen at fairs and country markets, and probably for some years the English common people (who deserved it) could find better fun than the King and his Court.

But now and again, the fashionable playgoers were in luck. So we find Pepys writing about a new play by Dryden:

> The truth is, there is a comical part done by Nell [Gwynne], which is Florimell, that I never can hope to see the like done again by man – or woman. The King and the Duke were at the play. But so great performance of a comical part was never, I believe, in the world before as Nell do this. . . .

We can understand why no king's mistress was ever such a favourite with the English people as Nell Gwynne. She was one of themselves: she had humour.

Many of the scenes in the Restoration Theatre were licentious in their texts, and they must have been much worse in their performance, with the players making the most of them. This could not go on. There were too many complaints from respectable people, as distinct from the rakes and women of the town. So censorship arrived, to pose problems down to our own time. Early in Anne's reign, in March 1704, came the following proclamation:

> Whereas many Great Complaints have been made to Her Majesty, of many indecent profane and immoral Expressions that are usually spoken by Players and Mountebanks contrary to Religion and Good Manners. And thereupon Her Majesty has lately given order to *Charles Killigrew, Esqre.*; Her Majesty's Master of the Revels, to take especial care to correct all such Abuses. The said Master of the Revels does therefore hereby require all Stage Players, Mountebanks, and all other Persons, mounting Stages, or otherwise, to bring their several Plays, Drolls, Farces, Interludes, Dialogues, Prologues, and other Entertainments, fairly written to him at his Office in *Somerset House*, to be by him perused, corrected and allow'd under his hand, pursuant to Her Majesty's Command. . . .

Low comedy actors like Will Bullock and Will Pinkeman were very popular indeed at this time, and more important still was Thomas Doggett, a manager as well as a famous comedian, whose Coat and Badge are still raced for by Thames watermen. It was said of him: 'On the Stage, he's very Aspectabund, wearing farce in his face, his

Thoughts deliberately framing his Utterance Congruous to his Looks; He is the only Comick Original now extant.'

This could not have pleased the ambitious Colley Cibber, though he was well removed from low comedy, specialising as he did in fashionable fops. He was an all-round man of the Theatre. For many years he helped to manage Drury Lane. He wrote several successful plays, in the new style, which he probably introduced, of sentimental comedy. He understood the taste of the town and in his later years was perhaps the most influential figure in the Theatre. He was personally unpopular because he was domineering, rude, and inclined to pontificate on matters he did not really understand. To have been openly ridiculed, in turn, by Pope, by Dr Johnson, by Fielding, to name no others, almost suggests a triumph of unpopularity.

A far more engaging character, certainly the greatest comedian during the middle years of the eighteenth century, was Samuel Foote, a genuine wit who could play the buffoon, a famous mimic and comic dramatist. The gossip of the time gives us many examples of his ready wit. Two will suffice here. He was once in company when the talk turned on the mutability of the world. 'Can you account for this?' said a master builder who was sitting next to him. 'Why, not very clearly,' said Foote, 'except we could suppose the world was built by contract.' He could never resist the temptation to use his wit. When his friend, Sir Francis Delavel, died, Foote was so overcome he saw nobody for three days. On the fourth day, his treasurer called to see him on urgent business, and Foote still tearful asked when Sir Francis was to be buried. 'Not till the latter end of the next week, sir,' the treasurer replied, 'as I hear the surgeons intend first to dissect his head.' 'And what will they get there?' Foote cried, his face still wet with tears. 'I am sure I have known Frank these five and twenty years, and I never could find anything in it.'

A well-educated man, who read for the Bar and spent some years in the Temple, he was such a spendthrift that he had to turn actor. But he was suited neither to tragedy nor to genteel comedy, so he finally invented a new kind of entertainment in which he could succeed as a mimic. His well-known victims had his burlesques suppressed, so Foote cleverly evaded the licensing laws of the Theatre. He invited his 'friends and the public' to drink tea with him at the Haymarket Theatre the next morning at noon: 'And 'tis hoped there will be a great deal of comedy and some joyous spirits; he will endeavour to make the morning as diverting as possible. N.B. – *Sir Dilbury Diddle will be there, and Lady Betty Frisk has absolutely promised.*' Foote then told his audience he was training some young actors, and, while tea was being made, he would give instructions to his pupils, and would then offer some uproarious satire and diabolical mimicry of celebrated persons. He did this for years. (Dr Johnson was to be one of the victims, but Foote changed his programme when he heard that Johnson had bought an enormous oak cudgel and proposed to sit in the front row.)

(*opposite*) Hayes (left) as Sir Jacob Jollup and Samuel Foote as Major Sturgeon
in *The Mayor of Garratt*, Haymarket Theatre, 1763

He wrote some farces for his company, with leading parts for himself, of course, and though these were hastily written one of them, *The Mayor of Garratt*, survived him. His part was Major Sturgeon of the Middlesex Militia, who is discovered here recounting his military experiences to his friend, Sir Jacob Jollup:

Major S. – Oh, such marchings and counter-marchings, from Brentford to Ealing, from Ealing to Acton, from Acton to Uxbridge; the dust flying, sun scorching, men sweating! Why, there was our last expedition to Hounslow; that day's work carried off Major Molassas. Bunhill-fields never saw a braver commander! He was an irreparable loss to the Service.

Sir J. – How came that about?

Major S. – Why, it was partly the major's own fault; I advised him to pull off his spurs before he went into action; but he was resolute, and would not be ruled.

Sir J. – Spirit; zeal for the Service.

Major S. – Doubtless. But to proceed: in order to get our men in good spirits, we were quartered at Thistleworth, the evening before. At day-break, our regiment formed at Hounslow, town's-end, as it might be about here. The major made a fine disposition: on we marched, the men all in high spirits, to attack the gibbet where Gardel is hanging; but turning down a narrow lane to the left, as it might be about there, in order to possess a pig-sty, that we might take the gallows in flank, and, at all events, secure a retreat, who should come by but a drove of fat oxen from Smithfield. The drums beat in the front, the dogs barked in the rear, the oxen set up a gallop; on they came thundering upon us, broke through our ranks in an instant, and threw the whole corps in confusion.

Sir J. – Terrible!

Major S. – The major's horse took to his heels; away he scoured over the heath. The gallant commander stuck both spurs into his flank, and for some time, held by his mane, but in crossing a ditch, the horse threw up his head, gave the major a douse in the chaps, and plumped him into a gravel-pit, just by the powder-mills.

Sir J. – Dreadful!

Major S. – Why, as Captain Cucumber, Lieutenant Puttyman, Ensign Tripe, and myself, were returning to town in the Turnham-green stage, we were stopped near the Hammersmith turnpike, and robbed and stripped by a single footpad.

Sir J. – An unfortunate day, indeed.

Major S. – But, in some measure, to make me amends, I got the major's commission.

Sir J. – You did?

Major S. – O yes. I was the only one of the corps that could ride; otherwise we always succeeded of course; no jumping over heads, no underhand work among us; all men of honour; and I must do the regiment the justice to say, there never was a set of more amiable officers.

(*opposite*) Study for the painting by George Clint, exhibited at the Royal Academy in 1833, of William Dowton as Falstaff with George Smith as Bardolph in the background, in *Henry IV Part One*

Sir J. – Quiet and peaceable.

Major S. – As lambs, Sir Jacob. Excepting one boxing-bout at the Three Compasses, in Acton, between Captain Sheers and the colonel, concerning a game at all-fours, I don't remember a single dispute.

Sir J. – Why, that was mere mutiny; the captain ought to have been broke.

Major S. – He was; for the colonel not only took away his cockade, but his custom; and I don't think poor Captain Sheers has done a stitch for him since.

Played by a comedian with a touch of genius, this part must have been irresistible. And indeed, Dr Johnson, in spite of his oak cudgel, admitted that Foote was irresistible.

A more versatile actor was David Garrick. We are apt to think of him now as a Shakespearean tragedian; but he could succeed in comic parts that other leading actors would have despised. Of these one of his favourites was the innocent Abel Drugger in Jonson's *Alchemist*.

The last years of the eighteenth century and those of the Regency that followed them appear to have been supremely rich in comic performers and performances. Even the actresses, in spite of their weakness for dubious liaisons and frequent pregnancies, could excel in comic parts. The best of them was probably Mrs Jordan, who somehow contrived to present her lover, the Duke of Clarence (afterwards William IV) with no fewer than ten children, while keeping her place as a star comedienne. Hazlitt, a keen playgoer, gives us a glimpse of this wealth of comedy in his essay on *Merry England:*

> The French cannot, however, be persuaded of the excellence of our comic stage, nor of the store we set by it. When they ask what amusements we have, it is plain they can never have heard of Mrs. Jordan, nor King, nor Bannister, nor Suett, nor Munden, nor Lewis, nor little Simmons, nor Dodd, and Parsons, and Emery, and Miss Pope, and Miss Farren, and all those who even in my time have gladdened a nation and 'made life's business like a summer's dream'. . . .

Oddly enough, Hazlitt does not include in the above list his own favourite comedian:

> Mr. Liston has more comic humour, more power of face, and a more genial and happy vein of folly, than any other actor we remember. His farce is not caricature; his drollery oozes out of his features, and trickles down his face: his voice is a pitch-pine for laughter. He does some characters but indifferently, others respectably; but when he *puts himself whole* into a jest, it is unrivalled. Munden with all his merit, his whim, his imagination, and with his broad effects, is a caricaturist in the comparison. . . .

(*opposite*) David Garrick as Abel Drugger (right) with William Burton as Subtle and John Palmer as Face in *The Alchemist*, Theatre Royal, Drury Lane, 1769. Painting by Johann Zoffany

And indeed Munden was often said to offer too many broad effects and to end in caricature, but is was he who captured the imagination of Charles Lamb, which conferred immortality upon the comedian. With Lamb's essay in front of us, we need not regret never having seen Munden, for his grotesque humour is caught and then enriched by that wild but delicate imagination:

Can any man *wonder*, like him? Can any man *see ghosts*, like him? or fight with *his own shadow* – 'SESSA' – as he does in that strangely-neglected thing, the *Cobbler of Preston* – where his alterations from the Cobbler to the Magnifico, and from the Magnifico to the Cobbler, keep the brain of the spectator in as wild a ferment, as if some Arabian Night were being acted before him. Who like him can throw, or ever attempted to throw, a preternatural interest over the commonest daily-life objects. A table, or a joint stool, in his conception, rises with a dignity equivalent to Cassiopeia's Chair. It is invested with constellatory importance. You could not speak of it with more deference, if it were mounted into the firmament. A beggar in the hands of Michael Angelo, says Fuseli, rose the Patriarch of Poverty. So the gusto of Munden antiquates and ennobles what it touches. His pots and his ladles are as grand and primal as the seething-pots and hooks seen in old prophetic vision. A tub of butter, contemplated by him, amounts to a Platonic idea. He understands a leg of mutton in its quiddity. He stands wondering, amid the commonplace materials of life, like primeval man with the sun and stars about him.

So there we are. But where are we? The point raised by the question is this: were Liston and Munden comedians of a quality beyond our experience, or is it simply that Hazlitt and Lamb were brilliant essayists with a lively sense of humour? What if there had been a Hazlitt to write about Dan Leno? Or a Lamb to appreciate Little Tich? Is broad comedy, its laughter dying out down the years, simply at the mercy of its critics – or, better than its official critics, the finest writers of its time? Clearly, chance plays its part here. We know for example that Charles Matthews (1776–1835) was the most original and gifted entertainer of his day, as fine a mimic as Foote, but less farcical, more thoughtful; and we know that Sir Walter Scott was among his admirers; but he had no Hazlitt, no Lamb, to celebrate his art. Or we can take a later example. J. L. Toole was a famous comedian-manager, the exception to the impressive list of tragedian-managers (incidentally, a close friend of Irving); and we know that he was equally good in farce and in humour touched with pathos; but his memory, though furnished with many amusing stories, is not illuminated by literature, as Liston's and Munden's were.

Indeed, as soon as we write about the Theatre of the past and its players, certain questions, some doubts, begin to tease us. How good were these players so much admired in their own time? If we were taken back to their famous performances, by some favour of the fifth dimension, would we be lost in admiration too or would we find them affected, clumsy, hopelessly overdone, not worth half an hour's attention? After all, during my own lifetime I have seen marked changes in styles of acting, first

Joseph Munden as Autolycus
in *The Winter's Tale*, Covent Garden, 1807

J. L. Toole as Barnaby Doublechick
in *Upper Crust*, Folly Theatre, 1880

the full-blooded and fully projected, then the fashion for understatement and 'throw-away lines', and now more recently a rather odd mixture of the two. What would I make of Garrick, Kean, Macready? Or, for that matter, of Liston and Munden? But I must confess I would be prejudiced in favour of the eighteenth-century actresses – Mistress Bracegirdle, Nan Oldfield, Peg Woffington, Kitty Clive – partly because of their enchanting names; but also because of some hazy delightful vision of their fluting away as Millamant, in a cloud of powder, or displaying their saucy legs in one of their 'breeches parts'.

However, we must return to the middle years of the nineteenth century, not a fruitful epoch for stage comedy. A little scene in *Bleak House* shows us what was going on then. It is the Harmonic Meeting at the Sol's Arms:

> The landlord of the Sol's Arms, finding Little Swills so popular, commends him highly to the Juryman and the public; observing that, for a song in character, he don't know his equal, and that the man's character-wardrobe would fill a cart.
>
> Thus gradually the Sol's Arms melts into the shadowy night, and then flares out of it strong in gas. The Harmonic Meeting hour arriving, the gentleman of professional celebrity takes the chair; is faced (red-faced) by Little Swills; their friends rally round them, and support first-rate talent. In the zenith of the evening, Little Swills says, 'Gentlemen, if you'll permit me, I'll attempt a short description of a scene of real life that came off here today.' Is much applauded and encouraged; goes out of the room as Swills; comes in as the Coroner (not in the least of the world like him); describes the Inquest, with recreative intervals of pianoforte accompaniment to the refrain – With his (the Coroner's) tippy tol li doll, tippy tol lo doll, tippy tippy lol li doll, Dee!

Something like this was happening in the singing rooms of taverns from London's East End to the factory towns of the North. The great glittering variety theatres were really born here. The very term *music hall* came from the larger taverns that added an extra-large room for music of a sort with a platform at one end and plenty of tables for drinkers. There was no admission charge at first, the profit coming out of the drink; but then when regular professionals were employed and arrangements were more elaborate, people paid a modest price for their seats. Charles Norton, called the 'father of the halls', began his career as the landlord of the Canterbury Arms in Lambeth, so popular that a special building was erected. Then came, increasing in size and splendour, invading the West End, the real 'halls', the variety theatres.

The first phase, belonging to the earlier 1880s, did not really begin to develop broad popular humour. It was the era of the 'Lion Comique', the apparent swell who celebrated the joys of 'going on the spree'. Champagne, nothing less, was their

(*opposite*) left to right: Miss P. Glover, Madame Vestris, Mr Williams and Mr Liston in *Paul Pry*, Haymarket Theatre. Engraving by Thomas Lupton after a George Clint painting of 1828

tipple, and there were times when they distributed it to more favoured members of the audience. 'Champagne Charlie is my name,' sang George Leybourne; while his rival, the 'Great Vance' had his refrain:

> For they always go a-rolling home,
> They always go a-rolling home,
>   A jolly lot are they!
>   Tra la la, Tra la la.
> Slap bang, here we are again!
> Slap bang, here we are again!
>   A jolly lot are we!

No humour here, just noise, impudence, determined silliness. Both Leybourne and the 'Great Vance' died young, after too many real sprees, but they left a tradition that lingered on the variety stage for many years. Immaculately dressed light comedians went on singing about Charlie Brown going on the Town. This represented the silly side of the 'halls', like the sternly patriotic song about the Navy, the Fighting Navy, and the sentimental ditties about their old Irish Mothers sung by adenoidal tenors who had probably never seen Ireland. Even when the music halls were at their best, you had to sit through a lot of rubbish.

They were at their best, I would say, roughly between 1890 and 1910, when the Moss Empires, with their twice-nightly shows, were conspicuous in every provincial city or large town. The management was able to offer artistes, including jugglers, acrobats, illusionists, from abroad, long reliable contracts, which might include appearances at the big London variety theatres, even though many great favourites would continually appear there. The humour, male and female, mostly had its roots in the urban working class, Cockney, Midland, North-country. It might be said to be a return, by way of the Industrial Revolution, to the clowning of long ago, giving the people what they wanted. It was a humour, vulgar but healthily coarse, coming from and going to the workers. It was the art, the only art, arriving from back to back houses in factory towns lost in smoke and grime. The stuff of it might be familiar and rather rank: red noses, battered hats, a blaring orchestra, and jokes about shrewish wives and drunken husbands, mother-in-law, the lodger, kippers, beer and cheese; but out of the strong came forth sweetness. It could flower into something that Lamb would have clapped his hands at, the humour of character. Touchstone and Sir Toby Belch and Sir Andrew Aguecheek and Dogberry and Ancient Pistol popped up again, came from dark side streets, put on big boots and concertina check trousers, red wigs and redder noses, sang inane choruses in hoarse strange accents, and, as they banged the stage with the ruin of an umbrella, took delighted thousands into their confidence, and might be said to have opened wide once more the doors of that Eastcheap tavern and unknowingly conducted pilgrimages to Arden and Illyria.

So it became possible once more for an essayist to pay tribute to a stage droll, as

E. V. Lucas did so generously and wisely to Dan Leno:

> That was, perhaps, Dan Leno's greatest triumph, that the grimy sordid material of the music-hall low comedian, which, with so many singers, remains grimy and sordid, in his refining hands became radiant, joyous, a legitimate source of mirth. In its nakedness it was still drunkenness, quarrelsomeness, petty poverty; still hunger, even crime; but such was the native cleanness of this little, eager, sympathetic observer and reader of life, such his gift of showing the comic, the unexpected, side, that it emerged the most suitable, the gayest joke. He might be said to have been a crucible that transmuted mud to gold.

We might remember too that a grave fastidious poet like T. S. Eliot could pay his tribute to naughty Marie Lloyd, who, with several Cockney comedians and singers, represented the sardonic wit, the gusty humour, all the rich vitality of the London streets.

The Moss Empires were run with great efficiency. With two complete shows a night, time was all-important. Both the order of the turns on the programme and the amount of time allotted to them were worked out in advance, and every local manager was instructed not to interfere with these arrangements. The variety artiste, even if a star performer, had to think in terms of minutes. The attention of the audiences had to be caught and held almost at once. A poor start, especially by one of the minor performers, could be a disaster. Even the favourites had to be careful, turning on their charm or humour like so many searchlights. Patrons of variety were often quite ruthless. An 'eccentric comedian' might come roaring on, to make the most of his ten minutes, to meet a terrible silence or the sight of men in the stalls hurrying out to the bar. Though associated in our minds with the warmth, the glitter, the coloured lights piercing the haze of smoke, all the catchy songs and the cheerful noise of the band, most of these people worked and lived under great pressure, hanging about all day, needing a few drinks (the pubs not closing at all then) but afraid to drink too much, waiting for the twice-nightly ordeal. More often than not, they could make it all seem like fun and games. But it wasn't.

I have just been going through a book dealing with half a century of music-hall artistes. The author chats and prattles away as if it were all pals sitting up late at the club. But his rosy glow fades as we give some serious consideration to his chronicles. Stars flash, smile in triumph, then vanish, not into cosy retirement, or very rarely indeed, but perhaps into more and more anxious visits to smaller and smaller agents, perhaps into obscurity and poverty, perhaps into hospital and an early death – all too common. A girl acquires two catchy songs, shoots up with them, then slumps down because she can't acquire any more. Anybody nearing fifty is an enduring ancient on these variety stages. At least two well-known 'eccentric comedians', beginning to weary their audiences, committed suicide. It was fun going to variety shows – as I can testify from my own youth – but in spite of the excitement, the applause, often the rapidly increasing salaries, it could be anything but fun waiting

(*right*) Programme for the New Sheffield
Empire Palace, Managing Director
Mr H. E. Moss

(*above*) Marie Lloyd singing 'What did she
know about Railways?, She had never had
her ticket punched before!'

all day to face and challenge audiences that might turn sulky and sour. Even if you 'topped the bill', as they used to say, you might be wondering if it was going to last, if this week's reception in Birmingham wasn't cooler than the week before in New-castle. Perhaps the stars who played three or four different 'halls' every night in London didn't worry in this fashion, but theirs was an exhausting existence, rushing from one stage door to the next, keyed up the whole time. Probably the best and most popular of them all, Dan Leno, broke down from overwork, went out of his mind, and was dead before he reached forty-five. No, for all its jolly reminiscences, I found this a rather melancholy book.

Managements could be even more ruthless than audiences. Before he accepted a Hollywood contract, Chaplin worked, very successfully too, for Fred Karno, who sent out very funny sketches. (The most famous of them was *Mumming Birds*, in which Chaplin played a drunk. I actually saw him playing this part, in my youth.) There is a revealing paragraph about Karno in Chaplin's *My Autobiography*:

> Karno could be cynical and cruel to anyone he disliked. Because he liked me I had never seen that side of him, but indeed he could be most crushing in a vulgar way. During a performance of one of his comedies, if he did not like a comedian, he would stand in the wings and hold his nose and give an audible raspberry. But he did this once too often and the comedian left the stage and lunged at him; that was the last time he resorted to such vulgar measures. . . .

A footnote on this same page of the autobiography makes an important point, telling us how long a company had to work together 'before we could perfect a tempo'. Both the troupes and individual clowns and comedians, playing the same act before demanding audiences week after week, month after month, were able to bring their timing to perfection. This largely explains why the best of their comic acts were so memorable. (Robbed of this experience, many comedians on TV and radio are almost playing charades.) It is worth noting that Chaplin took his highly disciplined sense of timing into films, where he took the eye almost at once.

But I have painted so far too dark a picture of variety. Its audiences could be generous as well as ruthless. They could give as well as take. As far as their darlings were concerned, they could suddenly nourish and inspire them. One of their darlings was Gracie Fields. One Sunday night, many years ago, I dined with Gracie, who wanted to discuss a film. She had not been long out of hospital and still looked frail, clearly unfit for work. I was, therefore, astonished when she suggested I should go along with her to the Palladium, where she had promised to appear in a Sunday night charity show. I couldn't see how she could ever make it, though naturally I didn't tell her so. We stood in the wings waiting for her act to be announced, and I remember feeling more dubious than ever. The announcement came, and immediately that sound of a gigantic rattle reached us, telling us that a large audience was eagerly applauding. The orchestra began one of Gracie's numbers. At once she seemed a different woman, erect, commanding, radiant. It was as if she had taken from the expectant audience some magic potion. The people out there, adoring her, were not demanding energy but bestowing it upon her. It was a dramatic example of what must have happened over and over again to the music halls' first favourites. They borrowed energy, confidence, radiance, from the audience. This created excitement that lingers in the memory but is hard to recapture in words.

Now I have to ask myself what these variety shows gave us in terms of real humour. This means I have to forget quite a lot of impudent rubbish that I yawned through so many years ago. When I think of the precious remainder, I face a difficulty at once, because I have already paid my tributes to the best clowns and comedians elsewhere. (Please see *Particular Pleasures*.) But I remember Wilkie Bard, discovered sitting on a swing as a policeman, singing 'I'm Here if I'm Wanted'; and Tom Hearne, billed as the Lazy Juggler, who would throw plates in the air and then saunter away from them, letting them smash on the stage; and Charlie Austin, a low coarse fellow but very funny, who ran his own police station; and the Brothers Egbert, apparently two solemn middle-aged men who headed a balloon-pig at each

(*left*) Harry Tate (*right*) W. C. Fields

other; and the comedian whose name I have forgotten who brought a little gate on to the stage and gravely walked through it; and all those wild daft sketches sent out by Karno and others, all of them fast, beautifully timed, and hilarious. (I can even remember W. C. Fields doing his cigar box and billiards act, though he of course was American. There were frequent exchanges then between American vaudeville and English variety.) How do I describe this humour? It was grotesque, refreshingly free from sentimentality, and much of it belonged to the earliest displays of surrealism. Yes, years before the intellectuals discovered and celebrated it in poetry and painting, the clowns and comedians were offering us surrealism twice nightly. And Chaplin earlier and Stan Laurel later exploited it in Hollywood slapstick.

What soon threatened variety at its best was the revue, first in London and afterwards in the provinces, where it was found cheaper and easier to organize than first-class variety bills. These had their comedians of course, but much of the old impudent drive and grotesquerie vanished: it was all easier and much less reward-ing. The London revues could be roughly divided into the Big, noisy and bustling, and the Small, quieter and more intelligent. The Big would have crowds of chorus girls, a ruthless large orchestra, and usually one outstanding comedian, perhaps Robey or Harry Tate. (Tate showing his son royal portraits: 'Is that Bloody Mary, Papa?' 'When I want your opinion, my lad, I'll ask for it.') But the small revues, especially in the 1930s, were much better. However, I have forgotten the date, though not the delectable thing itself, of the sketch in mock French played by Beatrice Lillie and Morris Harvey.

In the provinces it was the cinema that was taking over both legitimate theatre and the variety houses. Talking pictures, to be enjoyed in luxurious 'palaces', only heightened the threat. I remember one night drifting into what was left of a music hall, to see a poor little touring revue. It had a chorus of about ten teenagers, shrill but not convincingly defiant, who sang as best they could: 'Here's our reply to the Talkies – We're *alive* – We're *alive*!' But – alas – they and their show were only half-alive. The Talkies were winning every night. But our own English comic films of those years, even with the help of a good comedian like Will Hay, could not begin to challenge Hollywood, and offered a poor substitute for the rich and ripe humour of the old variety stage. Something had gone for good. Looking back now, I feel more strongly than ever that the years before the Great War belonged to an entirely different era, in which gusto and popular humour came out of a confidence afterwards shaken and darkened by those black casualty lists. How could it be the same, when there were so many gaps everywhere, when young men had been destroyed as if they had been swarms of locusts? Possibly I overpraise the quality of the humour we found in those old Moss Empires. But not only was I young in those days; my friends were alive then.

What I find it hard to remember now, at my age, is that the Second World War ended over thirty years ago, that solid middle-aged men were only children at that time, which now has a certain fascination for younger people. (Let me add here that in most respects English life in general was better then than it had ever been before – or since.) Arriving at the Second World War, we must now switch from stage performances to voices in the air. In most households – together with military mess rooms and the like – attention was concentrated on 'the wireless set' (still not *radio*, I think) through which came not only the war news but also the most readily available entertainment. If there was to be the dark nights cosily enlivened at home by *ITMA (It's That Man Again)*, surely the most popular humorous programme then on the air.

It owed far more to Kavanagh, its ingenious scriptwriter, and its producers, than it did to its star performer, Tommy Handley, whom I had seen several times on the variety stage and considered a rather routine performer. But his manner, jazzed up, was soon suitable for what became a fast programme. (An American radio man, visiting us, told me it was too fast for him; but I think that was probably because he was baffled by the variety of accents.) Repetition was an essential part of *ITMA*,

Dorothy Summers ('Mrs Mopp') and Tommy Handley as Leading Chair Woman and
Air Thief Marshal in an ITMA programme, 1944

rather as if its wartime audience found some kind of security in hearing the same
things over and over again, like children listening to bedtime stories. But the device
belonged to familiar pantomime humour too. Its stock characters – Funf, the idiotic
German; the charwoman with her 'Can I do yer now sir?'; the thirsty Colonel who
interpreted every remark as an invitation to have a drink; the melancholy diver
asking not to be forgotten; – these arrived every time with their respective pass-
words. Mixed with this was usually some sort of confused crisis, Handley shouting in
despair; and here, if we overlook the repetition of stock phrases, was something like a
return to the surrealistic humour so often found in the old variety shows. I cannot
pretend I always made sure of listening to *ITMA*, but I think it was a brave
programme, with genuine talent in every department.

As soon as we come to radio and television as humorous media, we must recognize
the difficult problem of the audience. There is first the gigantic remote audience
attending to its radio or television sets. These are very different from the audiences
that left their homes, paid their way into the plush and gilt, smoke and warmth, of
the old Moss Empires, and were sharp demanding judges of every turn, under great
pressure to hold their attention. Could something of the same atmosphere be created

by having the programmes played to audiences in the studio? Most comedians welcomed the idea; they liked playing to people and not to microphones; and they needed some help in timing the laughs. So there arrived the invited studio audience. And in my not-so-humble opinion (after all, I know about audiences), this was a mistake, offering more intelligent listeners and viewers hours of irritation or innumerable switchings off. Invited audiences feel they are being favoured and must be in for a treat, so they laugh too easily and loudly at bad jokes, and even applaud them. If they had stood out in the rain and then paid out good money, their attitude would have been very different, far more critical; and the performers, if they were any good, would have been helped not harmed, feeling they had something to play *against*, bouncing the ball of comedy against a wall and not into a heap of slush. Better to play the humorous programme, after some disciplined rehearsals, to the technicians in an otherwise empty studio, than give treats to invited people, who

Tony Hancock as a 'Ham' Radio Operator, when one day over his loudspeaker comes the urgent call 'May Day, May Day, May Day' – the international distress signal, 1961

often seem half out of their minds to the gigantic audience listening or viewing at home, perhaps putting the kettle on in despair.

One consistently amusing programme on radio was *Take It From Here*, written by Muir and Norden, the players being June Whitfield, Dick Bentley and Jimmy Edwards, a rumbustious comedian who would have held his own even in the early years of music hall. Even so, if I had a prize to award it would go to Henry Reed (a good poet too) for radio plays that are gloriously funny even when read in cold blood. (Four of them are published together by the BBC.) We should meet again on the air, as soon as possible, the idiot literary reseacher, Herbert Reeve, the determinedly miserable Stephen Shewin, the immensely formidable and shocking Hilda Tablet the composer, and the 'breadful' General Gland. I have just been reading these radio plays, first arriving in the 1950s, and they don't seem to me to 'date' at all. I doubt if genuine humour ever does.

So far on television I would suggest that the high peak was reached by the sketches from Galton and Simpson for Tony Hancock, who seemed to me to combine an unconscious despair and hatred of show business with more than a touch of genius for it (especially on television), finally giving him deep at heart a deathwish. The same scriptwriters have been successfully busy ever since, but never in such rare company and not to my taste. Of the humorous programmes since I had an affectionate regard for Michael Bentine's *A Square World*, which mixed absurdity with amiable satire, never turning sour. *Monty Python* has made me laugh, particularly when John Cleese, a fine comic actor, was its protagonist, but I found his colleagues much less attractive; too often there was a sense of strain and a certain brutality in the programme that seemed a long way from genuine humour. As I write this, Morecambe and Wise now appear to have claimed the jackpot, but I have written about them elsewhere.

We have come a long way indeed from the Elizabethan crowds, paying their pennies to roar at the clowns, to our own millions of viewers, through the medium of strange electronic equipment, laughing at Morecambe and Wise. The circumstances and setting of the respective performers could hardly be more wildly different. But is there really much difference at the heart and root of the thing? The people want to laugh at characters apparently even more foolish than themselves. And the clowns at the Globe and the television comedians have probably perfected the same skills. After some preliminary discussion, settling the language and technical difficulties, Richard Tarlton would understand and sympathise with Eric Morecambe, and Ernie Wise could discuss audiences with Will Kemp. As for me, going back in memory to the great era of variety, I can echo Middleton's Simon the Tanner: 'O, the clowns that I have seen in my time!'

(*opposite*) 'The Old Bedford Music Hall', by W. R. Sickert

This Song may be Sung in Public without fee on Licence, except at Theatres Music Halls & Variety Theatres.

OUR·STORES·LTD

EGGS
EGGS
EGGS.

WRITTEN BY
HARRY WRIGHT.

COMPOSED BY
FRED EPLETT.

Sung·by·the
Distinguished Shop-walker

DAN·LENO.

Copyright for all Countries.

Price 4/=

LONDON; CHARLES SHEARD & C.º Music Publishers and Printers, 192 HIGH HOLBORN, W.C.
The very latest issue of HEMY'S PIANOFORTE TUTOR, is the SEYMOUR SMITH EDITION.
☞ BUY·NO·OTHER.
BOSTON; MASS: U.S.A. THE WHITE-SMITH Music Publishing C.º 62 & 64 STANHOPE ST.
H.G.BANKS.Ltd.

CHAPTER 16

English Comic Art

In this chapter I am not going to be as sternly nationalistic about artists as I have been everywhere else about writers. Artists who have lived and worked in England, whose work is mainly associated with this country, will not be ruled out if they did not happen to be born here. But some of that work will have to be comic.

I cannot help feeling that with comic art, unlike humour in writing, personal taste varies widely, what is funny to some people being only a bore to others. Or is this simply because I am now away from my own familiar ground, where I make pronouncements with some confidence? I don't know. But I can still only say what I think, merely apologizing in advance if I outrage or at least irritate some readers.

We will begin with a great name, Hogarth. There can be no doubt here about Hogarth's stature as an artist. But we have to consider him in this chapter as a comic artist. Let us call to mind his most famous things, such as *Marriage à la Mode*, the *Rake's Progress* or the *Harlot's Progress*. They are magnificent of their kind, being at once realistic and dramatic, ingeniously contrived and designed, sharply pointing their moral conclusions. But, strictly

(*opposite*) Music front of 'Our Stores Ltd', sung by Dan Leno

speaking, are they and their sort contributions to comic art? I think they are not, and that we must look elsewhere, to less ambitious work of his. It is true that Hazlitt, whose judgment must be respected, would not agree with us. After praising Hogarth's 'passion for the *ridiculous*', he goes on to declare, 'Hogarth's pictures are a perfect jest-book from one end to the other. . . . In looking at Hogarth, you are ready to burst your sides with laughing at the unaccountable jumble of odd things which are brought together. . . .'

But, for the most part, it seems to me we not only do not burst our sides with laughing but in fact do not laugh at all. We may admire, as I do, but we do not find his most ambitious work laughable at all. Possibly a time element comes in here. Hazlitt was far closer to Hogarth than we are. He was, we might say, only half a world away, whereas we are several worlds away, looking out of a very different age. (I suspect that this time element is in general not sufficiently taken into account.) As it is, my own choice, with one exception, falls on smaller prints, in which varieties of character, comically observed and set down with great skill, are all-important.

Take, for example, *The Laughing Audience*, which gives us a whole theatre in a small space. The two rows in the pit are all cackling and guffawing, fulfilling the title. But in front

there are three members of the orchestra, who like so many of their kind are obviously bored stiff. Behind the pit the beaux are flirting – unless that is too mild a term – with the orange girls, possibly engaged in two different trades at once. In its close grasp of a familiar eighteenth-century scene and in its revelation of sharply contrasted character, this seems to me excellent comic art. Less ambitious as a drawing, but crammed with a wide variety of characters, all laughably delineated, is *Scholars at a Lecture*. We know that lecturer, whose mere profile suggests he is a self-complacent bore, and the scholars in attendance, their faces expressing everything from eager absorption through doubt to suffocating boredom, are a delight. We can laugh with Hazlitt here.

The Bench is confined to four large-scale figures, the leading one pompously attentive, his neighbour already dropping off, and the third fast asleep, while behind our pompous Worship a clerk or lawyer is busy reading something that may or may not be important. It is in the style that Daumier made so popular a century later. Daumier is perhaps a shade better, but Hogarth was there first. A far more complicated drawing, with eleven revellers in it, is *A Midnight Modern Conversation*, which appears to me marvellously contrived, full of zest and character. A great while ago I used to contribute to a weekly review, which held a monthly dinner; and, though we were not quite so riotous, I seem to remember faces not unlike some in this Hogarth print. My final choice – and there could have been a dozen others, not dissimilar – is *The Stage Coach* or *Country Inn Yard*, which is essentially comic in all its wealth of detail. I may not have been bursting my sides but I have certainly been smiling as my eye went from one end of the print to the other. Hogarth may have been more of a moralist than a humorist, but this great prolific artist was no stranger to the Comic Spirit.

In the second half of the eighteenth century there was a brisk trade in satirical scenes from

WILLIAM HOGARTH 'The Bench', 1758

WILLIAM HOGARTH 'Scholars at a Lecture'

(*opposite*) WILLIAM HOGARTH 'The Laughing Audience', 1733

(*opposite above*) WILLIAM HOGARTH 'A Midnight Modern Conversation', 1732/3

(*opposite below*) WILLIAM HOGARTH 'The Stage Coach' or 'Country Inn Yard', 1747

social life, but the first big name after Hogarth is that of Gillray. Any new print of his soon attracted crowds to St James's, where they were displayed and sold. He was a lucky man, not only because of his gifts of eye and mind but also because, unlike his rivals, he happened to be a master engraver, not having to entrust his work to clumsier hands. Though the boldest political cartoonist of his age, his own political beliefs and sympathies were rather ambiguous, veering rather than directly moving from the contemporary left wing to the right, from Whigs in Opposition to the Tory government. But then he was no ideologist; was always his own man; and certainly no respecter of important persons, royalty and all. He was not only bold but often downright ferocious. He did not avoid exaggeration; he loved it, piling it on though never losing sight of character. No other cartoonist of his time – or for many years afterwards – can display the same furious energy and imagination.

Many of his political cartoons do not lend

JAMES GILLRAY 'Hero's Recruiting at Kelsey's' or 'Guard Day at St James's', 1797

themselves to reproduction here; they deal with forgotten issues and often involve too much letterpress. But a good example of his comic social manner is his *Hero's Recruiting at Kelsey's*; or *Guard Day at St James's, 9 June 1797*. (Kelsey's was a well-known fruit shop, opposite Humphrey's, where Gillray's prints were displayed and sold.) The soldier standing in the doorway, though we only see the back of him, is to my mind a wonderful comic figure. *The Plumb-Pudding in Danger* dates from 1805, and shows us Pitt and Napoleon carving their respective areas of influence. Gillray's Pitt always seems to me superb, but his Napoleon, here as elsewhere, misses the mark, probably because Gillray never saw him. However, the earth as plum pudding is a happy invention.

JAMES GILLRAY 'The Plumb-Pudding in Danger', 1805

AFFABILITY.

"Well, Friend, where a'you going, Hay? – what's your Name, hay? – where d'ye Live, hay? – hay?"

James Gillray 'Affability', 1795

James Gillray 'The Gout', 1799

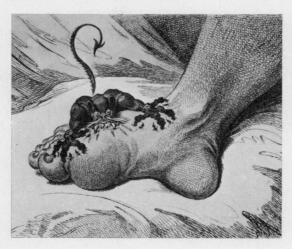

His George III, who always contrives to look innocent, complacent and inquisitive all at once, never fails us, and here in *Affability* (1795) we see him questioning a terrified rustic. Finally, perhaps because I have suffered from this ailment, I offer his highly imaginative print from 1799, *The Gout*. I do suggest, however, that the full force and wide range of Gillray cannot really be appreciated by taking him in small doses. We need to examine a collection of his prints, and fortunately they can be found in more than one volume. They make us understand his high reputation not only at home but also throughout Europe and in America, an astonishing reputation for an English cartoonist.

Thomas Rowlandson, whose name suits him, was born sometime in the middle 1750s, and died in 1821. In spite of his fertility and superb talent, somehow he vanished from public notice and regard until our own time, when collectors and then galleries began to hunt for his scattered work, recognizing at last that here was a great draughtsman, one of the greatest in English Art. Both his career and his character are odd. Until his last years his work sold briskly, often to influential patrons, yet he never made a lot of money. And we may be sure he liked money, being fond of gaming, convivial company, and – we must suppose – women. We can gather this, not from any record of his private life – though we know he never married, but also know his last housekeeper called herself (and good luck to her!) Mrs Rowlandson – but from the eye he had in his work for opulent feminine charms. Even his pretty young girls are mostly voluptuous, destined to turn fairly soon into big blowzy creatures, whose various roundnesses he drew to offset his perpendiculars and diagonals. All his delicacy was captured by his pens, pencils, brushes. In his life outside work he was a rather coarse-grained type, a tough extravert, an excellent companion for a long evening or a tour, abroad as well as at home, in search of new subjects. He had plenty of humour of a

THOMAS ROWLANDSON 'The Chamber of Genius', 1810

somewhat commonplace sort, and comic touches can be found almost throughout his art, including his complicated fine designs, such as his *Vauxhall* (see the plate facing page 49).

I am less concerned here with his infinitely pleasing watercolours than with his broad comedy expressed in splendid draughtsmanship. The first example, *The Chamber of Genius* (fairly late work), is perhaps too brutal. The painter has upset the chamber pot; his bare-bosomed wife is asleep; his two young children are busy misbehaving: a crowded composition, with studio, bedroom, kitchen all one. *Bookseller and Author* is a much earlier satirical drawing, and a triumph of line and character; the bookseller (also a publisher) so fat, haughty, patronising, the wretched author so humble, stooping, ill-nourished. Rowlandson was very fond of these sharp

THOMAS ROWLANDSON 'Bookseller and Author', about 1780–4

(*opposite above*) THOMAS ROWLANDSON 'The French Hunt', 1792
(*opposite below*) THOMAS ROWLANDSON 'The Runaway Horse', 1790–5

contrasts, making use of them over and over again: the fat and the thin, the young and the old, the pretty and the ugly, the proud and the humble. *The Runaway Horse*, a remarkable action sketch, could belong to tragedy and not comedy, but somehow the furious diagonal of the gig and the galloping horse, together with the two contrasted figures, compel us to take this as a comic episode.

Rowlandson visited Paris several times and appears to have felt at home there; but he had neither affection nor respect for the French in general, adopting a familiar John Bullish attitude. We can discover this in his *The French Hunt*, at once tremendously energetic and absurd, with all that cracking of whips and the

hounds running between the legs of the man on the ground. But there is much else that is ridiculous here, and the pen and wash drawing is worth a close examination. And so of course is one of Rowlandson's most famous drawings, the brilliant and impudent (technically as well as sexually) *Exhibition 'Stare-Case'*, with its shallow spiral, dangerously close to the vertical, of tumbling figures, and its fashionable women sightseers turning into sights themselves. There is a large helping of Rowlandson here, both in his art and out of it, and so in this place we can leave him.

Now for the Cruikshanks. Isaac Cruikshank was the contemporary of Gillray and Rowlandson, though not equally gifted, even if some

A Scene at the London Museum Piccadilly, or a peep at the Spoils of Ambition taken at the Battle of Waterloo being a new Tax on John Bull for 1816 &c &c

GEORGE CRUIKSHANK '*A Swarm of English Bees hiving in the Imperial Carriage*', 1816

of his political cartoons – 'on the radical side' says the *Dictionary of National Biography* – were very successful. After drinking too long and hard, he died in his fifties.

His eldest son, Isaac Robert Cruikshank went to sea but returned to work in various arts, notably serious miniatures and caricatures of dandies, fops, fashionable women. But it was his younger brother, George (1792–1878) who became by far the most famous member of the family, immensely popular as an illustrator. (Versatile too, he painted quite a number of ambitious oils, exhibited at the Royal Academy.) A tremendous worker, he seems to have illustrated almost everything that could be illustrated. Most of us know him best for his Dickens drawings in *Sketches by Boz* and *Oliver Twist*.

That Dickens then turned away from him – though they remained friends – is not surprising. Cruikshank was twenty years older than Dickens; he was self-assured, combative, apt to be dictatorial, and Dickens did not intend to be dominated. (After Dickens's death, Cruikshank, an old man now, claimed to have largely created *Oliver Twist*, which was absurd.) In his later years, Cruikshank (though still 'a jolly old gentleman') became a fanatical teetotaller and non-smoker, spending most of his time and energy denouncing drink and tobacco. But his enormous popularity as an illustrator now belonged to the past.

After some deliberation, I have chosen three very different examples of Cruikshank's art. The first and earliest is a satirical crowded drawing, entitled *A Swarm of English Bees hiving in the Imperial Carriage*. (Napoleon's carriage was taken at Waterloo and sent to London, where it was put on show.) The second example consists of four plates illustrating

George Cruikshank Four etchings from *German Popular Stories*, by M. M. Grimm, 1823

171

GEORGE CRUIKSHANK illustration to *Oliver Twist*,
by Charles Dickens, 1838

impressive. A comparison with Rowlandson at all points – though he was flourishing and famous when Rowlandson was forgotten – firmly establishes his inferiority.

Well then, what about Hablot Knight Browne, otherwise Phiz? I have a better opinion of him now than I had fifty years ago, when I wrote that his people did not seem to be made of bone and solid flesh, that they looked like marionettes, and usually very fragile marionettes. Why was I so severe with him? I think that then, being young myself, I was determined to resist any influence he had had on me when I was still younger, going through Dickens in my boyhood. Now, taking a long look back at him in my old age, I feel there is a great deal more to Phiz than I once imagined, when I could even declare 'there is little real humour in him'. Follow him through, drawing the great comic characters, from Sam Weller to Mr Micawber, and one finds he has plenty of genuine visual humour. Dickens was no fool and if he called on Phiz time after

PHIZ 'The friendly Waiter and I', illustration to *David Copperfield*, by Charles Dickens, 1850

Grimm's fairy tales. The third, which most of us will remember, is the scene in which Fagin and Monks are looking through the window at Oliver. It is a situation perfectly suited to Cruikshank's style and temperament. This is true of the German fairy tales, for which he was probably the ideal illustrator. It is not true of his crowded *Swarm of English Bees*, which lacks both style and real humour and relies on a display of grotesque energy. Cruikshank has force, dramatic power, and an imagination that could cope with fantasy and horror. He can be striking but is hardly ever pleasing, as Rowlandson is. Something can be put down to his shaky draughtsmanship, but over and above that there is something in the man himself, a personal essence coming through into the work, that damps my own enjoyment of most of it. He was, I feel, greatly overrated in his own time, and recent attempts to restore his reputation have not been

Phiz 'Light', illustration to *Bleak House*, by Charles Dickens, 1853

time to illustrate him, he knew what he was doing. A point often missed is that as Dickens matured, so did Phiz. This is obvious as soon as we compare the plates for *Pickwick* (1836–7) with those for *David Copperfield* (1849–50).

No doubt the early plates for *Pickwick* are faulty. But then Boz and Phiz were two young men in a hurry. (Dickens was twenty-five, Browne twenty-two.) *Pickwick*'s first illustrator, Seymour, had committed suicide; Buss had been dropped after two drawings; so Dickens asked Browne and Thackeray to submit samples. Fortunately for everybody (including Thackeray) he chose Browne, who soon became Phiz, illustrating novel after novel. (He also worked with Charles Lever, Harrison Ainsworth, and a few others, but it is the Dickens association that is important.) He was not naturally a good draughtsman – he had done little drawing from life – and even though he greatly improved, too many

of his figures are either too stiff or too limp. There is something oddly theatrical about the majority of his scenes, but then this is Dickensian too: Boz and Phiz are in agreement here. However, he was not incapable of drawing and etching an occasional powerful scene, as we can discover in *Dombey* and *Bleak House*. He never used models, leaving everything to memory and a strong imagination. He securely captures most of the Great Drolls; he is very effective with the small innocents, so often found in Dickens; unlike Cruikshank, he can draw a pretty girl (horses too: he was a hunting man); and where he is weakest is with the middle range of characters, neither hugely absurd nor pretty or small and innocent.

In his Phiz capacity, it seems to me that Browne, with all his limitations, matches and keeps in tune with Dickens as no other contemporary artist – or, for that matter, anybody later – could have done. I am ready to

JOHN LEECH 'How to Clear a Carriage for a Cigar'.
Ferocious Looking Passenger (to Old Gent who objects
to smoking): 'That's a pretty knife ain't it? That's the
sort of thing we use in California! Jolly thing to stick
into a fellow, eh?' (Old Gent fears his companion is
not 'quite right' and changes his carriage at the next
station)

declare that a person who really dislikes Phiz
is never really at ease in the special Dickens
world. It is significant that when Browne
offers us a *Pickwick* illustration, done in 1874,
after Dickens's death, it is an excellent drawing, technically an improvement on the original plates, but somehow the old comic magic
has gone out of it. Browne was a quiet humorous fellow, his own man, but not a powerful
personality, unlike the magnetic Dickens,
and I think the lesser man responded to the
spell of the greater man. Even so, however,
Phiz offered something better than a mere
reflection; he had something of his own to add
to his illustrations, especially an odd comi-
cality. And this secures him a respected place
in any history of English Comic Art.

In the summer of 1841 *Punch, or the London
Charivari*, an illustrated comic weekly, made
its first appearance. There had been periodicals of this sort before; there were to be a good
many afterwards; but *Punch* remained supreme of its kind. (It was very radical at first
but gradually modified its outlook and moved
closer and closer to the Establishment.) Its
first real editor was Mark Lemon, and its staff
soon included Thackeray, Hood, Leech and
then, later, Tenniel and Keene. The importance of *Punch* presents us with a problem
here. Somehow we have to distinguish between contributions to Comic Art and what
are merely adequate illustrations of unusually
good jokes. This makes my task much harder,
and I am bound to displease some readers
along the way.

JOHN LEECH 'A Day's Amusement'.
Driving Lady: 'Oh, Frank dear, only fancy, George
has got so tipsy at the Archery Meeting that we've
been obliged to put him inside and drive home
ourselves – and poor Clara has pinched her fingers
dreadfully putting on the drag coming down Blunsden
Hill'

I may do this at once, when considering
John Leech. He was almost a national in-
stitution during the middle Victorian years. It
is astonishing to discover that he was only
forty-seven when he died in 1864, after contributing about three thousand humorous drawings and cartoons to *Punch* as well as supplying
etchings and woodcuts to dozens of odd volumes. He spent a lot of time in the hunting
field, which means that he must have worked
prodigiously long and hard at his art. A big
amiable man, well liked by almost everybody,
he was more nervous than he appeared to be,

and his early death may be attributed to prolonged hard work, too much hunting, and the
street noises that he came to dread more and
more. He had a happy domestic life; he was
one of Thackeray's closest friends; he must
have been a friend of Dickens, otherwise he
would not have agreed to join Dickens in those
rather rash amateur theatricals. He was also a
friend – as it was said over and over again – of
the whole British middle class, whom he
amused without ever offending.

So Ruskin, for one, heaped praise on Leech
and his work. But Ruskin was not writing
about English Comic Art. To go through a
large album of Leech's drawings, as I have
just done, is to be mildly entertained by a
panorama, on the funny side, of Mid-
Victorian life and manners: cheeky small
boys, characterless sweet misses, 'dwawling'
whiskered swells, French and American
visitors (heavily patronised), the inevitable
hunting scenes, railway and cab jokes. But this

(*above*) EDWARD LEAR 'Lear at the Academy Schools'
(*below*) EDWARD LEAR Caricature

is quantity without noticeable quality. Where is the equivalent of Rowlandson's or Keene's draughtsmanship, Cruikshank's force, even the comic individuality of Phiz? What is Leech contributing, apart from fertility and good nature? It seems to me – though I am sure I would have liked the man himself – really very little in strict terms of comic art. Though I will confess a prejudice against hunting jokes, which were to bedevil *Punch* for three-quarters of a century.

Before we return to *Punch* I must mention Edward Lear. When he was writing his nonsense verses, he seems to have had a habit of drawing, probably at high speed, comical little sketches. They are hardly more than bits of 'doodling', yet some of them are worth reproducing because they are funny and as characteristic of Lear as his verbal nonsense.

I now propose to take two famous *Punch*

artists together, because by comparing them we shall understand them better. They are Keene and du Maurier. They are not exact contemporaries, Keene being older by eleven years; and we might say that when Keene, plagued by rheumatism and dyspepsia, was fading out, du Maurier was just coming in. They were very different characters. Keene, a sober, hard-working, Tory Bohemian, not unsociable but always prepared to be solitary, was a born bachelor. Du Maurier was a born husband, father, family man, though again a hard worker, until his eyes gave him trouble. (His best-selling novel, *Trilby*, brought him a larger reward than all his drawings.) Keene liked to draw the middle and lower classes while du Maurier concentrated on the upper class and the fashionable aesthetes. They were equally popular with *Punch* readers, but their reputations among their fellow artists were very different, Keene being regarded as the supreme black-and-white artist of his time, not only in London but also in Paris. Both did a great deal of work outside *Punch*, as illustrators, but while du Maurier soon joined the

(*above*) George Du Maurier Drawing for *Punch*, 1885
(*below*) George Du Maurier Drawing for *Punch*, 1888

(*above left*) CHARLES KEENE 'Aesthetics of Dress'
(*above right*) CHARLES KEENE Drawing for *Punch*, 1887

staff of the paper, Keene always worked as a freelance and had no particular liking for the convivial meetings to which he was often invited. Du Maurier is by far the better social historian (much influenced by his worship of Thackeray), while Keene is by far the better artist, a master in his own chosen field, with a marvellous grasp of character and of all its fleeting expressions. To this we might add that in general du Maurier did adequate illustrations of rather good jokes and Keene did superb drawings for what were often rather poor jokes.

To do justice to Keene in our reproductions, I am taking him away from his *Punch*

jokes to show individual figures. It may be argued that while these are magnificent examples of draughtsmanship, they are not contributions to comic art. But I cannot agree with this. They show that marvellous grasp of character and of all its fleeting expressions, mentioned above. Moreover, they belong to pictorial comedy, these characters being seen as comic figures. And I feel there is nothing to come near them in du Maurier.

However, the truth is that du Maurier was encouraged to approach his *Punch* drawing, right from the first, in quite a different way. Mark Lemon, the editor, had told him to let others be funny; *his* task, as a member of the staff, was to be graceful, poetical, showing readers 'the Beautiful'. The du Maurier we know best clearly obeyed this command. While he could afford to laugh at some aspects of English upper-class life, in his drawings he flattered its members by *deliberately elongating* them. Either instinct or experience told him that these men and women loved to think of themselves as being taller than the common herd, and that is how he represented them. (A long time ago I knew a very impressive aristocratic old lady who was related to Swinburne. She told me, quite seriously, that the family was rather ashamed of him: 'He was such a *little* man,' she explained.) We now have to ask ourselves this question: was du Maurier

(*above*) CHARLES KEENE 'In the City'
(*left*) CHARLES KEENE 'A Scavenger'

trying to obey Mark Lemon's instructions or can we see in his work a sly element of comic art? Readers who own old volumes of *Punch* must supply the answer themselves.

Quite apart from his talent and the amount of work he did, John Tenniel cuts an extraordinary figure in the annals of English Comic Art, for he was born in 1820 and died only a few months before the Great War. He exhibited and actually sold an oil painting, at the Society of British Artists, a year before Victoria came to the throne. His earliest cartoon for *Punch* was in 1851 and his last in 1901. It was his political cartoons, good of their kind and not without humour, that made him

JOHN TENNIEL 'Alice and Humpty Dumpty', illustration to *Through the Looking-Glass and What Alice Found There*, by Lewis Carroll, 1872

Happy Families –'Mr Bones the Butcher', and the rest – a game that should be played even now with all young children.) But let us consider his drawings for *Wonderland* and *Through the Looking-Glass*, which have taken him round and round the world for over a century.

If I declare these *Alice* illustrations to be both unique and ever-delightful, I must also admit to being deeply prejudiced. I knew them first in childhood and they have never lost their hold on me. If a distinguished black-and-white artist of today, perhaps longing to try his hand on the *Alice* books, pointed out firmly Tenniel's limitations – a certain cartoon element, a lack of imaginative atmosphere, a stiffness in the drawing – I doubt if I could successfully oppose him (or her – we must remember that). I would have to say, first of all, that the Tenniel drawings worked for me as a child and that they still seem to work for me. We must assume they worked for

famous and brought him a knighthood. But he shall be honoured here – and greeted with a cheer – because he lives in *my* affection, and has done for the past seventy years, as the illustrator of the two immortal *Alice* books. (Incidentally, it was he who drew the original

John Tenniel 'Leg of Mutton', illustration to *Through the Looking-Glass* . . .

(*below*) John Tenniel 'Tweedledum and Tweedledee', illustration to *Through the Looking-Glass* . . .

hindered him in this task. He drew as firmly and sharply as he could what he felt Lewis Carroll wanted him – and us – to see. Another kind of artist might have wanted to add fantasy to fantasy – and would have gone wrong. Unlike his inimitable Humpty Dumpty – one of his triumphs, I think – Tenniel kept his feet on the ground. And he is my man for the job, whether I am staring again at his terrible Jabberwock or at his superb sketch of the leg

Lewis Carroll too because he gave the later and (in my opinion) better book, *Through the Looking-Glass*, also to Tenniel. The fact that Tenniel is so definite and downright is all in his favour when he is illustrating these fantastic stories. His cartoon experience helped not

of mutton being introduced to Alice, who is her sober little self throughout every fantastic adventure. Bravo, John Tenniel!

It is time we entered the Nineties. Now is there any single figure that might best represent this picturesque and lively decade? I

Cockney low life (displayed in verses, short stories, music-hall turns, and so forth), and it was Phil May who drew so many pearly costers and their befeathered 'donahs'. It was a Bohemian age, and Phil May both in his poverty and in his prime was nothing if not Bohemian, never achieving anything that looked like bourgeois respectability. The town was full of sporting characters, and though Phil May was no sportsman he was fond of dressing up like one. Both in his life and in his work, we might say he was *more like the Nineties* than any other single figure. Finally, and tragically, he did not long survive this time, dying, a wreck reduced to five stone, before he reached forty.

He was neither an Australian nor a Cockney, as many people thought he was, but a Yorkshireman, born in Leeds. There was no money in the family, and he never went near an art school, but after a sketchy education he kept himself going by doing various odd jobs, but always drawing and trying to sell his drawings. He was completely self-taught, unlike every other artist in this gallery, never having had a drawing lesson in his life. If,

PHIL MAY 'The Pot and the Kettle'. 'Ow, I sy, look at 'is bloomin's 'at

think there is. Not, I feel, Aubrey Beardsley, Oscar Wilde, Ernest Dowson, nor Dan Leno, Henry Irving, Ellen Terry, Albert Chevalier, nor any of the 'Pink 'Un' roisterers. No, my chosen representative figure would be Phil May. And not simply because he was the best and the most popular comic black-and-white artist of those years. The Nineties seemed to be fascinated – for no reason I can discover – by

PHIL MAY
'Gladstone', 1893

BROWNS COFFEE HOUSE

PEAS PUDDING 1ᵈ

HOT JOINTS 4ᵈ

Bloater Mackerel & Cup of Tea or Coffee 2½ᵈ

TRIPE 3ᵈ

PUDDING 1ᵈ

TO WINS,
KIPPER 1ᵈ
ECLI ½
TEA ½ᵈ 4ᵈ
PEA C½ᵈ

PHIL MAY

TANTALIZING!

when he was successful, he enjoyed drawing the poor, with a humour not without compassion, it was because he had known poverty. Never robust, always threatened with lung trouble, and already married, he accepted a contract to go to Australia and draw cartoons for the *Sydney Bulletin*. But here we need some dates: he sailed for Australia in 1885, and as Philip William May he was born in 1864; so he was still only a mere youth, untaught, unsophisticated, but, in spite of his health, a prodigious worker, for ever drawing and drawing, sketching the life around him, no cartoonist (he never was really) but already beginning to understand what black-and-white might be able to do. An anecdote from his stay in Sydney proves this point. His editor complained that his drawings were 'not finished up' like those of his fellow artists.

May's reply to this showed how his mind was working: 'When I can leave out half the lines I now use I shall want six times the money.'

Five years later, after visits to Rome and Paris (subsidised by a generous patron), Phil May in London was beginning to leave out more and more lines and was soon earning more than six times the money. He joined *Punch* but was never at heart a *Punch* man, preferring more space in other periodicals and his own less laborious jokes. He published a number of albums. Money came quickly but it vanished faster still. May was naturally a generous man, but he was also 'a soft touch', pursued by spongers and parasites. As he spent more, he had to earn more, and this at least, in spite of all the booze and late hours, kept him hard at work. And here, in his work, he was one of the most fortunate of artists: his

BITS & SCRAPS.

PHIL MAY

tributes to him as a witty charming companion – he drove a delicate constitution too hard, and he died in 1903, aged thirty-nine. For a few years after his death there were still reprints of his work and original sketches were eagerly collected. But then, as the Twenties passed into the Thirties, he was largely forgotten, except by a few connoisseurs of black-and-white drawing. However, there are signs now of a renewed interest in a man who is really a master of his chosen art, the greatest we have had since Keene. And he will remain for some of us the representative figure of the Nineties.

Going forward ten years beyond Phil May's death, I have been going through a bound volume of *Punch* for 1913. The jokes – some good, many dreadful – are for the most part adequately illustrated, with drawings ranging from the boisterous to the elegant. But adequate illustration, with the fun of the letterpress, adds nothing to comic art. And this was hard to find. It is there at times in Belcher; and almost always in George Morrow and Jack B. Yeats (appearing as 'W. Bird'); both of them to stay in *Punch* for many years. But one man who never went near *Punch* is to my mind the representative comic artist of this era, that literary man, Max Beerbohm.

It may seem surprising but we have it from Max Beerbohm himself that he wrote reluctantly, regarding it as a task, whereas he enjoyed drawing, especially caricatures. 'I can draw caricatures at any moment,' he once told his future wife, 'and how I rejoice in them! *They* are what I was put into the world to do.' Yet I think most of us see him as an author first, with writing as his profession, and keep the artist in the background, amusing himself – and of course the rest of us too. His drawing begins in the Nineties and ends somewhere in the Thirties, but the bulk of his work – and the best of it – belongs to what we roughly call the Edwardian Age. (I knew Max only when he was an old man, but even then I thought of him as an Edwardian

technique and his temperament were perfectly matched. His economy of effect and wonderful sureness of line perfectly expressed his sense of character and bubbling humour. He had also a gift for swift economic portraiture, often based on photographs. (See his drawing of Gladstone, from his Winter Annual of 1893.) But even better is what he could do with that superb line of his to capture characters and situation in a flash. (For example, his *At 'Appy 'Ampstead on Easter Monday*, from his *Sketchbook 1895*.) A whole volume, *Phil May's Gutter-Snipes*, was devoted to his sketches of East End kids and their Mums, and there was more than a trace of compassion underlying the humour of these drawings. (This is particularly true of the women and children lining up at the shop for *Bits & Scraps*.) He understood the life of the poor.

Really his only enemy – for there are many

GEORGE BELCHER 'When she's 'ad a couple she speaks under 'er breath, *blotto voce*, as the sayin' is', drawing for *Punch*

figure.) There may be literary prejudice here – so many of Max's subjects being literary – but he does seem to me the most distinguished and the most amusing of the cartoonists and caricaturists among the Edwardians. I cannot help feeling too that he was the boldest of them, even though he did postpone the exhibition and publication of some works involving royal personages.

An example, which I insist upon reproducing here, is the delicious cartoon entitled *The Rare, the Rather Awful Visits of Albert Edward, Prince of Wales, to Windsor Castle*. I doubt if he

(*opposite*) MAX BEERBOHM 'The Rare, the Rather Awful Visits of Albert Edward, Prince of Wales, to Windsor Castle', 1921

MAX BEERBOHM 'A Memory of Henry James and Joseph Conrad conversing at an Afternoon Party, circa 1904'

MAX BEERBOHM 'Mark Twain', 1908

MAX BEERBOHM 'Osbert and Sacheverell Sitwell', 1925

ever did anything better. It seems to me a masterpiece of comic cartooning. It enables us to take in at a glance a royal relationship extending down the years, a huge lump of social history. Unlike many of Max's more elaborate cartoons, which tend to look laboured and amateurish if they present us with a number of figures, it is technically very accomplished, with the two massed-black figures so effectively and admirably composed. It is very funny at first sight and yet will repay careful study. Here, for once, Max created a full-size cartoon that rivals the brilliant immediacy of his caricatures, so dear to him – and so pleasing to us if we relish a

bold and ironical impudence, essential to caricature, in the artist.

There are scores of these to choose from, and I cannot undertake to please everybody. One I particularly like is comparatively quite late (1926) but revives *A Memory of Henry James and Joseph Conrad conversing at an Afternoon Party – circa 1904*. The Conrad is superficial but the Henry James seems to me superb. So too, in a different manner, is the Mark Twain of 1908. Again, in a very different manner, going forward to 1925, is the caricature of Osbert and Sacheverell Sitwell. There is some work to be done yet, assembling for print the best of Max Beerbohm's cartoons and

(*above*) E. T. REED 'No Bathing To-day', from *Mr Punch's Prehistoric Peeps*, 1896
(*below*) J. A. SHEPHERD original drawing to *Zig-Zags at the Zoo*

caricatures. Together they would make an original and very rewarding contribution to our Comic Art. Both verbally and pictorially Max may be a dandy little master, but that still leaves him a master.

We are now in the Twenties and the whole field seems to widen. Names come rolling out that were affectionately familiar to those of us who were around – and probably young and eager to be amused – in those years. Let me recall offhand some of them, in no order of merit, simply those who float into memory. There was J. A. Shepherd, whose sketches of birds and animals, really inimitable, seemed good-natured satires on the human race he chose to ignore. There was E. T. Reed and his *Prehistoric Peeps*; Heath Robinson, with all his solemn fantastic machinery, designed by quietly mad professors; H. M. Bateman, so

(*opposite*) W. HEATH ROBINSON 'Inspecting Stockings on Christmas Eve'

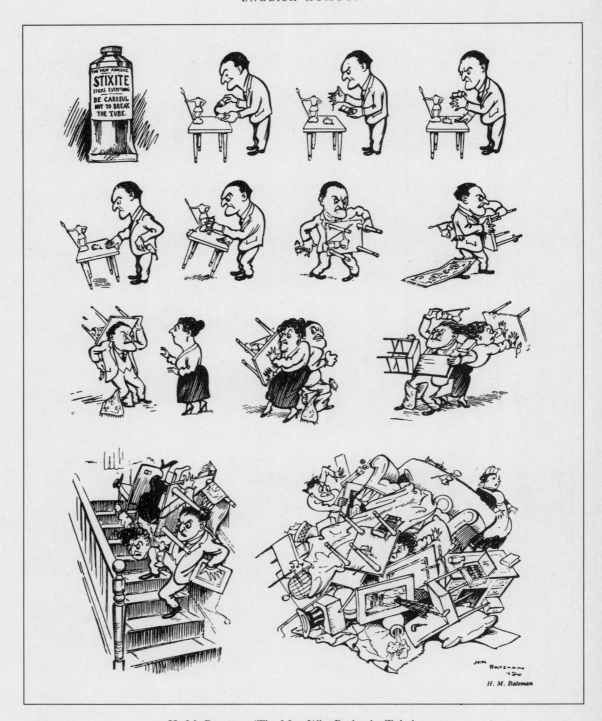

H. M. BATEMAN 'The Man Who Broke the Tube', 1920

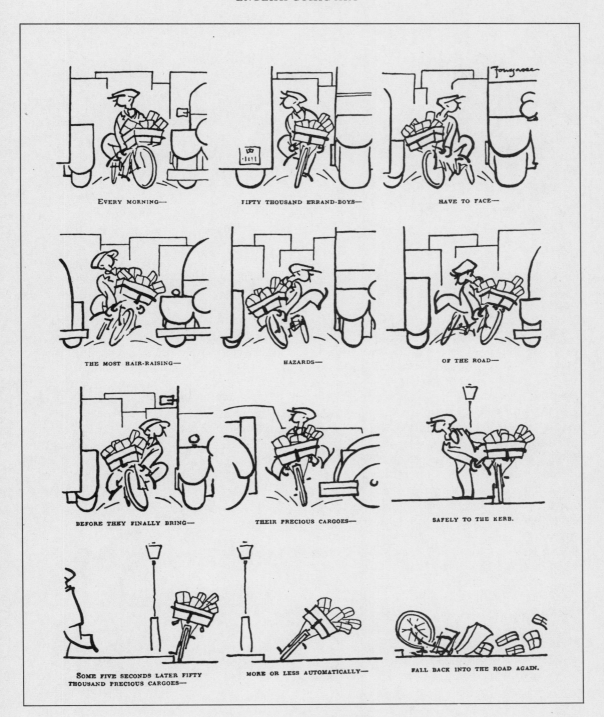

Fougasse Drawing for *Punch*

PONT

a pack-mule trip. We were all very fond of him. As a comic cartoonist he is a genuine original. The experts on *Punch* were quick to recognize this, and as he was developing and deepening all the time, both technically and as a humorist, this makes his early death all the more cruel. Had he been able to fulfil himself completely, I believe he would have been one of the great masters of comic art. As it is, he left us work that is unique of its kind. And going again through Bernard Hollowood's splendid volume of it, I have been surprised and delighted to notice how little of it 'dates', how fresh and rewarding it all seems.

I have called him already in print – 'an unusually attractive young man, handsome and friendly, merry and modest, with that unsleeping sly sense of humour which peeps out of the smallest drawing by him'. I am quoting myself here, before discussing his work, because I feel that his essential quality as a person comes through to us in that work. I can imagine a competing comic artist, perhaps jealous of Pont's vogue, declaring that the drawing is not as brilliant and up to the minute as his own, and that the humour is not as sharp and pointed as his, really rather old-fashioned and banal. And the criticism would not be completely so much jealousy and bad temper. But it would have missed something essential, both in the drawing and

full of energy and the spirit of wild burlesque; Fougasse and Arthur Watts in their different worlds of droll mini-men; and Belcher and George Morrow again, and G. L. Stampa. Though no sportsman, I remember rejoicing in the wild but shrewd draughtsmanship of Tom Webster, who could bring both surrealism and sharp comment into the sporting world. Only one of these Twenties comic artists, Arthur Watts (see pages 132–3), was a friend, cut off in his prime by, I think, an air crash in Italy. But a closer friend suffered a crueller fate still; though it is not personal prejudice but appreciation of a rare talent that makes me consider him at some length.

Graham Laidler, who signed his work 'Pont', died at the appallingly early age of thirty-two. He had no trouble with his health during his schooldays at Glenalmond, and it was not until the end of his course at the London School of Architecture that he was taken ill, though he managed to pass his finals. After that he had to leave England every winter, usually for somewhere high in Austria or Switzerland. In the winter 1937–8 he went to Arizona, staying at Wickenburg, a small desert resort, where my family and I were fellow guests. He showed no trace of being an invalid, and went with us on various expeditions, even going as far as Rainbow Bridge –

PONT

PONT 'The Importance of not Being Intellectual', 1937

the humour (though the two cannot really be separated). Until the last two or three years, when development was rapid and there were gains all round, this was the work of a very young and unsophisticated artist. There is about it *a kind of innocence*. It is the very opposite of the ultra-sophisticated, the fashionable, the cleverness that is becoming jaded. It suggests a fresh start. And with all due respect to his instinctive feeling for character, his basic wit, the sheer competence of his pen, I believe that in this idea of a fresh start we can discover the secret of the public's eager response to Pont.

Once he was sure of that response, Graham went from strength to strength, employing fresh media, using the joke element with more and more economy (often using single figures), and revealing new depth. Selecting drawings to be reproduced here has been a teasing pleasure. The first comes from 1937 and the British Character series: *The Importance of not Being Intellectual*. Like much of Pont's wit, it is double edged. We laugh at the impressed, bewildered, retreating guests. Pont was fond – perhaps overfond – of stupid, intimidated, upper-middle-class females. At the same time we laugh at the Intellectual himself – straight out of the Thirties – half-sulky, half-self-important. The next drawing, a superb specimen, takes us to the summer of 1940, and is a

PONT '. . . Meanwhile, in Britain, the entire population faced by the threat of invasion, has been flung into a state of complete panic . . . etc., etc.'

pictorial reply to the propaganda of Goebbels and Lord Haw-Haw (on the radio that the landlord, bored, is switching off) – *Meanwhile, in Britain, the entire population faced by the threat of invasion, has been flung into a state of complete panic . . . etc., etc.* If the landlord is bored, his two customers, with their pipes and pints, are completely immobile, sunk deep into some rustic reverie. The cunning drawing makes Nazi propaganda look silly, which indeed it mostly was. But isn't there a touch of double-edged wit here too? Aren't those three too complacent, content not to use their minds at

all? And hadn't that been a British weakness for years?

My final choice was Pont's last piece of work for *Punch* and appeared in it after his death. There are two middle-aged women at the breakfast table, and one is saying to the other, 'Must you say "Well, we're still here" every morning?' It is more a picture than a pen drawing, *Pont* wanted to make us appreciate the morning sunlight after another long dark night. It is a splendid thing in itself and is also important because it suggests the way in which Graham Laidler would probably have developed if he had lived. Indeed, he might have soon come to the end of his Pont phase. But it is as Pont that he remains with us, to win our admiration, gratitude, affection. Going through the whole *Punch*

PONT 'Must you say "Well, we're still here" every morning?'

range of his work, I for one naturally realised that some drawings, some jokes, are weaker than others, and might be left out of some future collection. But the remaining majority seemed to me, after all these years, to do what he wanted them to do. Time dealt cruelly with Graham Laidler. But as Pont, secure in print, he may be outwitting Time.

So far I have said nothing about the political cartoon, *Punch*'s star performance down its long years. Now and again, these *Punch* cartoons came close to being comic art. (After all, they had Tenniel for a long time.) Then daily papers began to employ regular cartoonists

and pay them handsomely. Sooner or later, a master had to appear – and he did. Though there were some good political cartoonists at work during the Thirties and Forties, the man who dominated the scene was David Low. I knew him well and met him quite frequently, even though, being a very thorough careful person, he spent long hours at his drawing board. Arriving here from the Antipodes, he had no reverence for tradition, not even in political cartooning. So he was a daily-paper artist, no *Punch* man. Moreover, he *was* an artist, something more than an amusing draughtsman. His best cartoons are pleasing compositions in line and mass, so that they can be enjoyed long after the political events involved in them have been forgotten. (But he was very much aware of and responsive to

(*left*) DAVID LOW 'The Dream and the Nightmare'

(*below left*) DAVID LOW 'Security by Col. Blimp'

(*opposite*) DAVID LOW 'The Right Honourable David Lloyd George, M.P., O.M.'

those events.) We must add to this that he had a very sharp eye for characters and public faces, and he was successful as a caricaturist and, perhaps to a lesser degree, as an occasional illustrator. His wide and rich talent entitled him to dominate the cartoon scene.

After some hesitation, there being so much to choose from, I have selected for reproduction one of his cartoons from the earlier Forties. It shows Mussolini hesitating about declaring war in 1940. It is in his grander pictorial manner, with a cunning use of dead-black, for the uniform, and deepening shadows for Musso's dubious haunted imagination.

I have also included what seems to me his most successful caricature, that of Lloyd George, so brilliant and richly comic that I have laughed – and I mean *laughed* – every time I have caught a glimpse of it. There is a fairly long tradition of this kind of humorous portrait-cum-caricature, going back to the Victorian Ape and Spy; but this seems to me to head the list, with L.G. so comically foreshortened and full of life and devilment: a little masterpiece. It was a fortunate day for us when a man so superbly gifted, so capable of

(*on this page*) Edward Ardizzone Three illustrations to *Sugar for the Horse*, by H. E. Bates, 1957

illustrative artist in the Phiz tradition. In general, however, I suspect too much American influence. And I am rather tired of what I might call 'the scribble technique'. In front of me here, as I write, is a recent drawing going across the whole width of a newspaper page. It has a number of points to make, and it makes them without hesitation. But *as a drawing* it offers me no pleasure at all. Its affected simplicity takes away but adds nothing of its

swift development, as David Low set sail from Sydney to arrive in Fleet Street.

I may have been out of luck but I have not seen any caricatures here – even including our too frequent imports from America – that could match Low's version of Lloyd George. (Vicky, a witty cartoonist, had lots of fun with Macmillan in his own sketchy style.) But I think I am too old, too full of prejudice and general grumpiness, to do justice to the work of the last twenty years, even though I have been entertained by Ronald Searle and his colleagues, and Edward Ardizzone is a skilful

own; I have seen its sort too often before, and I find it boring. This is not to condemn a whole generation of humorous draughtsmen; but surely among all this activity, there is a lack of unique, sure, startlingly triumphant talent?

But I must not be too negative. I have no doubt that Giles is the most popular of all our regular English cartoonists today. His popularity is well-deserved. He represents the

(*opposite*) Ronald Searle 'Hand up the girl who burnt down the East Wing last night'

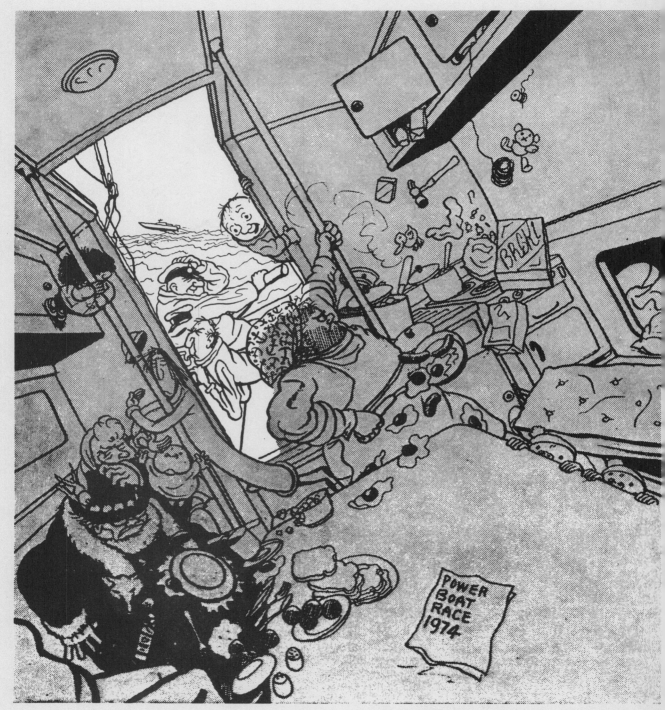

GILES 'That was a 42-footer with six Mercruiser 950 h.p. engines', caricature published in the *Daily Express*, August, 1974

robust tradition of English comic art; he combines a topical appeal with his own sardonic humour; he offers an immediate sense of character with a feeling for appropriate composition and design, as in the example I have chosen, bursting with energy. Notice how the reeling cabin shows us some of his familiar figures, notably that formidable Grandma and those mini-monster kids. It is good Giles and first-class cartoon work.

It may be – and the doubt has already occurred to me – that while all the work we see around us today is up to the minute I on my side am dropping out of date. Even so, I might be allowed to make a point, after going through two centuries of comic art. It is this.

The minor work is defeated by fashion and the passing of time. What made our great-grandparents laugh often now makes us yawn. But this seems to me not true of the major work, coming out of great talent. We may not enjoy it in exactly the same way as our forebears did; it may be revealing different aspects of itself; but the technical mastery remains the same, and the underlying sense of humour is never far removed from ours. Because of my own profession, I may be prejudiced in favour of verbal as against pictorial humour – believing that it lasts longer and brings more depth – but there is a sudden glory of fun and the instantly laughable about comic art that instantly wins and then keeps our affection.

Illustration Acknowledgments

Half-title Six caricatures by Pont, illustrated from *Pont*, by Bernard Hollowood, Collins, 1969

frontispiece 'How to Dispense with Servants in the Dining Hall', by W. Heath Robinson. British Museum, London

11 'Canterbury Pilgrims', painted about 1809, by William Blake. Glasgow Museums and Art Galleries, Stirling Maxwell Collection, Pollok House

15 Scene from *The Knight of the Burning Pestle*, Greenwich Theatre, 1975. Stephen Moreton Prichard Photography

16 Henry Woodward as Bobadill in *Every Man in His Humour*, Theatre Royal, Drury Lane, 1751. Mander and Mitchenson Theatre Collection, London

22 Ralph Richardson as Falstaff and Laurence Olivier as Justice Shallow in *Henry IV Part Two*, Old Vic, 1945. Photograph John Vickers, London

28 Judi Dench as Mrs Margery Pinchwife in *The Country Wife*, by William Wycherley, Nottingham Playhouse, 1966. Mander and Mitchenson Theatre Collection, London

facing 32 Illustration by Rex Whistler to the 1930 edition of *Gulliver's Travels*, by Dean Swift. Collection Laurence Whistler. Photograph Derrick Witty

facing 33 Designs by Lovat Fraser for the production at the Lyric, Hammersmith, of *The Beggar's Opera*, 1920, from the edition of the work published by Heinemann in 1921. Mander and Mitchenson Theatre Collection, London

33 John Gay. Mander and Mitchenson Theatre Collection, London

34 Mrs Peachum, costume design by Lovat Fraser for *The Beggar's Opera*, 1920, as above. Mander and Mitchenson Theatre Collection, London

35 Polly Peachum, costume design by Lovat Fraser for *The Beggar's Opera*, 1920, as above. Mander and Mitchenson Theatre Collection, London

36 Scene from John Gay's *The Beggar's Opera*, Lyric, Hammersmith, 1920. Mander and Mitchenson Theatre Collection, London

39 'Partridge interrupts Tom Jones in his protestations to Lady Bellaston', engraving by Thomas Rowlandson, from the 1791 edition of *Tom Jones*, by Henry Fielding. British Museum, London

41 'Parson Adams's miraculous escape', engraving by J. Hulett from *The Adventures of Joseph Andrews and his friend Mr Abraham Adams*, by Henry Fielding, 1743. British Museum, London.

45 Laurence Sterne, by Sir Joshua Reynolds. City Art Gallery, Manchester

facing 48 Four watercolour drawings for *Tristram Shandy*, by John Nixon, 1786. Collection J. C. T. Oates

facing 49 'Dr Johnson at Vauxhall', exhibited 1784, watercolour by Thomas Rowlandson. Victoria and Albert Museum, London. Photograph Cooper-Bridgeman Library

53 Charles Lamb, 1798, by Robert Hancock. National Portrait Gallery, London

61 Thomas Love Peacock, about 1805, by Roger Jean. National Portrait Gallery, London

65 'Mr Jorrocks has a Bye Day', illustration by John Leech to *Handley Cross, or Mr Jorrocks' Hunt*, by Robert Smith Surtees, 1854. British Museum, London

67 'First appearance of Mr Samuel Weller', illustration by Phiz to *Pickwick Papers*, by Charles Dickens, 1837. London Library

69 'Meekness of Mr Pecksniff and his charming daughters', illustration by Phiz to *Martin Chuzzlewit*, by Charles Dickens, 1844. London Library

72 'Restoration of mutual confidence between Mr and Mrs Micawber', illustration by Phiz to *David Copperfield*, by Charles Dickens, 1850. British Museum, London

75 'Theatrical emotion of Mr Vincent Crummles', illustration by Phiz to *Nicholas Nickleby*, by Charles Dickens, 1839. London Library

84 'Lady Jingly Jones and the Yonghy-Bonghy-Bo', about 1867, by Edward Lear, from *The English Comic Album*, edited by Leonard Russell and Nicolas Bentley, Michael Joseph, 1948

86 The 'Walrus and the Carpenter', illustration by John Tenniel to *Through the Looking-Glass and What Alice Found There*, by Lewis Carroll, 1872. British Museum, London

87 'The Mad Hatter's tea party', illustration by John Tenniel to *Alice's Adventures in Wonderland*, by Lewis Carroll, 1865. British Museum, London

88 'The Beaver brought paper, portfolio, pens', illustration by Swain after Henry Holiday to *The Hunting of the Snark*, by Lewis Carroll, 1876. British Museum, London

95 'The greengrocer's boy . . . who pushed into my hands two cabbages and half-a-dozen coal-blocks', illustration by Weedon Grossmith to *Diary of a Nobody*, by George and Weedon Grossmith, 1892. London Library

97 'Mr Farmerson smokes all the way home in the cab', illustration by Weedon Grossmith to *Diary of a*

Nobody, by George and Weedon Grossmith, 1892. London Library

98 'Mr Padge', illustration by Weedon Grossmith to *Diary of a Nobody*, by George and Weedon Grossmith, 1892. London Library

104 Ivor Novello in *The Happy Hypocrite*, by Max Beerbohm, His Majesty's, 1936. Mander and Mitchenson Theatre Collection, London

109 Jacket for *Full Moon*, by P. G. Wodehouse. Collection Mr and Mrs A. G. Sanders

111 'Dr Strabismus', illustration by Nicolas Bentley to *The Best of Beachcomber* (alias J. B. Morton), 1963. London Library

118 Mr Collins's proposal to Elizabeth Bennet. Illustration by Hugh Thomson to *Pride and Prejudice*, by Jane Austen, 1894 edition. British Museum, London

120 Mr Collins's proposal to Charlotte Lucas. Illustration by Hugh Thomson to *Pride and Prejudice*, by Jane Austen, 1894 edition. London Library

126 ... after tea.... 'Hush, ladies! if you please, hush!', illustration by Hugh Thomson to *Cranford*, by Mrs Gaskell, 1891 edition. London Library

129 Miss Matty, illustration by Hugh Thomson to *Cranford*, by Mrs Gaskell, 1891 edition. London Library

132-3 (left to right) Mademoiselle, the Rector, 'Very, very distinguished novelist' and Cissie Crabbe, all illustrations by Arthur Watts to *Diary of a Provincial Lady*, by E. M. Delafield, 1930. Collection J. B. Priestley

139 Will Kemp. Mander and Mitchenson Theatre Collection, London

140 Richard Tarlton. Mander and Mitchenson Theatre Collection, London

143 Hayes (left) as Sir Jacob Jollup and Samuel Foote as Major Sturgeon in *The Mayor of Garratt*, Haymarket, 1763. Mander and Mitchenson Theatre Collection, London

facing 144 Study for the painting by George Clint exhibited at the Royal Academy in 1833, of William Dowton as Falstaff with George Smith as Bardolph. Mander and Mitchenson Theatre Collection, London

facing 145 David Garrick as Abel Drugger (right) with William Burton as Subtle and John Palmer as Face in *The Alchemist*, Theatre Royal, Drury Lane, 1769. Painting by Johann Zoffany. From the Castle Howard Collection

147 (*above right*) Joseph Munden as Autolycus in *The Winter's Tale*, Covent Garden, 1807. Mander and Mitchenson Theatre Collection, London

147 (*below*) J. L. Toole as Barnaby Doublechick in *Upper Crust*, Folly Theatre, 1880. Mander and Mitchenson Theatre Collection, London

149 (left to right) Miss P. Glover, Madame Vestris, Mr Williams and Mr Liston in *Paul Pry*, Haymarket Theatre. Engraving by Thomas Lupton after a George Clint painting of 1828. Mander and Mitchenson Theatre Collection, London

152 Marie Lloyd singing 'What did she know about Railways?' Mander and Mitchenson Theatre Collection, London

152-3 Programme for the New Sheffield Empire Palace, Managing Director Mr H. E. Moss. Mander and Mitchenson Theatre Collection, London

155 The Egbert Brothers. Mander and Mitchenson Theatre Collection, London

156 Harry Tate. Mander and Mitchenson Theatre Collection, London

156 W. C. Fields. Mander and Mitchenson Theatre Collection, London

158 Dorothy Summers ('Mrs Mopp') and Tommy Handley as Leading Chair Woman and Air Thief Marshal in an ITMA programme, 1944. BBC Copyright Photograph

159 Tony Hancock as a 'Ham' Radio Operator, 1961. BBC Copyright Photograph

facing 160 'The Old Bedford Music Hall', by W. R. Sickert. By permission of the Syndics of the Fitzwilliam Museum, Cambridge. Photograph John Hadfield

facing 161 Music front of 'Our Stores Ltd', sung by Dan Leno. Mander and Mitchenson Theatre Collection, London

162 WILLIAM HOGARTH 'The Laughing Audience', 1733. British Museum, London

163 (*above*) WILLIAM HOGARTH 'The Bench', 1758. British Museum, London

163 (*below*) WILLIAM HOGARTH 'Scholars at a Lecture'. British Museum, London

164 (*above*) WILLIAM HOGARTH 'A Midnight Modern Conversation', 1732/3. British Museum, London

164 (*below*) WILLIAM HOGARTH 'The Stage Coach' or 'Country Inn Yard', 1747. British Museum, London

165 (*above right*) JAMES GILLRAY 'Hero's Recruiting at Kelsey's' or 'Guard Day at St James's, 1797. British Museum, London

165 (*below left*) JAMES GILLRAY 'The Plumb-Pudding in Danger', 1805. British Museum, London

166 (*above*) JAMES GILLRAY 'Affability', 1795. British Museum, London

166 (*below*) JAMES GILLRAY 'The Gout', 1799. British Museum, London

167 THOMAS ROWLANDSON 'The Chamber of Genius', 1810. Reproduced by Gracious Permission of Her Majesty the Queen

168 THOMAS ROWLANDSON 'Bookseller and Author', about 1780-4. Reproduced by Gracious Permission of Her Majesty the Queen

169 (*above*) THOMAS ROWLANDSON 'The French Hunt', 1792. British Museum, London

169 (*below*) THOMAS ROWLANDSON 'The Runaway Horse', 1790-5. Courtesy of the Boston Public Library, Print Department

170 GEORGE CRUIKSHANK 'A Swarm of English Bees hiving in the Imperial Carriage', 1816. British Museum, London

171 GEORGE CRUIKSHANK Four etchings from *German*

Index